We Were Berliners

We Were Berliners

From Weimar to the Wall

Helmut & Charlotte Jacobitz
and Douglas Niles

For our family, and for Berlin
– Helmut & Charlotte Jacobitz

For my father, Donald Niles,
who brought me up to love the stories history has to tell
– Douglas Niles

First published 2012

The History Press
The Mill, Brimscombe Port
Stroud, Gloucestershire, GL5 2QG
www.thehistorypress.co.uk

British Library Cataloguing in Publication Data.
A catalogue record for this book is available from the British Library.

ISBN 978 0 7524 6461 9

Typesetting and origination by The History Press
Printed in the EU for The History Press.

Contents

Preface

I didn't know Jason Jacobitz when he telephoned me one day in 2009 with an interesting proposition. Throughout his life the young Californian had listened to his grandfather, Helmut, talk about his experiences during the Second World War, and Jason wondered if those remembered stories might form the content of a book. Helmut, now a German-American in Los Angeles, was a Berliner by birth, and had been drafted into the Luftwaffe – the German air force – during the war.

Although he hoped and expected to become an aircraft mechanic, Helmut had instead been given a rifle and was informed that he would be a paratrooper. His subsequent path took him to Normandy, France, where he and his battalion arrived shortly after several hundred thousand British, American and Canadian soldiers had pushed their way on to the European mainland over the D-Day beaches.

The genesis of this book, as much as anything, is Jason's determination to see the story told. I learned that he picked me as a co-author because he'd enjoyed one of my adventure novels, a story written nearly twenty years ago; and that he'd been disappointed with the several experienced ghostwriters he'd already interviewed. In his frustration, I gather that I became something of a last resort.

The idea of the book was intriguing to me, and I leapt at the opportunity. I have always been fascinated by the history of the Second World War, and have written numerous articles and designed several military simulations on the topic. The chance to tell the true story of a man who had been there was irresistible. We agreed that Jason would record extensive conversations with his grandfather, send me the recordings, and I would turn the interviews into an autobiographical narrative.

Jason started the project by spending several weekends at his grandparents' kitchen table, listening and recording while they both reminisced, and a funny thing happened. Jason and I realised that this is not just a Second World War story – in fact, it is not just Helmut's story. For one thing, Helmut's wife (and Jason's grandmother) Charlotte was every bit as much of a Berliner as Helmut. She, too, had a compelling story of her experiences during the war years. (During one of the interviews, an astonished Jason tells her 'You saw more of the war than Grandpa did!') Secondly, the Jacobitzs were present for many of the most significant events of modern German and European history, events that occurred before, during and after the Second World War.

Berlin is far more than just the largest city in, and the capital of, Germany. It is a symbol of German history, pride and hubris; and it has paid the price, in spades, for its part in that history. It is the place where Hitler seized power; where the Nazis planned their most dastardly acts; where the Allies – Britain and the United States through the air, the Soviet Union on the ground – took their ultimate revenge against the Third Reich; and the place where the Cold War became focused like a laser beam, and very nearly turned hot. Finally, when the Communist Empire collapsed like a house of cards, Berlin was the first and most crucial card pulled from that deck.

So the book expanded to become the story of both Jacobitzs, from their childhoods, through the war, to marriage and parenthood and eventual emigration. And it expanded again when we realised that the story called for context, for historical perspective of events occurring beyond the immediate scope of Helmut and Charlotte's lives and memories. To that end, I have framed the autobiographical sections with passages in the mode of popular history, so that the personal events are placed against the backdrop of epic happenings.

For more than a year, Jason made many trips from San Diego to Los Angeles to interview his grandparents, compiling dozens of hours of recordings, ferreting out details long buried. Occasionally his cousin Nicholas would join him for the recording sessions.

Near the end of the writing process, I travelled from Wisconsin to Los Angeles to meet and be charmed by the Jacobitzs. They are in their mid-eighties now, but they were energetic and personable as we chatted at their kitchen table, in a beautiful home high in the foothills of the San Gabriel Mountains. We talked for hours on end, several days in a row as they shared with good humour and insight more of their experiences, answering my questions and filling in the blanks of the story. They both speak English well, but when they put their heads together to discuss, in German, some aspect of the story they recalled from different perspectives, a listener gets a clear picture of the Berliners they were, and will always be.

To transcribe the recorded interviews I used the able assistance of Andrea Roberts, a young lady whose accurate transcripts became my invaluable working tools. She put in many hours with headphones on her ears and keyboard at her fingertips, wrestling with German terms and, occasionally, Helmut's accent, as she created the clean, crisp copy that made my job immeasurably easier.

Another fortuitous occurrence moved us forward when my friends Matt Forbeck and Stephen Sullivan put me in contact with their associate Steven Savile, who in turn connected me with Jay Slater, at The History Press. Jay embraced the concept of the book from his initial look at the idea, and has been an enthusiastic supporter in moving this project toward publication. My good friends of the Alliterates Writing Society have also been very helpful, as always, in listening to sample sections read aloud, and providing me with astute criticisms. Stephen Sullivan gave me further help when he rendered my two hand-drawn maps into the versions published in this book.

However, mostly this book exists because two wonderful people were willing to share their story with the world, and because they had a grandson who cared enough to make sure that it happened. To all the Jacobitzs, I can only say thank you, and it is a privilege to be involved in your story.

Douglas Niles
Delavan, Wisconsin

Maps

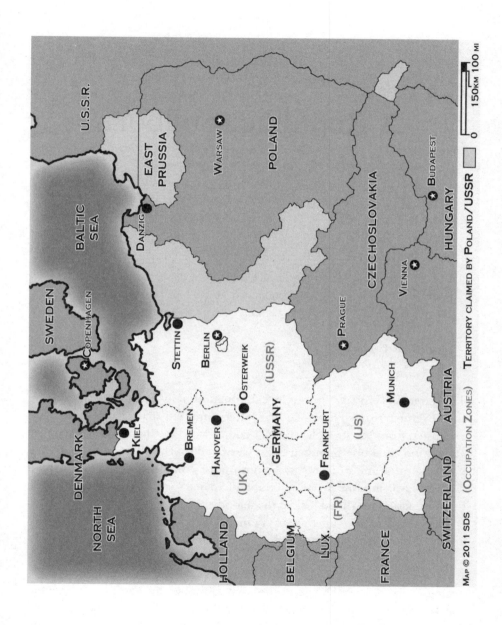

MAP © 2011 SDS   (OCCUPATION ZONES)   TERRITORY CLAIMED BY POLAND/USSR

1

A Republic, Stillborn

My father pushed me along in my stroller, running as fast as he could. Fascists and communists were shooting at each other right down the street, and he was terrified. I was too young to be frightened. He told me later that I laughed and clapped my hands the whole way home.

– Charlotte Jacobitz

The First World War's four-year cannonade finally faded into silence on 11 November 1918. The Great War left a continent shattered, battered and exhausted from the struggle that had commenced in August 1914. An entire generation of young men had been sacrificed on the altars of barbed wire, machine guns and poison gas. A communist convulsion had transformed Tsarist Russia into the fledgling Union of Soviet Socialist Republics; in 1918, that vast nation remained locked in a bloody civil war.

The Allied nations of Britain, France, Italy and the United States had emerged bloodied but victorious. One half of the defeated Central Powers, Germany's erstwhile ally in the First World War, had been the long-standing Austro-Hungarian Empire. With the final defeat, that empire simply ceased to exist. At war's end the sprawling monarchy, also remembered as the 'Habsburg Empire', which had always been made up of feuding ethnic minorities, was broken by the victorious Allies into newly formed nations, including Czechoslovakia, Hungary, Austria, Romania, Bulgaria, Albania and Yugoslavia.

Even the major European victors of that awful war, Britain and France, staggered out of the conflict weary and exhausted. Only one of the powerful Allies, the United States, had emerged from the war with population and territory relatively unscathed. And the US had been a latecomer to the conflict. Following numerous sinkings by German U-boats of merchant ships in the Atlantic, the American Congress finally declared war on Germany on 6 April 1917. The entry of the USA had proven decisive in Europe, but damaging in the New World as the American government subsequently fell into the hands of isolationists who wanted nothing to do with the troubles 'over there'.

However, in all the terrible aftermath of the conflict that was termed 'the War to End All Wars', no single nation, no people, had suffered as much and been as soundly punished as Germany and the Germans. Under the autocratic rule of the monarch Kaiser Wilhelm II and his powerful industrialist advisers, the nation had committed some 11 million men – 18 per cent of the population – to the struggle by the middle of the war. About 2 million of these men died in a conflict that exhausted the country physically, emotionally and financially. By the winter of 1916–17, Germany was virtually out of food, with civilians subsisting near starvation levels.

In the last year of the war, the German army had tried a new tactic, employing elite storm troopers in small units to infiltrate and finally break through the stalemate of the trenches in spring 1918. By then, however, the nation lacked the men, ammunition, equipment and economic power necessary to exploit that breach. As new machines like tanks and aircraft flexed their muscle on the battlefield, Germany didn't have the resources to produce enough of these modern weapons to matter. When American troops began to arrive in Europe in great numbers – eventually some 2 million 'doughboys' would be deployed to France – the tide turned for the last time.

In late summer 1918, Germany faced revolts among the working class and mutinies in the armed forces. Beginning with the navy, the Kaiser's troops simply refused to fight. Facing the inevitable, Wilhelm II abdicated his throne and the de facto rulers of the nation, Major Generals Erich Ludendorff and Paul von Hindenburg, finally gave up the struggle. It was Ludendorff and von Hindenburg who had decided to embark upon the total unrestricted U-boat war in the Atlantic – authorising submarines to sink, without warning, any ships they encountered. They gambled that to cut off supplies to Britain and France would offset the certain entry of the USA into the war. It was a gamble they lost.

As a national power, Germany had marched on to the world stage much later than centuries old states such as England, France and Russia, all of which had possessed a national identity for a thousand years or more. With the Teutonic states, it wasn't until 1871 that a confederation of monarchies, duchies and baronies – aligned by culture, language and ethnicity to the militant and powerful state of Prussia, with its capital at Berlin – was forged into the German Empire. That empire's course was planned and plotted by the iron will of its first chancellor, Otto von Bismarck.

Although she arrived late on the scene, Germany wasted no time in trying to catch up to the rest of Europe. Since Prussia had trounced France, Russia and Austria in a series of short, dramatically successful wars, Bismarck proceeded to secure his nation's place in the first rank of the world's Great Powers. In the 1870s and 1880s, Germany became a leader in diplomacy, defusing several potential flashpoints between Turkey, Russia and the rebellious Balkan states of the slowly withering Habsburg Empire. German factories powered forward with industrialists gaining ever-increasing influence until the country was producing more armaments than any European rival. Krupp steel became the benchmark of high-performance metal, and Krupp gun barrels were known to make the best cannons in the world.

Bismarck's influence waned in the last decade of the nineteenth century as Wilhelm II, the son of the original emperor, secured more power for himself. Adopting the title of 'Kaiser', young Wilhelm was a bellicose and insecure wildcard on the international scene, one who was determined to dominate European politics. He maintained the alliance with Austria–Hungary originally forged by Bismarck, but regarded the other major powers as distinct rivals.

Naturally, Tsar Nicholas II – virtual dictator of Russia – and the parliaments of Britain and France regarded the German rise with alarm. All of these countries devoted huge segments of their economies to armaments, and when 1914 rolled around the various empires were armed to the teeth, and each was confident of ultimate mastery. By the time a Serbian terrorist assassinated Archduke Ferdinand, the heir to the Habsburg throne, in Sarajevo, Europe was on the fast track to war.

The specific causes of the First World War were complex and will forever remain controversial; suffice to say that the conflict had become virtually inevitable. Too many nations had invested too much money and influence on modern arms and industrial development. Too many leaders were utterly convinced of their nation's own physical and moral superiority, and of the vulnerability and venality of their rivals. During the years of bloody conflict, the mobility provided by extensive rail networks and the lethality of machine guns, barbed wire and poison gas dramatically increased the horrors of battle, raising the carnage to previously unimaginable levels.

There is no debating the outcome, however: the Germany of Kaiser Wilhelm had been defeated, worn down to a state of economic ruin, forced to sign a humiliating treaty to end the hostilities. The Treaty of Versailles, inflicted upon Germany by a vengeful tandem of Britain and France, would leave wounds that would only be closed after another, even more destructive, war.

My father had been a German soldier in World War I, but he never talked about it. We all knew it had been a very dark time, and like most other Germans he wanted to forget about it.

I was born on 10 February 1926, the last of my father's four children. My oldest brother was Hermann, and he was around 10 when I was born; my next oldest brother was Karl, and he was six years older than me. They were the sons of my father's first wife.

She died when Karl was 2 years old. She was pregnant again, and times were really hard so she didn't want to have another child. She tried to have an abortion – on the black market, like in an alley. They used something that I heard was called 'black soap', maybe glycerine, and it killed her. That was in about 1922, which was a really bad time for Germany.

So then my father married my mother, Anna Weber, who was about nine years younger than him. She had my sister Gretel, and then two and a half years later she had me, Helmut. My brother Hermann had a lot of trouble adjusting to a new mother. He was at a bad age to lose his own mother, and he never really accepted my mother in her place.

We lived in a Berlin neighbourhood called Prenzlauer Berg. It was an older area, just north and east of the city centre. The Tiergarten Park, for example, was about 4 miles away. The place where we lived was middle class, but kind of low. Still, it was better than the lower-class areas. People were employed, and many of them had salaried jobs.

It was getting a little better when I was born than it had been during the First World War and right after. I remember hearing that during that war they used to make everything out of cabbage – that's how people stayed alive. I guess they even made coffee out of cabbage! We learned about that war in school. They didn't tell us that Germany was good or bad in the war, just that the prince from Austria got shot in Sarajevo.

My father was a *Buchstaben Klempner*, a 'sign hanger', which was a very specific job in the sign business. There were several companies involved in each sign. The first was the sign painter, who does a drawing, in colour, of the sign. Those drawings go to the sign maker – that was my job when I was older – who cut out the pictures, usually from pieces of sheet metal.

And then there was the guy who mounted the signs on the posts or buildings or towers or whatever. That was my dad. In fact, it was kind of his dream that someday one of his sons would make the signs that he hanged. He owned his own business – he even did some work in the United States for a while, when I was a boy. He never really talked about it, except to say that everyone had a car in America – too many people had cars!

In Germany, things had been tough for the years after the first war. There was a flu epidemic right after the war ended that killed millions of people. I guess more than 1,000 people died every day, just in Berlin.

And when that passed, there was still no money. Inflation was terrible. I heard about people who got paid on Monday and right away went to cash their pay cheques – because they would only be worth half as much by Friday! So you would earn your money, and then stop at the shop or market right away to spend your earnings, since they'd be worth only half as much, maybe less, by the next day.

When I was little, before 1933, people still used to go and vote. They would go to the pub to vote, and I remember the Nazis in their uniforms, carrying their swastika banners, would be outside the pub with their signs and they'd push people pretty hard to vote for the Nazis. At that time, the economics were still pretty lousy, with lots of unemployment. Those guys were called the *Sturmabteilung* (storm troopers); but we all knew them by their uniforms as the 'brownshirts', and they were really just a bunch of bullies. But they marched and were loud, and were pretty frightening.

Some people voted for the Nazis because they believed they would do something about the terrible times and the tough economy. At that time we were still supposed to be paying a lot of money to Great Britain and France. The Nazis said, 'No, to hell with that! We're not paying!' They played on people's feelings, like the deal that the treaty after the First World War was really unfair to us. They always claimed that Germany was destined to be a great country, and they also blamed the Jews for just about everything that was wrong. They were blaming Jews from the very beginning.

I think that's partly why inflation got so bad, because of that money Germany was supposed to pay. But the country didn't have the money, so they just started printing more and more of it. When 1-mark bills didn't have any value they'd print 10-mark bills, and then 100 marks, and 1,000, and so on.

They didn't win those elections in the 1920s, but when there got to be more Nazis they would march through the street in their uniforms, with their flags waving. Everybody was supposed to salute the flag. If someone refused to salute, a couple of guys or maybe even more in the front of the parade would come over and beat up the person who didn't salute.

– Helmut Jacobitz

The Legacy of Versailles

It was on 'the eleventh hour of the eleventh day of the eleventh month' (11 November 1918) that the treaty was famously signed in a railway carriage parked on a siding in Versailles, France. The Treaty of Versailles ended the First World War at last, and it imposed sanctions of unprecedented harshness on defeated Germany. The repressive and humiliating settlement would leave vicious scars in the national pride of the German nation, scars that would neither be forgotten nor forgiven. In fact, when the Nazis forced the surrender of France in 1940, Hitler would require his enemies to submit to him in that very same railway carriage.

The victors , naturally enough, blamed the losing side for the war, though an objective observer can see that there was more than enough blame to go around. Not surprisingly, the treaty required that Germany make territorial concessions – to France, Poland and the newly created nation of Czechoslovakia, most notably (see Map 1). France made good on her losses in the Franco-Prussian War of 1870, reclaiming the territories of Alsace and Lorraine; these provinces lay on the southern edge of the border between France and Germany, and had been the focus of conflict for many centuries. They would remain so for several more decades, and as the Nazis rose to power the grievance with France would frequently be cited as a gross indignity. Another part of Germany, the Sudetenland, was torn away and given to Czechoslovakia. This enforced change, too, would provide Hitler and the Nazis with a strong rallying cry for justice and retribution.

Probably the most galling change in borders from the German point of view occurred when the Allies restored the nation of Poland as an independent state. Poland had been fought over and divided by Prussia and Russia for a very long time, but it remained a national entity with its own language and a sense of identity that demanded independence. The restoration of Polish sovereignty rankled the Russians as much as the Germans, but as that great Slavic state was still engaged in its own civil war in 1918, one that would soon see Lenin's communists victorious, the eastern power did not have a strong voice in the settlement details. Since it was deemed right that Poland have access to a major port – the city of Danzig – East Prussia was split from the rest of Germany, leaving a gaping slash in the country that before long would provide the most powerful fodder for Hitler's ambitious, nationalist proclamations.

German overseas colonies were stripped away, with her African colonies going primarily to Britain and her islands in the Pacific, notably the Gilbert and Marshall chains, handed over to Japan – which had been aligned with the Allies in the Great War. The latter provision was one that the Americans, in particular, would come to very much regret since, when the Second

World War began, those islands had already been developed into powerful Japanese bases.

Further restrictions were designed to keep Germany from ever becoming a great military power. German troops, army and air installations were banned from the Rhineland – a large German province west of the Rhine River and adjacent to France. The defeated nation was limited to an army of only 100,000 men, with a drastically curtailed navy. She was not allowed to build or operate submarines, military aircraft or tanks. As a final nail in the coffin of German militarism (or so it was hoped) the German General Staff, developed from the Prussian model and the clear gold standard for all professional militaries in the world, was ordered to disband, never to be formed again.

The treaty was rounded out with some so-called 'honour clauses', designed mainly to humiliate the defeated nation. Germany was forced to admit responsibility for starting the war – a 'fact' that was debatable, at best – and to pledge to make financial reparations to the victors. These reparations, if fully enforced, would have placed Germany in a state of abject poverty for the foreseeable future.

Despite the harsh terms of the treaty, the nation began the post-war period with a very modern constitution. The traditional aristocracy, long rulers of the hodgepodge of territories making up Germany, knew that a king or emperor would be unacceptable to an increasingly modernised populace. They settled for a constitutional republic, established in the city of Weimar (hence the 'Weimar Republic', as it would be known in later years), in which a great deal of political power remained in the hands of the wealthy aristocracy, but a lower house, the Reichstag, would be populated by lawmakers elected with nearly universal suffrage.

At the same time, the victors in the Great War were already bickering among themselves. France and Britain had ever been historic rivals; and Russia was going through a complete transformation of government and society. Each was proud of its own place, and suspicious of all potential rivals. One of the leaders among the Allies, American President Woodrow Wilson, presented a visionary plan of 'Fourteen Points', including a proposal for the establishment of a League of Nations, an international body to mediate differences. Though the European countries eventually adopted the league, Wilson suffered a stroke and became an invalid before he was able to convince conservative American senators to ratify the treaty required for US participation. These early isolationists essentially killed the League of Nations even as it was created, for without American involvement it could never be more than a symbol.

Even so, the German people, hungry, defeated and humiliated, did not prove easy to govern. The years 1920–23 were wracked with turmoil, as communists struggled to gain power and conservative elements, many of them ex-soldiers, organised right-wing militant groups called *Freikorps* and acted violently and ruthlessly to repress the liberal and socialist elements of society. During the early years of the twenties, inflation raged out of control, and the country veered from one extreme to another.

I was born on 31 January 1927. I soon had two younger brothers, Paul and Gerhard. I was the oldest, with Gerhard coming eleven months after me, and Paul four years younger. Together with my parents we lived, the five of us, in a small apartment in Berlin. The neighbourhood was called Berlin Wedding, and it was a lower-middle-class area – mostly what we would call 'blue-collar workers'. My parents were Paul and Martha Wolff; my mother's maiden name was Kirchoff.

Wedding is just north of the heart of the city, and just west of Prenzlauer Berg. It was known for having being an area with many residents who leaned toward the communists. There were a lot of Catholics living there, and also a lot of Jews – later, it was one of the areas that suffered a lot when the Nazis did all that damage during the Kristallnacht.

The apartment we lived in was really tiny, but it did have a decent-sized kitchen, which made it a nice place compared to a lot of others in the same neighbourhood. I slept in the corner of the kitchen. There was one other room that was the living room and bedroom together.

It was small, but better than the neighbours' place! They just had one room; the kitchen was in the same room as the rest of the space. It was a neighbourhood of working people, mostly pretty poor. You had to be rich to have a big apartment. All kinds of people were mixed up together. I wouldn't want to show it to my family now – they would think 'Oh my God, where did my grandmother come from?'

Later, because our last name, Wolff, sounded like it might be Jewish, we were worried about trouble from the Nazis. So my father looked up to find out where our forefathers came from. His father was Polish – he was an architect, and I heard that he designed many famous buildings in Poland. He, my grandfather, was disinherited from his family because he married a woman who was not wanted in the family.

And maybe his family was right about that woman! I don't know why they didn't want him to marry her, but he married her, they came to Berlin, had six children, and then he drank himself to death. That was my father's father – he drank himself to death when he was 42 years old. I never knew him.

I did meet my grandmother, his wife, once. She died when she was 70. Her name was Catarina Piotrowvich. It sounds Russian, but it's a Polish name.

I remember meeting her for a very good reason: my mother took me to see her on my birthday, when I was 5 – so that would have been 1932, almost a year exactly before Hitler came to power. My grandmother gave me a bar of chocolate for my birthday. You didn't see much chocolate in those days. My mother told me to take the chocolate home and share it with Gerhard. Now, I really loved my little brother, but I said, 'No – I want to eat all the chocolate!'

And Catarina said, 'Let her eat the chocolate, it's her birthday.'

So I'll never forget her. I can't remember what she looked like, but she let me eat all the chocolate. And of course, I got sick! Even then I felt sorry that I didn't share it with Gerhard; and of course, after what happened to my little brother after the Nazis took over, I have felt guilty about that chocolate for the rest of my life.

That's about all I remember about my grandparents. My father worked pretty hard. He had a job in a factory, at least for a while. But he was still working in 1928, 1929. By that time, the communists and the fascists were already fighting. The Nazis had started in Bavaria and were not popular in Berlin, which was more full of communists than fascists. But by the time I was a few years old the Nazis were getting more powerful, and they would battle right in Berlin.

There were several times I heard about this happening: gunfire would start up nearby when I was out with my dad on some errands, or for a walk. My father pushed me along in my stroller, running as fast as he could. Fascists and communists were shooting at each other right down the street, and he was terrified. I was too young to be frightened. He told me later that I laughed and clapped my hands the whole way home.

That happened more than once! He said I loved it, that I was laughing my head off because I wanted him to run.

He didn't work in that factory too long because he got lead poisoning, and couldn't work. He was sick for many years, and for a lot of that time he couldn't even walk. He was in the hospital for a long time. They were going to open up his brain, but he wouldn't let them do that. He put on his pants and his coat and somehow he walked out of the hospital and went home.

But he couldn't work, so he was sick at home. My mother collected welfare, which I guess was about 14 marks a week. I remember that our rent was 20 per month, and we had to pay for electricity, coal for heating and food also out of that.

My father could be stubborn, but really he was quite a softie. He was very affectionate with us children, and, maybe because he was staying home so much, he did a lot with us. My mother was the opposite: I would say she was kind of hard. She was unhappy about a lot of things in life, and she had a bad temper. She had a paddle, with seven leather straps hanging off of it – it was called a *Seibenstream* – and she would use it to spank us. She used it so much that the leather straps wore away!

I got sick, when I was about 5 years old, with diphtheria. Near our apartment there was this big hospital, called the Kinder Hospital. They had a lot of good doctors there. This was before the Nazis took over, when I got sick and went there. The doctors put me in a glass room, a sterile room, all by myself. Visiting time was for one hour each on Wednesday and Sunday, and my Mom could come and only look at me through the window. I got chicken pox when I was recuperating from diphtheria, but I got better, and after four or maybe six weeks they let me go home.

– Charlotte Jacobitz

A Storm Out of Bavaria

In south-west Germany, aligned beside Austria and Switzerland, the province of Bavaria had long been a remote and conservative counterweight to the prosperous and technologically advanced nation of Prussia. Bavaria's great cities, including Munich and Nuremberg, were more old fashioned and traditional than modern, cosmopolitan Berlin. In fact, with its heart in towns and small villages, and the Alps at its back, Bavaria was as far from Berlin both culturally and physically as it was possible to get without leaving the country. Bavaria is a realm of dark, impenetrable forests – think the Brothers Grimm – and of fairy-tale castles, of Alpine foothills and boisterous beer halls.

It was in Bavaria that the scattered organisations known as the *Freikorps*, militant groups made up primarily of angry and bitter First World War veterans, began to coalesce around what would become a single leader and a single party. The nationalist movement began with the deep-seated belief that Germany had been badly wronged by the Treaty of Versailles, and that the country was destined to regain its ascendancy. The most prominent of these *Freikorps* was called the *Deutsche Arbeiterpartei* (DAP, or German Workers' Party) and it was rallied by the words of a fiery speaker named Adolf Hitler.

Ironically enough, Hitler – who would become known as the vocal proponent of the Aryan, purely German, 'master race' – was not German at all, but rather an Austrian, from Vienna. His family moved to Bavaria when he was a young boy, and he grew up speaking the (low) German dialect of the province. He spent some time at a school run by monks, where the walls were inscribed with many images of a cross with each of the bars turned at a right angle; later, he would use this symbol for his party, and the world would come to recognise it as the Nazi swastika.

He served with the German army in the Great War as a mere corporal, and by all accounts he was courageous on the battlefield as he performed the unusually dangerous role of a military courier. In 1914 he earned an Iron Cross (Second Class) for bravery, which was followed by the Iron Cross (First Class) in 1918, Germany's highest award for military bravery, very rarely bestowed upon a soldier ranking as low as a corporal. During the course of the war Hitler fought in major engagements, including the First Battle of Ypres and the battles of the Somme, Arras, and Passchendaele.

Following the war he settled in Munich, where he became one of the early members of the group initially known as the German Workers' Party (DAP). He participated in the smashing of the Bavarian Socialist Republic, a fledgling provincial government that vanished as quickly as it had arisen, and by 1919 Hitler was embracing a right-wing agenda that blamed Germany's problems on the Treaty of Versailles, and a vast conspiracy perpetrated by 'International Jewry'.

Always a fractious organisation, the DAP wavered between socialist and fascist leanings. Hitler's influence, supported by his matchless oratory, soon made him the most important and influential member of the party. When the socialists made an attempt to take control, he threatened to resign, and the members realised that his absence would effectively mean the end of the party. After a vote of 543 for Hitler, one against, his position as leader of the DAP was secure.

In April 1920 the party was renamed the *Nationalsozialistische Deutsche Arbeiterpartei* (National Socialist German Workers' Party), commonly short-ened to 'Nazi' Party. On 29 July 1921 Hitler was installed as the absolute leader, or Führer, of that party. He continued to speak and gather support-ers using Munich's ubiquitous beer halls as his auditoriums. His speeches focused bitter accusations against Jews, social democrats, monarchists, com-munists and capitalists; and these attacks resonated with many of the most bitter and humiliated of the German people.

The Nazi Party grew steadily in membership and influence, attracting some famous members, such as the former air force fighter pilot Hermann Göring and a captain in the army named Ernst Röhm. Röhm soon became the leader of the Nazi street army, called the *Sturmabteilung* (SA). Distinguished by their brown shirts and their unified, marching swagger, the SA were in fact little more than an organised gang of bullies and thugs. However, they were very well organised indeed, and each man was sworn to follow the orders of Hitler and Röhm. At the same time, the Nazis gradually became more mainstream, at least in Bavaria, with Hitler being welcomed into Munich society and being courted by many prominent businessmen. (Obviously, the latter did not see themselves as the 'capitalists' he routinely attacked in his vitriolic speeches.) Even the great hero of the First World War, General Erich Ludendorff, allowed himself to become known as one of Hitler's associates.

During the same period of the early 1920s, Benito Mussolini's fascist party in Italy had gained increasing control of that nation. The Nazis eagerly mimicked the Italian fascists in policy and even styles of dress. When Mussolini rallied his followers into a grand 'March on Rome' to seize control of Italy, Hitler was truly inspired. He felt that the same thing could be accomplished in Germany, with the fascists taking control of Bavaria and igniting a spontaneous national revolution that would allow him to take over the central government in Berlin.

Believing that they had the support of Bavaria's most influential politician, Gustav von Kahr, Hitler and Ludendorff conspired to make their move in November 1923. At the head of a column of his SA loyalists, Hitler burst into a large Munich beer hall where von Kahr was presiding over a large public meeting. At gunpoint, the young Führer demanded that Kahr support him, and declared that Ludendorff would command the new government that would replace the republic currently presiding in Berlin.

Not a Nazi supporter after all, Kahr threw his influence behind Hitler's opposition as soon as he got out of there. The next day the SA marched on the Bavarian War Ministry, intending to overthrow the provincial government and begin the march on Berlin. The Nazis were met by a phalanx of well-armed police who didn't hold their fire: sixteen party members were killed and Hitler was arrested and soon found himself being tried for high treason.

Fortunately for Hitler (and unfortunately for the rest of the world), the Nazi Führer was allowed to speak for many hours at his trial. Ever a gifted orator, he used his new national forum to rally many more disillusioned Germans to the Nazi cause. He was sentenced to five years in Landsberg Prison, where he quickly became a favourite of the guards and received a steady stream of mail from his admirers. He was pardoned by the Bavarian Supreme Court before the end of 1924, having served barely a year of his sentence, and emerged from prison far more famous and influential than he had been when he was convicted.

Furthermore, he put his time in prison to very good use, writing a book that he called *Mein Kampf* ('My Struggle'). He used that forum to expound upon his racist beliefs, and to articulate his claim to Germany's destiny as masters of Europe. A key element of that claim was his declaration that the Aryan people would need *lebensraum* – that is, space in which to grow and expand their population. Implicit in that claim was that the land would have to come from someone else, and already the Nazis were turning their attentions, ambitions and plans to the fertile steppes of Poland and Russia.

However, when Hitler emerged from prison conditions in Germany were better than they had been since the Great War. By 1927 industrial production was back to pre-war levels, and though unemployment was still rife, the jobless were by then being provided with compensation by the government. Things were going so well that, in national elections in 1928, the Nazis could only muster 2.5 per cent of the vote, compared to 10.5 per cent for the communists.

I remember that my father let me climb up one of his ladders when I was really little, maybe 3 years old. He had one of his tall ladders against the side of the apartment where we lived, and I started climbing up. He let me go up for a while, and then he followed me and caught up, so that by the time I was two stories up, I was right in his lap. Then he took me down again, but even then I wasn't afraid of heights. I guess I was always supposed to be a sign maker!

Actually, it was amazing what my dad used to do. His longest ladder was 14 metres (about 44 feet)! It was made out of wood, and was very heavy. But when he had to hang a sign really high he would put up that long ladder, then drag a 6-metre (18 feet) ladder up to the top and tie that on to the 14-metre ladder. If he needed to, he would take a 4-metre (12 feet) ladder and lash it to the top of the other two. He'd put braces against the whole thing so it wouldn't swing. Still, it seemed crazy to me!

My brother Hermann did some work with my father, but he wasn't happy about it. I think because his own mother had died when he was so young, he never really felt that close to the rest of our family. My mom, Anna, wanted Hermann to call her 'mother' but he wouldn't do it. Hermann was one to get in trouble – he stole a lot of stuff, I remember. He was so much older than me that we didn't know each other very well, at least until after the war.

There's a lot of water in and around Berlin, with the Rivers Havel and Spree flowing through the city; in lots of places those rivers spread out and became wide enough to be called a lake (*See*, in German) such as the Tegeler See, Langer See and Grosser Wannsee. There were also huge tracts of woods and forest. Some, like the Tiergarten Park in the middle of the city, had roads and paths and formal gardens, kind of like Central Park in New York. In other places, like the Grunewald Forest and the Spandau Forest, the areas were really pretty wild.

In Berlin, the communists were more popular than the fascists. Hermann belonged to a local youth sports club in the early thirties. I remember he used to go kayaking with that group. The communists ran those clubs, and they tried to let us know that the fascists were trouble. But by then the Nazis were getting stronger, even in Berlin.

Even before Hitler came to power, we could tell that it wouldn't be too much longer before they took over the whole country. By the early thirties they were always having marches in the street, and the brownshirts would beat people up who didn't give the Nazi salute. Everyone was afraid of them.

– Helmut Jacobitz

A World Depressed

The New York Stock Exchange crashed on 19 October 1929, and within a matter of weeks the economy of the entire world ground to a halt. The Great Depression swept across the globe with a wave of job losses, business bankruptcies, and famine, despair and hopelessness that seemed to paralyse the planet. By 1930, unemployment in Germany had reached 3 million, and it would be six million by 1932. Under the pressure of those numbers, the republic could not maintain compensation to those who were out of work. Gradually succumbing to this growing despair, the entire government collapsed.

The coalition that had more or less successfully seen Germany through the latter part of the 1920s could not sustain an alliance under the bleak shroud of the depression. Monarchists vied with democrats, while communists always challenged the right-wing fascists. With the ageing Paul von Hindenburg in the primarily symbolic post of president, new chancellor Heinrich Brüning hailed from the predominantly Catholic Centre Party, but could not gain a majority and form a government. By 1930, with no legitimate political presence taking the reins, it became the norm for Germany to be ruled by decree – an ominous stepping stone for the coming authoritarian regime.

Also in 1930, the Nazis finally began to make some headway in the polls. In a September election with no clear winner, the Nazis gained some 18 per cent of the vote, rising from the seventh-largest party to the second-largest. Hitler continued to gain influence and followers. He spoke at the trial of two army officers who were charged with membership of the Nazi Party – at that time illegal – and his impassioned defence won him many converts among the military.

His speeches resonated with many industrialists, workers and farmers, all of whom were increasingly despairing of the nation's course. In 1932 he ran against von Hindenburg for president, and won a respectable 35 per cent of the vote. As the economy and the nation continued to collapse, Brüning was forced to step down. With no viable alternative for the office of chancellor, and under heavy pressure from the powerful industrialists who still formed the backbone of German society, President von Hindenburg yielded to the fate that was beginning to seem inevitable.

On 30 January 1933, by decree of the President, Adolf Hitler was appointed Chancellor of the German Republic. The era that would be called the Third Reich had begun.

2

Under the Swastika

It was early on, right after Hitler took control, that some storm troopers came for my brother Hermann … I remember them, in their uniforms – they broke into our apartment with guns. They took Hermann and beat him up really bad – they nearly killed him – trying to get information about the communists.

– Helmut Jacobitz

Germany's transformation from a nominal republic to a brutal authoritarian regime happened with dizzying speed. Appointed chancellor at the end of January 1933, Adolf Hitler immediately authorised decrees that would change the order and fabric of German life. Since no single party had a majority in the government, Hitler persuaded President Hindenburg immediately to dissolve the Reichstag – the parliamentary body that was supposed to represent the voting populace. This occurred in February, with new elections slated for March. The Nazi, Communist, Social Democratic and Centre parties were all vying for votes as their candidates campaigned for the new legislative body.

However, on 27 February 1933 the Reichstag building, one of the prominent government edifices in Berlin, was ignited by an arsonist. A communist of Dutch citizenship was discovered in the building, and the Nazis immediately declared that the fire was the result of a communist plot. In this case, Hitler's claim might actually be true – no proof or contradicting evidence was ever found, so history must remain vague on the point, but there is no doubt that the fire provided a very convenient excuse for the Führer to advance his authoritarian plans.

The very next day, 28 February, the government issued the Reichstag Fire Decree, which suspended most personal liberties, including the right of accused prisoners to a trial. The decree also outlawed a number of organisations and associations. Hitler had been chancellor for less than a month, and already the Communist Party was banned, with its members subject to arrest, imprisonment and, not infrequently, outright murder. Also in the immediate wake of the fire, the storm troopers of the SA and Heinrich Himmler's newly organised *Schutzstaffel* (SS) commenced a programme of blatant and violent intimidation of political opponents.

On 21 March, less than two months into the Nazi era, a new Reichstag body was sworn in at Potsdam, a Berlin suburb. Thanks to the SA men who had prevented Social Democrat candidates from campaigning by harassment and had barred their supporters from reaching the polling places, the Nazis now had a large plurality, though it must have galled them that they still hadn't been able to gain 50 per cent of the seats. Nevertheless, Hitler immediately proposed the Enabling Act, which would grant him and his government essentially limitless powers. The Nazis had still not been able to attain a popular majority in the election, but they secured an alliance with the Centre Party by assuring that sternly Catholic organisation that the government would leave the Church alone and allow the Centre Party to remain in existence. With the communists already banned, only the Social Democrats resisted the Enabling Act. The act passed, and the Social Democrats joined the communists on the banned list. Brown-shirted troopers of the SA stood outside the temporary Reichstag building when that body convened on 23 March; they effectively (and physically) barred members of any opposition party from even entering the chamber.

Between the Reichstag Fire Decree and the Enabling Act, the Nazi regime had granted itself absolute dictatorial powers. The government wasted no time in moving forward. In April, the civil services and university staffs were purged of Jews, socialists and democrats. In May, SA troops ransacked and destroyed the offices of every trade union in the country. In June, the small State Party was ordered to disband and the following month the Centre Party – notwithstanding the agreement made only four months earlier – was also outlawed.

Thus, the Nazis became the only legal political party. Everywhere Röhm's SA men roamed the streets and countryside, brown-shirted bullies who enforced the regime's decrees and ruthlessly proved its prejudices. In Bavaria, Himmler's SS, which within a year would become the state's primary security organisation, continued to rise in influence, while in Berlin and the eastern German territories Hermann Göring organised the traditional Prussian police force into the *Geheime Staatspolizei*, more commonly known as the Gestapo.

In fact, Himmler, a relative latecomer to the Nazi hierarchy, was making great strides in his efforts to become Hitler's right hand man. Another Bavarian, Himmler had been a minor party functionary during the days of the Beer Hall Putsch. In the late 1920s he was appointed captain of one small company of SA men, numbering fewer than 300. By 1933 he had expanded the SS to 52,000 men, and enforced racial rules of membership even more stringent than required for Röhm's SA. Men of the SS wore black, as opposed to the SA's brown, and had to prove beyond any shadow of a doubt that they sprang from pure Aryan stock. Small and slight, polite and apparently benign, Himmler's face became an image of evil that was perhaps more pleasant than Hitler's, but represented a power every bit as brutal and immoral. As he exerted his control over the SS and every aspect of Nazi life, the repercussions of his activities would be proved in the network of death camps and crematoriums that would eventually stretch across the heart of the Third Reich.

I was 6 when the Nazis took over. We were just moving into a slightly bigger apartment than the place where I was born. This one had a bedroom, living room, a kitchen and another small bedroom where my older brothers Hermann and Karl slept. My sister Gretel and I still slept in the room with my parents; we were both pretty small. Even with those rooms, the apartment wasn't big – maybe 1,000 square feet.

It was hard to get an apartment. They had some kind of government department you had to go to – like a Department of Apartments. If you had an apartment to rent, you told them about it and the Nazis would pick who would live there. But the manager of this apartment was someone my dad dealt with all the time – I think my father was renting space in the courtyard to store his ladders and cars, and other equipment from his business. He was able to get some priority from that guy, so we got to move into the apartment.

Actually, it was just plain cheating a lot of the time, but that's kind of how things operated. My dad used to write bills and get paid by that manager, but sometimes he didn't even do any work. They were drinking buddies, now that I think about it. My dad was drunk quite often.

The district was a nice one, mostly professional office workers, not day labourers like where we used to live. It wasn't rich, not like Beverly Hills or anything, but better than where we had lived before. We lived there until after the war started, until 1941 or '42 I think.

There were lots of good little stores nearby. It's not like today, with supermarkets; they had a butcher's shop with meat, where the butcher made his own sausages, all kinds of them; there was a dairy store with cheese and milk; and also a fish shop; and a liquor store. You didn't buy beer in a store – you bought that in a pub. If you wanted beer at home, you gave your kids a bucket and they would take it to the pub and say, 'Here, fill it up.' So the kids would bring the beer home.

We actually had a dairy right in the back of our building. The farmer had maybe twenty cows and he milked them right there, twice a day. He sold his milk in the front of the building, and made his own cheese, mostly like cottage cheese.

They called those apartments high-rise, but for us that was about five or six stories. Each apartment building had its own courtyard – if it was a poor place, the courtyard would be really small and would hardly get any sunlight.

So right away, when Hitler got power, he kicked out the communists and socialists. He started the concentration camps too. You always think about the Jews going to the camps, and they did, but it wasn't just the Jews. Anyone who disagreed with the Nazis would get taken away – it happened to a lot of communists, even Jehovah's Witnesses. They would take them into the camps and beat them, and keep them there for a long time. When people came out of those camps, they would never say one word about what happened there.

It was early on, right after Hitler took control, that some storm troopers came for my brother Hermann. We didn't have a good lock on our door – nobody did in those days – and they knocked and called out for Hermann. My father didn't open the door, so they picked that cheap lock with a piece of wire or something. I remember them, in their uniforms – they broke into our apartment with guns. They took Hermann and beat him up really bad – they nearly killed him – trying to get information about the communists who ran the sports club, and other stuff. But Hermann didn't tell them anything, and finally they let him go. I guess he was lucky he didn't get sent to a concentration camp.

Early on when the Nazis started they had three levels of jails, or prisons, they would send you to. The simplest was called the *Gefaengis*, and it would be kind of like a city or a county jail. The next level was the *Zuchthaus*, which was more of a prison where they sent people for some of the serious crimes. Finally, they started making all of the *Konzentrationslager*, or KZ, which we call concentration camps. They were used for political prisoners, for people who weren't Aryan enough, like Jews, and sometimes just for people who got denounced by their neighbours or something, and didn't even do anything wrong. Under the Nazis, they usually didn't give you a trial or anything, especially if they were putting you in one of the camps. The only time there was a trial was if they wanted to make a public example out of a person's crime.

In school they were always telling us how great the Nazis were. They said that after the First World War there was lots of unemployment, and the socialists were taking over and nobody was working. But according to our lessons,

then the Nazis came, and everybody was working. Some people were happy
about it. There were a lot of soldiers from the first war who were bitter about
the way Germany lost. They were glad that the Nazis had come into power.

– Helmut Jacobitz

An Iron Grip

Even though Berlin was now the centre of the Nazi government and the
heart of the German state, Hitler and his lackeys remained suspicious of the
bustling and cosmopolitan city. Propaganda Minister Josef Goebbels wrote
scathingly of the capital in a published essay. His lurid descriptions included
observations like: 'Harlots smile from the artful pastels of fashionable wom-
en's faces; so-called men stroll to and fro, monocles glinting, while fake and
precious stones sparkle.'

Before Hitler could feel completely secure in his dictatorship, he had a
few matters of housekeeping before him. The first of these he accomplished
with a typically ruthless display of violence. Ever since the Führer had gained
legitimate control of the state, he had been worried about the thuggish street
fighters of Röhm's SA. Not only did they make many of the industrialists –
wealthy, powerful men Hitler needed on his side – nervous, but under the
leadership of the ambitious Röhm they might one day prove a threat to Hitler
himself. Of further embarrassment to the Nazis, Röhm was an admitted and
practising homosexual, which was a clear contradiction of the Nazi ideal.

To prevent Röhm or his men from making any kind of power grab,
Himmler's SS and Göring's Gestapo embarked on a three-day orgy of violence in the summer of 1934. This purge became known as the Night of the
Long Knives, during which a hundred or more of Hitler's political opponents
were murdered and several thousand were arrested. Röhm's power, as well as
that of the SA, was shattered, and Himmler ascended to complete mastery of
the state security apparatus. With rival Nazis out of the way, the SS was free to
go after those whom Hitler had long declared to be the true racial enemies
of the German people.

By this time, the concentration camp system was well established, and
expanding. One of the first of these had been created near Munich, under
Himmler's direct control, outside the scenic little village of Dachau in 1933.
A former chicken farmer, Himmler had ascended to control of the Munich
police when the Nazis attained power. Even before the Jews were rounded
up, the camps held communists and other liberals. Later on, Jews would
become the most numerous prisoners, but people of other groups, including

Gypsies, religious groups including Mormons and Jehovah's Witnesses, and homosexuals would be sent to the camps in great numbers.

The ultimate goal of the Nazi Party, articulated by Hitler and Minister of Propaganda Goebbels, and actively pursued by Himmler and the SS, was called *Volksgemeinschaft*. This was nothing less than the purification and expansion of the German, or Aryan, race. A key to the success of this process was the complete removal of Jewish blood from the culture of the Third Reich, a process that the Nazis embarked upon with ruthless determination.

However, Jews were not the only threats to the Aryan superman that was the Nazi ideal. In July 1933, the government had passed a 'Law for the Protection of Hereditary Health', allowing for the sterilisation of people deemed unworthy of reproducing. A parallel law passed in the same month was called the 'Marriage Subsidy Law'. This legislation attempted to increase the population of 'pure' Germans by making loans available to newly married couples; the amount of loan repayment could be steadily reduced as the couple produced more children. In fact, the Nazis idealised motherhood and celebrated the 'special service' of mothers to the Reich.

Not satisfied with removing Jews from positions of public service and education, the regime passed the infamous Nuremberg Laws in 1935. These statutes forbade marriage and sexual relations between Jews and other Germans, and created a lower class of citizenship for the Jews. By 1938, about 50 per cent of the Jewish-German population in 1933 (about half a million) had emigrated. Fortunately for the rest of the world, these refugees included uncountable numbers of brilliant scientists (Albert Einstein was only the most famous of them; there were many others, a number of whom would go on to teach and study in American universities), as well as professors, doctors, engineers and many other skilled professionals. It remains a source of shame, however, that the US government made it very difficult for Jews of more ordinary skill sets to enter the country. Furthermore, those Jews who fled Germany to Poland, Czechoslovakia, Holland, France and many other countries were not escaping; they were only postponing the moment when they would fall under Nazi control.

At the same time as he was perfecting repression and control as public policy, Hitler was rebuilding the German economy. He banned unemployment compensation, and created massive public works projects, including a revolutionary network of limited-access highways called the *Autobahns*. (When Allied Supreme Commander Dwight Eisenhower saw these roads in 1945, he filed the idea away and emulated it by creating the United States Interstate Highway system during his presidency in the 1950s. Like the *Autobahns*, one of the integral objectives of the interstate system was to allow the fast movement of military forces around the country.)

Most dramatic of the Nazi labour initiatives, however, was the move to restore immediately Germany's military might. Beginning secretly in 1933, Hitler authorised the creation of an air force (the Luftwaffe) and the design and construction of a modern fleet of warplanes. He also organised a fledgling armoured force for the army, and authorised a massive expansion of the armed services – swiftly moving far beyond the 100,000-man maximum imposed by the Treaty of Versailles. The latter expansion was accomplished with typical German organisation and efficiency: the existing soldiers were used as cadres and became the non-commissioned officers for the rapidly growing Wehrmacht, or German army.

In 1935, Hitler removed the veils from his rearmament programme, displaying his modern aeroplanes to the world in public aerial shows. He negotiated a treaty with Britain that allowed the Germans to build surface ships equalling 35 per cent of the tonnage of Great Britain's Royal Navy. Even more shocking (at least, from today's vantage point) is that the British agreed to allow Hitler to develop a submarine force, even though that single type of warship, used with deadly effect against merchant shipping in the Atlantic, had almost brought them to their knees during the First World War. By the 1930s, submarine technology had advanced by leaps and bounds – modern U-boats would be larger, have longer range and carry much more lethal weaponry than their relatively primitive First World War predecessors.

The truth was that Britain, and France as well, remained traumatised by the memories of the First World War. Both western democracies were afraid of Soviet power, and were also occupied with increasingly restive colonies in Africa and Asia. The leadership of neither nation was in any mood to confront an immediate threat, or even to admit that one could exist in the very heart of war-torn Europe.

However, that threat existed, and it was growing stronger every day, every week, every month and every passing year.

Hitler didn't really like Berlin, because most of the people there were not on his side. The communists were the most popular party in Berlin before Hitler came to power. He came to the city and had his office there because he was chancellor, and that's where the government was, but he preferred to be in Bavaria. He had a beautiful house there which he liked to use for most of his business, and we all thought that he didn't want to have anything to do with Berlin.

But he sure changed life for everyone in Germany. My father had been sick with lead poisoning for a long time. He couldn't work and they wanted to operate on him, but he wouldn't let them. So he stayed at home and my mother took care of him.

When the Nazis took over, there was no more welfare, no unemployment money. They told my father he had to go to work. Fortunately, he was good at lots of different things, even though he wasn't strong. He went to work in the Berlin city parks, taking care of gardens, so he had a job again.

The city sent him a letter before he could get that job. They made him prove he was Aryan, and that he didn't have any Jewish blood. He worked raising plants, like flowers, that were used for celebrations that the Nazis had. Then later, during the war, times got harder and they used those gardens to raise carrots, salad and potatoes. For a while my father was able to keep a few potatoes that he brought home to us. The rest of the food they grew they sent to the hospital, which was a good thing.

The other thing my father did with his little garden was raise tobacco. He was addicted to it! Our whole apartment smelled of tobacco so much that it was terrible. It wasn't just the tobacco smoke: he would hang the leaves all over the apartment to dry them out. To this day, I still can't stand the smell of tobacco.

The Nazis were really careful to find out about where you came from, and who your ancestors were. I had a little schoolbook that I had to sign saying I was Aryan, and I did. But I was also supposed to sign it 'Heil Hitler' and my mother wouldn't let me do that.

My mother was a Jehovah's Witness. We all know about the Jews in the concentration camps, but did you know they sent Jehovah's Witnesses there too? Hitler hated the Jehovah's Witnesses, because he said his Reich would last a thousand years, and they said, 'No, the world is not going to last that long.' So he had them put in camps, if they found them. But they never found out about my mother.

My mother got sick the same month that Hitler took over. That was a hard year for my family. She went to the Jewish Hospital for a little while. That was a great hospital, and it was right in our neighbourhood. She slowly got better, over a few weeks. She came home, but she was still weak.

But then a month or two later my little brother Gerhard got sick, with scarlet fever. By this time, the Nazis were really in power. My mom went to take him to the Kinder Hospital, but by then Hitler had kicked all the regular doctors out, and replaced them with Nazi doctors. They were young and inexperienced, and they didn't know what they were doing.

So these Nazi doctors took all the sick little kids and they moved them to a hospital very far away, on the other side of Berlin. They put the patients in a huge room all together. My mother was afraid Gerhard was dying, and she couldn't even go to see him. It cost too much money to get a ride, and one time she walked, but she had to walk the whole day to get there and come back.

One day I remember I was sleeping, and my father woke me accidentally by talking loudly to my mother, upset and saying that an angel had flown in and told him that Gerhard had died. My father and my mother got dressed and said they had to go to the hospital. I was only 6 or 7 years old, but I was there alone, or I guess with my little brother Paul, about an hour later when the police came and told me that Gerhard had died. I still remember that his funeral was on 8 June 1933, which was not even half a year after Hitler had taken over the country.

My brother was the first one dead in our family that my mother blamed on Hitler. She said, 'How can you put all the sick kids in one room?' Those doctors didn't know anything!

And you couldn't go and talk to the doctor, not in those days. They didn't give a damn what you thought – the only thing that mattered was what they thought. The next one to die was my cousin, one of my father's sister's daughters. She was 10 years old, and she had blood poisoning or something, but the doctors couldn't figure out what it was, so she died.

Then my great-grandmother died, and then my grandmother Catarina died. And not long later an uncle died. He was a *Loetse*, a harbour pilot who guided ships in and out of port. He worked up by the North Sea, in Bremen I think, but his wife lived in Berlin so he came home to see her often. He got very sick, with a terrible fever. They put him in a room in a hospital, with a nurse who was supposed to watch over him. But he opened the window and – I think he was so sick he didn't know what he was doing – he jumped out and died.

– Charlotte Jacobitz

A Public Face

By the third year of Hitler's reign, he had already engineered massive changes in the way Germans lived, and their nation was governed. He was making plans for a war of aggression against Poland and, eventually, Russia, while developing a strong enough military to stand against any possible challenges from Germany's First World War foes in the west, Britain and France. However, he was not ready to reveal these intentions to the rest of the world.

One key event allowed the Third Reich to present its best face to the entire world, when the Olympic Games were held in Berlin, in late summer 1936. The city had been selected for the event in 1931, well before the Nazis came to power, but Hitler and his henchmen embraced the opportunity provided. In preparation for the event, many of the overt images of the Nazis' harshest policies were carefully hidden. The signs forbidding Jews from entering public places were (temporarily) removed, and all the Gypsies that could be located were rounded up and moved to a special camp to keep them out of the way. A great stadium was dedicated, and Hitler paraded for the international masses, welcoming them as a gracious host.

Government officials put on a full-court public relations press to assure the many journalists and luminaries who came from around the world that Nazi Germany was undergoing a happy renaissance of productivity, peacefulness and culture. Behind the scenes, however, Jewish and other non-Aryan athletes were banned from participation on the German team; those barred included Gretel Bergmann, who just a month before had equalled the German national record in the high jump. Goebbels proclaimed that 'German sport has only one task: to strengthen the character of the German people, imbuing it with the fighting spirit and steadfast camaraderie necessary in the struggle for its existence'.

One of the most acclaimed athletes at the event was the African-American Jesse Owens. Though Hitler privately expressed the opinion that those athletes whose ancestors 'came from the jungle' had an unfair advantage and should be banned from future competition, the Führer was in the stands during many of Owens' outstanding performances in the track events. Ironically enough, Owens and other black athletes had the freedom to ride public transportation around Berlin and to enter any nightclub or hotel they chose to attend at a time when these freedoms were not available to these men and women in much of the United States.

I didn't start school until I was almost 7 years old. For some reason I was really afraid of going, even though 6 was the usual age when you started. To try and get me to go despite being scared, my father used his whole vacation, two weeks, to take me to school every day for the start of the term. He would stay in the back of the room all day, each day, but I told him I wouldn't stay if he wasn't there.

On the last day of his vacation, I still wouldn't change my mind. He put me over his knee and paddled me, right in front of the whole class! That was really unlike him, but he must have been really frustrated. I can't blame him. He only got two weeks of vacation in a year, and he used them to get me to go to school, and I wouldn't go!

But the next year, I started, even though I didn't want to go. My teacher was really nice to me, and she helped me become a very good student, which I was for the whole time I went to school. She would give me a penny from her purse, at first, when I stayed in school all day. Later on, she even bought me a flute.

I became a very good student, but I always worried about making mistakes, so much so that I became kind of a perfectionist. I would worry myself sick when there was going to be a test. My classmates couldn't understand that – they all expected I would still get the best grades in the class. But my teachers were kind of hard on me, because they knew I could do good work. I remember one time I wrote a ten-page essay. Of course, I wrote with a fountain pen, which I had to dip all the time, and there was no way to fix mistakes. I did an almost perfect job, but I made one mistake, and my teacher rebuked me: he asked, 'How can you be so stupid?' right in front of the whole class. There was another girl who made something like twenty mistakes, and he never said a word to her!

One of my favourite things was writing, and I used to write long stories and essays just for the fun of it. I don't remember too much about when the Olympics came to Berlin, except that in school we all had to learn to draw those five rings, the Olympic symbol, until we got pretty good at it.

We had a neighbour named Max Sprengel, and he was crazy about Hitler. He looked kind of ridiculous. He grew a moustache just like Hitler's, and wore a uniform that was too big for him – the tunic and pants would just hang off of him because he was kind of a little person. He was always going to Nazi meetings, and he would give the 'Heil Hitler' salute every time he saw me or anyone from my family.

His wife, Frau Sprengel, was a friend of my mother's. They lived in the same building as we did. The two women referred to each other in the familiar form – they used '*Du*' instead of '*Sie*' for the word 'you', which meant they were really good friends. Herr Sprengel wanted me to call him 'Uncle Max', but I could never bring myself to do that.

Still, he wasn't as bad as he could have been. He knew my mother was a Jehovah's Witness, and they used to argue – he would try to get her to become a Nazi, she would try to get him to be a Witness. He could have gotten her in big trouble if he had turned her in, but he didn't. There was also a man named Erich on the top floor of our building. We all knew he was half Jewish, but he never got turned in either. I think he hid out later during the war, and he got tuberculosis and died right after the war ended.

One of my friends, named Vera, was really fond of Hitler. I remember she told me once that she loved Hitler more than she loved her own father. I couldn't believe that, but she said it was the truth.

– Charlotte Jacobitz

There were lots of signs and banners to be hung during the Olympics, and my father got a lot of those jobs. He was really busy during that time, and his company made lots of money.

Because of Hermann being in that kayaking club, I was a big fan of the rowing events. My brother Hermann, as a matter of fact, was an alternate for one of the German crews, though he didn't actually compete in the Olympics. Still, he was that close to being an Olympian.

At that same time, I was in the Hitler Youth, which all boys had to join. It was every Saturday, and also Wednesday nights. Saturdays were called *Staatsjugendtag*, which means 'State's Day for Youth'. I was only about 10 years old, so I didn't have to work or build the *Autobahn* or anything. But they did make us march and drill, and told us all how great Hitler was. They said Germany was going to be the greatest country in the world, and we were all going to be a part of it.

– Helmut Jacobitz

3

A Nation Resurgent

I saw that she was crying, one day, and I wondered why, so I asked her why she was upset. She said that the Nazis had made her go to a doctor, and that he had done an operation on her so that she could never be a mother.

'I wanted to have babies!' she told me. That just about broke my heart.

– Charlotte Jacobitz

Shortly after the conclusion of the Berlin Olympics, in October 1936, Adolf Hitler signed a treaty with his fellow dictator, Benito Mussolini. The Rome–Berlin Axis created a bastion of fascist territory across central Europe, though for now the two nations did not share a border because Austria and Switzerland intervened. Mussolini's aggressive eyes looked south, where he desired to control significant parts of North and East Africa, including Libya and Abyssinia (modern Ethiopia). He also had territorial ambitions in the east, including Albania right away and, later, Greece. Mussolini wanted to create a modern version of the Roman Empire, and desired control of most, if not all, of the Mediterranean Sea. Il Duce's territorial avarice made him a perfect accomplice when compared to Hitler's similar intentions toward so many other nations of Europe. (At least, he seemed like the perfect accomplice, until Italian military forces proved incapable of matching their dictator's extensive objectives.)

At about the same time as he signed the Axis pact, Hitler revealed his military power to the rest of the world in a series of stunning developments.

Single-wing aircraft designed by Willy Messerschmitt, most notably the sleek all-metal fighter designated as the Messerschmitt Me 109, were displayed to aviators from around the world. The Me 109 set a new speed record for an aeroplane, a development that must have been alarming to Britain and France. Still, peace and appeasement remained the orders of the day in London and Paris.

At the same time, the Führer announced that the German army was expanding to thirty-six combat divisions. As if to prove that the Versailles Treaty was dead once and for all, he sent many of those divisions marching into the previously demilitarised province of the Rhineland – German territory, to be sure, but territory that was supposed to remain free of any military presence. The Führer's own generals opposed this move on the grounds that France would certainly intervene; and when there was no objection from Paris, the influence of those reluctant generals was again curtailed in the light of Hitler's audaciously successful gamble. In fact, when Britain and France made no effort even to challenge this complete violation of an important Versailles provision, Hitler felt comfortable throwing off the shackles of that punitive agreement for good.

In addition to single-seat fighters, German aircraft companies began to design an array of modern military bomber aircraft. Drawing on the extensive experience of the civilian airline, Lufthansa, companies such as Junkers, Heinkel and Dornier introduced fast twin-engine bombers, with skins of sheet aluminium, not the fabric that had been the standard coating on older designs. The Junkers Corporation modified its reliable civilian airliner into the Junkers Ju 52, a ubiquitous military transport that would serve the Third Reich on all fronts during the Second World War.

Germany also copied a new tactic that had been developed by American aircraft designers and pilots, primarily within the US navy. During the 1930s, the Grumman Corporation introduced a series of small bombers, single-engine planes typically crewed by a pilot and a rear gunner, that could plunge seaward (or earthward) from high altitude at a very steep angle and deliver individual bombs on to targets with unprecedented accuracy. The 'dive-bomber' would become a staple of the American and Japanese navies because of its efficacy in striking ships at sea, but the Germans put the concept to a whole new use. Employed mainly by a clunky-looking aircraft produced by Junkers, the Ju 87, Luftwaffe dive-bombers would terrorise opponents on every battlefield in Europe during in the early years of the war. The Ju 87, more commonly known as the Stuka, was ungainly, slow and under-armed; but with its pinpoint accuracy it was also lethal against a fixed enemy position.

Nor did the Nazis neglect the development of armoured fighting vehicles, including not just tanks, but half-tracks, armoured scout cars and other vehicles required for mechanised warfare. These initial models were not the powerful armoured behemoths like the later Panther and Tiger panzers of Second World War fame; instead, the Panzer Mark I and Mark II were small, light vehicles. The Pz1 didn't even have a cannon in its turret – it was armed with a heavy machine gun. Yet when these early-style armoured vehicles rolled into action against Poland and France, their speed and relative immunity to rifle fire rendered them into terrifying and successful weapons of modern war.

The German military also made plans, unlike anywhere else in the world, for the effective use of these modern machines. Though banned by the Treaty of Versailles, during the 1920s and early 1930s, the German General Staff and War College had not disappeared so much as they had gone underground. With the blessing of the Nazis, they emerged into the light of day and immediately began to develop plans and concepts for the next war. Inspired by brilliant tacticians and strategists, like General Hans Guderian, the father of modern armoured warfare, the Wehrmacht concentrated its tanks and half-tracks into panzer (armoured) divisions, in which the entire large formation was capable of moving quickly and delivering a powerful and explosive punch. No other nation's military would take this step in any significant way until the German offensives of 1939 and 1940 proved the dominance of armoured formations on the modern battlefield.

The Germans were also ahead of the curve when it came to co-ordinating their air forces with their ground forces on the battlefield. Indeed, the whole series of Luftwaffe bomber designs was crafted with the intent of quickly delivering ordnance on to a precise enemy position. This stood in stark contrast to American philosophy, especially during the pre-war years, as the United States Army Air Force (USAAF; the air force was part of the US army until 1947) formed its operational plans around a vast fleet of massive four-engine 'strategic' bombers, machines suited for plastering an enemy city into rubble, but ill-designed for nimble use in the support of ground troops.

Even in the mid-1930s, it seems apparent that Adolf Hitler had clear ideas about the kind of war he wanted to fight. The lessons of the First World War were ingrained deeply: he knew that Germany could not afford to fight and could not prevail in a protracted war of attrition, especially one in which the nation faced enemies both to the east and the west. The German economy was not structured to handle such a war; Germany's supply of natural resources was much more tenuous than its rivals'; and Germany's potential enemies were many and lay to every side.

So the Führer planned accordingly. His goals, most specifically the need for *lebensraum*, were immutable. However, they could not be obtained through peace. He recognised that war was inevitable. Every fibre of the national industrial plant was directed toward this goal with laser-precision focus and absolute central control.

Additionally, Adolf Hitler wanted to make certain that Germany would fight his kind of war. He viewed this tactic as bold and decisive, a gambling style that was capable of providing dramatic victories even as it entailed massive risk. He thought of the new method as a 'lightning war'.

The world would come to know it as blitzkrieg.

The Nazis, when they came to power, needed a lot of signs, and flags, and posters — and they wanted them hung way up high. So my dad was the guy they asked to put all those signs up. They would have signs and flags all along the route of a big parade, and my dad would hang all of that stuff. He had a lot of people working for him, but he himself would do the jobs where he had to lash the ladders together and put something up really high. He never seemed to be afraid of heights.

He was making a lot of money doing it, too, since they would pay him for twenty-four hours straight some times. There was a lot of work just putting up all the banners and flags, and my father needed a large crew to help him do that. But then he'd have to keep a few guys, and himself, on the payroll during the whole march and celebration, in case something came loose and had to be repaired. Many times those events lasted far into the night, with all the Nazis getting together to drink beer and champagne. Then, the next day, my dad needed a big crew again to take everything down.

But when they told him he had to join the Nazi Party or lose all that work, he wouldn't do it. The Nazis were angry about it, even told him that the Führer himself was mad, and if my father didn't join the party he wouldn't get any more pay from them. The guys that worked for my dad were pretty upset too, because they liked the work and the income. Maybe some of them sympathised with the Nazis, I don't know. But my father still wouldn't join the party, and he told his workers to go find another job if they didn't want to work for him.

And of course the Nazis told him, 'Okay, we'll find someone else to hang the signs.'

They got the fire department to hang many of the banners for a big parade, but there was one tower on the city hall that was too high up even for the fire department.

The city hall was a huge building, about four stories high, but this tower was in the middle of the roof and extended really far up from rest of the structure. There was another small tower at the very top of the flag tower, almost like a steeple, and even with the fire department's longest ladders and biggest trucks, they couldn't get up to the base of that top tower, much less the top. And of course, the party needed to have their banner hanging from the very highest place on the parade route.

The Nazis came back and told my dad they'd pay him to put the flag up on that really high tower, since he could reach it by putting his ladders together like I described earlier. But he said, 'No. You either pay me to put up all the flags, or none of them. I won't do just that one. Give me the whole job, or nothing.'

They didn't like it, but they finally gave in. My dad got a lot of work from them, and he hired a big crew every time they staged a march (which was a lot), but he never joined the party.

I was still a young kid, going to school, but my brothers had to go to work. Hitler made everybody work – and if you didn't have a job, you had to go pick hay. Other guys they put in labour camps and work corps, where you had to build the *Autobahn*, or work on army bases and new airfields. There was a lot of work going on in the country during those years, with construction happening in the cities and out in the farm fields. People had money to spend again, and to many folks it seemed like times were good again.

Hermann went to work for the Heinkel Werkes Company, making aeroplanes. That was a good job, not only because he got paid well, but because it kept him from being drafted. I guess the Nazis needed aeroplanes even more than they needed soldiers! Heinkel made lots of types of planes, but the two most famous were twin-engine bombers. They looked kind of strange, almost like giant bugs, because they had nothing but glass around the front of the cockpit.

My other brother Karl, I don't remember too well, but he was kind of a lazy bum. He was supposed to build signs, to help my dad, but he just did some work for a different company hanging them. So one day my dad came home drunk and tried to kick Karl right out the window. My mother told me to go get Hermann, which I did, and he came and made sure Karl didn't go out the window.

But my father kicked him out of the apartment. I didn't see him much after that. I don't know what he did before the war, except I know he had a girl-friend he wanted to get married to. But he couldn't do that, either.

And even before the war started, we knew things were going to get tough. They gave us ration cards, for bread and meat, even things like soap. My mother must have guessed what was coming, because she was saving those pieces of soap. They were tiny pieces, each one light as a feather. But my mother had it stored up when the war came.

– Helmut Jacobitz

First Moves

In March 1936, Hitler had put his militant words into action when he ordered troops of the Wehrmacht to reoccupy the Rhineland. Between this event and the start of the Second World War in Europe (1 August 1939), the leaders of the other powerful nations in Europe, most notably France and Britain, had many opportunities to stand up to the Nazi leader and stop him in his tracks, short of igniting a war. Until the very outbreak of hostilities there remained a significant likelihood that a united and determined Allied front against Hitler would have emboldened German military leaders such as Colonel General Baron von Fritsch and General Werner von Blomberg to initiate a coup that would have ended the Nazi regime and prevented the Second World War.

Unfortunately, all of those opportunities slipped by with scarcely a notice or a second thought. Hitler had gained a sense of his enemies' level of resolve when he sent his troops into the Rhineland and French leaders Pierre Laval and Édouard Daladier gave voice to only a token objection. As Adolf Hitler drove ever closer to armed conflict, his highest-ranking military commanders grew ever more fearful of the course upon which their leader had embarked. However, the Führer's power was absolute, and these venerable soldiers never mustered the courage to stop him. It wouldn't be until 1944 that some German soldiers rebelled, and then it was a group of younger officers, not generals, who would try a desperate, doomed plot against their ruler.

Based on proximity – the two nations shared a long border – and military strength, France was best poised to resist her neighbour's belligerence and even to bring the Third Reich's expansion to a halt, but Britain also had reason to fear a resurgent Germany. Yet such resistance was nowhere to be found, even though in 1936 Germany had only begun the process of rearmament. The Third Reich as yet had no air force nor mechanised ground forces capable of facing an enemy, and even the German infantry units were not up to full strength, created as they were from units formed mainly of older survivors of the campaigns of the First World War. In contrast, France held a relatively strong military hand, with hundreds of thousands of trained troops and much superior strength in artillery.

However, France also felt reasonably safe behind a heavily fortified border, and the Gallic nation was Germany's clear inferior when it came to military spirit and daring. As events unfolded, Hitler used French timidity to justify many of his actions to his military leaders. Such was his power and charisma that few of his own generals questioned him, even though they feared that the Nazi dictator was leading the nation to disaster. A Wehrmacht high commander would later describe his colleague's objections as 'straws in the wind' when placed against the power of Hitler's will.

Hitler also played with great skill upon British, French and American fears of the growing power of Josef Stalin's Soviet Union. He managed to convince the western democracies that a Nazi Germany could be useful to them by serving as the strongest, best and perhaps only bastion against the advance of Soviet communism. The German ruler reminded them how the Soviets had nationalised industries, abolished private businesses and put an end to so many kinds of commerce – all ideas that were anathema to these devoutly capitalist societies.

With each subsequent success, the Führer would become more convinced of his own infallibility, and more aggressive in his behaviours, ambitions and plans. The German population remained deeply resentful of the Treaty of Versailles, even nearly twenty years later, and they increasingly united behind Hitler's explanations. Josef Goebbels, the Nazi Minister of Propaganda, kept repeating the same simple lies and racist rants, viciously attacking the Jewish people as the source of almost all of Germany's problems; Goebbels added, almost as an afterthought, that foreigners were to blame for everything else that was wrong with Germany.

Hitler soon articulated his goals in a specific plan, presented to his most influential advisers in a secret meeting on 5 November 1937. Finally he let them know exactly what he meant when he referred to the idea of *lebensraum*. He believed and proclaimed that certain lands belonged to Germany virtually as a birthright, and he would claim these lands by diplomacy, using the threat of military force – and the growing power of the German army – to persuade the foreign powers to let him have his way.

Among his targets were lands adjacent to the current German borders, where a great number of people of German ancestry resided. Austria was one such country, and one that was already sympathetic toward the resurgent German ideal. The portion of Czechoslovakia known as the Sudetenland, a border area in the west of that country, was another. And, of course, East Prussia would have to be physically reconnected to the rest of Germany, which meant that forces of the Third Reich must occupy the Polish Corridor and the city of Danzig. Further plans, already written but closely held as secret, included a war of conquest to seize the fertile growing regions of Poland and the Ukraine. Hitler also coveted the productive oil fields of Romania. He assured his generals that Britain and France would not go to war to protect these eastern realms, and he used the western democracies' passivity in the face of the Rhineland remilitarisation to justify his contentions.

These plans appalled the German generals who learned of them. To a man, they foresaw these schemes leading to the same result as occurred during the First World War – that is, a catastrophic defeat for Germany. However, as always, these fears were held privately, and even though a military revolt, once again, could have forestalled the Nazis, the German General Staff showed no more stomach than did France or Britain when it came to standing up to Adolf Hitler.

I did a lot of writing in school, and I really liked to make up stories, and do reports and essays. I guess I was pretty good at it; my teachers told me so, anyway. I was still getting very good grades, pretty much a straight 'A' report card every time. But I think I was aware that things were not good in Berlin.

One of my favourite styles of writing was fiction, short stories. I wrote a lot of these, sometimes not even for an assignment but just because I liked to do it. I'd show them all to my teacher.

She told me that she liked my stories, and that I was a good writer. But she had to ask me a question: 'Why do you always have someone die in your story?'

I didn't realise that I was doing that, but it was true. When I thought about it, there had been a lot of people from my family who had died in the last few years, all of them after the Nazis took over. My mother, and I think me, too, blamed those deaths on Hitler. I think I was putting that anger and blame into my stories.

The Nazis did so many things that were not fair, that were cruel even on the surface. Remember, we didn't know anything about what was happening in the concentration camps; but we did know that all the Jewish doctors were gone, and lots of shops run by Jews had been closed up. The newspapers, and that awful Goebbels on the radio, were always going on about how the Jews were to blame for everything.

But again, it wasn't just the Jews that the Nazis made trouble for. One of the saddest stories I knew happened to one of the girls from my school. She wasn't a really smart person, but she didn't seem like she was mentally handicapped or anything. She was friendly, and I liked her. I guess she was a couple of years older than me; I was maybe 12 when this happened, so she was about 14 or 15.

I saw that she was crying one day, and I wondered why, so I asked her why she was upset. She said that the Nazis had made her go to a doctor, and that he had done an operation on her so that she could never be a mother.

'I wanted to have babies!' she told me, and she started to cry again. That just about broke my heart.

They were starting to ration everything by then. We had cards for food, and even for new clothes, and shoes and things. My mother used to save up her coupons and use them to buy clothes for me, at least as much as she could afford, which wasn't an awful lot. She said she wanted me to 'look nice' for school. Later on, when I went to work during the war, she did the same thing for me.

– Charlotte Jacobitz

'Peace for our Time'

In March 1938, Germany laid claim to Austria, and overnight the country meekly accepted membership in the Third Reich and mastery by the Nazi Party. A great many Austrian citizens, still mourning the loss of the great Habsburg Empire, supported this regime change, which they called the Anschluss. Since the Austrians were, at least publicly, supportive of this takeover, there was no point in Britain or France resisting it – not that they were ready to take a stand against Hitler, in any event.

Austria was a key acquisition for the Third Reich because it provided a broad overland link between Germany and Italy. Now the Axis really did control the wide belt of central Europe, from German ports on the North and Baltic Seas to Mussolini's bases far in the south of the Italian boot, as well as the entire large island of Sicily.

It is probably true that some conservative leaders in both Britain and France actually welcomed the German military resurgence under Hitler. They still believed that they were more powerful than Germany, and that Germany would be foolish to go to war with the west. Even more significant, however, is the fear they felt for the growing muscle of Stalin's USSR. Germany was viewed as a significant obstacle standing in the path of Soviet westward expansion.

One lonely but influential voice trying to awaken the world to the Nazi menace was British Foreign Minister Anthony Eden. Prime Minister Neville Chamberlain's continued insistence upon appeasement infuriated him and he refused to be quiet about it. Eventually he became so irritating that Chamberlain, reportedly, ordered him to 'go home and take an aspirin'. Another dissenting opinion came from a venerable politician, formerly the First Lord of the Admiralty, Winston Churchill, who eloquently tried to raise the alarm about the spectre of Nazi power. However, Chamberlain was the leader of the Conservatives, and to this point he still had the support of a majority of the party's voters.

Eden finally had enough of Chamberlain and resigned in February 1938. The Prime Minister replaced him with Lord Halifax, who shared many of his leader's ideals. Halifax went to Germany and privately told Hitler that Britain understood the Nazi leader's challenges, and that, basically, the British government knew that Germany needed to do what was right for Germany.

Hitler clearly took away from this meeting the idea that Britain would not object to his ambitious plans, so long as Germany did not directly threaten British interests. This is not entirely what the British Foreign Minister was trying to communicate, but the failure to make clear even a little bit of the

British resolve was a catastrophic failure in diplomacy that certainly helped pave the way to war.

The Führer's next demand came in the late summer of 1938, when he declared to the world that the Sudetenland territory of Czechoslovakia must be returned to Germany. Unlike the Austrians, however, the Czechoslovakians didn't want to turn their lands over to the Nazis. Furthermore, the country had a large and well-trained army, and made it clear that it was willing to fight to retain its territory as established by the Treaty of Versailles. The Czechoslovakians appealed to Britain and France for help.

The western response was to schedule a conference with Hitler, to occur in Munich in September 1938. Chamberlain himself would attend, as would Prime Minister Daladier of France. Poland sent a delegation, as did a few other European countries. Not surprisingly, the Soviet Union was not invited to attend.

If the Czechoslovakians had expected support from Daladier and Chamberlain, however, they were rudely surprised. The two prime ministers instead decided to agree to Hitler's request – that is, they virtually handed over the Sudetenland to the Nazis – so long as the Führer promised that this time he really was finished making territorial demands. The Munich Conference, rightly, has gone down as one of the most shameful acts of appeasement in the history of international diplomacy. When Hitler agreed to turn over a small bit of the Sudetenland to Poland, even the Poles – very short-sightedly, it soon turned out – went along with his plans.

After the conference, Neville Chamberlain returned to Britain and ignobly boasted that he had attained 'peace for our time'. With its resonating reminder of Britain submitting to Nazi belligerence at Munich, the phrase remains one of the most ignominious remarks in the long history of the United Kingdom. Apparently, though, the Prime Minister was sincere for, despite the agitation of other British leaders such as Churchill, Chamberlain determinedly declined to initiate any upgrade in the woefully unprepared British military.

Despite clear evidence of the Luftwaffe's growing strength, the RAF remained constrained by a peacetime budget and lack of will or plans to begin the construction of a modern fighter force. Churchill and other conservatives, members of Chamberlain's own party, loudly protested this inactivity, but could not move the country any closer to rearmament. Meanwhile, the Luftwaffe and other branches of the German armed forces continued to flourish and grow.

In November 1938, the Nazis enacted a violent pogrom, or anti-Jewish assault, that came to be known as the Kristallnacht, named after all the broken glass that littered the streets following this nationwide orgy of vandalism, theft and looting. The alleged trigger was the assassination of a

German diplomat in Paris, by a Polish Jew whose family had been robbed and exiled from Germany with no possessions or money. Hitler himself authorised the pogrom, which extended across the nation and also through much of Austria. Members of the SA storm troopers and run-of-the-mill thugs were encouraged by Goebbels' announcement in a nationally broadcast speech, during which he said that 'demonstrations should not be prepared or organised by the party, but in so far as they erupt spontaneously, they are not to be hampered'.

Strict but secret guidelines were sent out to local leaders, ordering that non-Jews and foreigners be spared, but that any activities directed against Jewish homes, businesses and synagogues should not be interfered with. Nearly all of Germany's 200 synagogues were destroyed, as were more than ninety in Austrian Vienna. Some 30,000 Jewish men were hauled off to concentration camps, where many of them were tortured and thousands died. Further edicts, including the banning of Jewish children from public school and the complete shutdown of Jewish publications, set the stage for the Holocaust that would commence, lethally, in but a few more years.

The events of Kristallnacht were widely reported around the world, and provoked universal horror and condemnation. Himmler himself lamented the event as a public relations fiasco, no doubt because it proved the influence of his main rival, Goebbels. For the Jews of the Third Reich, it was the most stark and terrifying warning of Nazi intentions, and even more horrible events still to come.

Even by 10 March 1939, Chamberlain still believed that Europe was looking at a peaceful future. That was the same day that Hitler, barely six months removed from the Munich Conference, broke his promise by sending his army from the Sudetenland into the rest of the Czech portion of Czechoslovakia, which included the provinces of Bohemia and Moravia. The remainder of the country, Slovakia, was absorbed more gradually, but soon it, too, became cemented into the pre-war borders of the Third Reich.

It wasn't until 1 April that Chamberlain finally abandoned the appeasement policy. At that point he ordered that the British military begin preparing for war, as did Daladier in France. The RAF, finally facing the real threat presented by the Luftwaffe, began ordering modern fighter planes and training the men to fly them.

However, for much of Europe and the world, this rearmament would prove to be too little and too late.

We had a little stationery store in our neighbourhood, right around the corner from our apartment. It was run by a lady who sold cards, and paper, and lots of little gifts. I didn't realise that she was Jewish until the Kristallnacht, when these young men came by and smashed her window.

They were going to break in and steal her stuff, when my brother Hermann happened to be driving by. He stopped his car right in front of her store and got out and chased those Nazis away. Then he helped her pull down the metal shutter so that she could cover it up, and he stayed there in front of that store for a long time. No one else came by to bother her.

A little bit later, after it was over, she came by and brought my brothers and me little gifts from her store. She was really grateful. I wish I could remember what happened to her.

– Helmut Jacobitz

I was horrified by how crazy and violent the people got during the Kristallnacht. It made me cry, and made me very afraid of the people who were running our country. The Nazis were really out of control, and nothing seemed too awful for them to do.

My friend Vera, the girl who said she loved Hitler more than her father, was pretty shaken up when she saw all the damage that was done on the Kristallnacht. 'I just don't know how they could do that,' she told me. 'I don't know if Hitler is … I just don't know what to think.'

– Charlotte Jacobitz

4

Blitzkrieg

Sometimes you could talk to your neighbours about it, but even then you had to be careful. We had a neighbour who was put in a concentration camp for telling people that Germany was going to lose the war … When he got out, we used to ask him what was going on in those places, but he wouldn't say a word about it.

– Helmut Jacobitz

Hitler's first true military objective should have been obvious to everyone in the world who was paying attention. Poland had been a vexing thorn in Germany's side since the end of the First World War. Any person who looked at a map could see the Polish Corridor as a physical insult to Germany's border, with East Prussia off by itself along the shore of the Baltic Sea and the rest of the Third Reich sprawling to the west and south of the Polish state.

In fact, the existence of that corridor served Hitler strategically in two vital ways, one political, one military. In the first instance, the humiliating loss of German territory imposed by the Treaty of Versailles was an example that Hitler had long used to whip up his adoring crowds into a hysterical desire for vengeance. The corridor was clear, tangible proof that Germany had been wronged, and Hitler could argue that he was the man to right that wrong.

In the second case, the Polish Corridor ensured that the borders of Poland were virtually indefensible against an attack from Germany. East Prussia provided a base of operations north of that low-lying country, with no natural boundaries in the way of an attack. Germany proper lay to the west, and here, too, the border consisted of flat, frequently open ground, unfettered by natural military obstacles. Also, with the Nazi annexation of first the Sudetenland and soon afterward all of Czechoslovakia, the whole of Poland's southern border was now exposed to German attack. Although that border did include some ranges of rugged mountains, cruel fate had placed those mountains mainly outside of Poland, where they were of no use to the defenders. The effect made Poland resemble a fat morsel sitting between widespread German jaws – jaws that were eager to snap shut.

Poland had strong political disadvantages as well. The country took heart from the British and French guarantees made half a year earlier, when those nations told Hitler that war with Poland would mean war with them as well. Perhaps the Poles believed that pledge, but Hitler didn't. He was certain that the Western Allies would stay on the sidelines while he made yet another territorial grab. The British and French, furthermore, made that pledge not because they were ready to go to war with the Third Reich – they most definitely were not – but because they naively thought the threat would deter Hitler from his chosen course.

One final, brutal truth put the last nail in Poland's coffin: less than a month before the war, Nazi Foreign Minister Joachim von Ribbentrop arranged a secret treaty with his Soviet counterpart, Vyacheslav Molotov. The two dictatorships agreed not to interfere with each other's operations as they divided Poland between themselves; the pact covered every detail, right down to the establishment of a new border.

A last dirty trick opened the conflict: the SS put Polish army uniforms on convicts, and ordered those convicts to attack a German radio station near the Polish border. The convicts blew up the station before being killed by SS troops, and Goebbels loudly broadcast the lie that an aggressive Poland had invaded a peaceful Third Reich. The falsehood was so transparently blatant that it would have been laughable, except for the long and tragic conflict that would follow.

The war started with a surprise attack at dawn, on 1 September 1939. Air strikes against the Polish air force were the first order of the day. Poland began the war with a force of some 200 fairly modern warplanes; yet by the end of the first day virtually every one of them was a smouldering wreck, bombed on the ground before flying a single mission. By the second and third day of the war, with the enemy air force a complete non-factor, the Luftwaffe concentrated its attacks on the Polish rail network.

The well-trained, courageously led Polish army was not an inconsequential force. Numbering nearly a million combat troops, it was a proud and confident military, having soundly trounced its opponent – Soviet Russia

– in a brief war in 1920. In that conflict, a Polish offensive had pushed the Russians all the way to Minsk before the fledgling Red Army capitulated. Now the Poles boasted that they would do the same to the Germans, with some officers believing that their elite cavalry force would be able to ride all the way to Berlin.

However, a lot of truths about war had changed in the last twenty years, and the Poles had not kept up with the times. They had no armoured vehicles, no anti-tank or anti-aircraft weapons, and relatively weak and immobile artillery. The vast bulk of the army relied upon feet and trains to move around. As the officer corps believed in offensive war, the Poles had made little attempt to fortify their borders. They had no permanent defensive installations, and even disdained the trenches and barbed wire that had proven so effective in the First World War.

When the Germans attacked, their panzers sliced through the immobile Polish infantry and plunged quickly into the heart of the country. Of the sixty German divisions participating in the attack, only nine were motorised or armoured, but these were the formations that essentially won the war within the first few days of the campaign. With their rail network destroyed by bombing from the air, the Poles had no manoeuvring capability, and their large army was quickly reduced to isolated pockets. Some of the Polish cavalry got into the fight, but the futility of sword-wielding horsemen riding against tanks quickly, and fatally, became obvious.

Fifteen days after the German invasion, the Red Army attacked Poland from the east. By that time, the Nazi spearheads were closing in on the capital, Warsaw, and over the next few weeks the infantry finished the job, destroying the surrounded pockets of the defending army. Warsaw capitulated at the beginning of October, and by 5 October, thirty-five days after the invasion, Poland was conquered and that part of the war was over. The new style of offensive war, employing concentrated armoured formations and tactical air forces fighting in close co-ordination with the ground troops, had been a stunning success. It was this revolutionary approach that earned it the new name blitzkrieg.

From October 1939 until mid-spring 1940, the war between Germany and the Allies went through a lull that came to be known as the Phoney War, or, mockingly, '*Sitzkrieg*'. The western democracies had essentially remained passive while Germany gobbled up Poland. Though France and Germany shared a long border, and the large French army was poised along that line, the French had only made a tiny, very tentative advance of a few miles into German territory. At a time when the vast bulk of the Wehrmacht was occupied in overrunning distant Poland, the French army had no stomach for even the most limited of offensive operations.

When Goebbels came on the radio and announced that Germany had gone to war with Poland, my mother immediately started to cry. I asked her why she was so sad. She said, 'This war is going to be terrible, even worse than the last one!'

Of course, she turned out to be right. But at first all the news about the war was good. Everyone seemed to be excited about it, at least when you met them in public. Boys who were 14 or older were trying to volunteer to join the army. Everyone at school was supposed to give the 'Heil Hitler' salute. My mom didn't want me to do that, though, so I didn't.

I know I mentioned that my mother was a Jehovah's Witness. She joined that religion after my little brother Gerhard died, in 1933. She would be talking to these other people who were also Jehovah's Witnesses, and they were supposed to go around and convince other people to join. That was dangerous, because the church was outlawed.

My mom didn't do that part of it too much, but even so I was worried that she belonged to that religion. I didn't believe in it myself – there were too many strange things they thought were true, like the world would end on a certain day, and that only a certain small number of people were going to be allowed into heaven.

It was about when the war started when I noticed they were even passing laws about the language. Maybe they'd started that earlier, but that's when I became aware of it in school. Hitler wanted to 'purify' the German language, like he wanted to do the same thing with everything else about Germany I guess. So they started to ban words that they decided had come from French, especially, but also English and other languages. It seems kind of silly, but that's how much they wanted to control how everyone thought, and talked.

And still Hitler remained popular, not just with people like my neighbour Max Sprengel. My own grandmother, my mother's mother, lived on a farm in Pomerania, which was north, near the Baltic Sea and also near the Polish border. She used to keep a picture of Hitler on the wall in her living room. My grandfather didn't think much of Hitler or the Nazis, but he didn't make her take it down. He just said, 'Ach, let her have her picture.'

– Charlotte Jacobitz

Hitler Turns West

As soon as Poland was conquered, the Germans rushed hundreds of thousands of soldiers across the country to garrison the border in the west, while the Western Allies didn't even try to interfere with these movements by air. Gradually Britain put together a field army, the British Expeditionary Force, and shipped her men across the English Channel to northern France. From their position on the border with Belgium, the British troops were not even adjacent to German positions.

In fact, the Low Countries – the collective name for Holland, Belgium, and Luxembourg – were in a very awkward position. These small states bordered Germany, and stood squarely across the expected invasion path of the Nazi armies. Yet their two influential monarchs, King Leopold in Belgium and Queen Julianna in Holland, worried about antagonising Hitler, so they would not even allow their military staffs to engage in combined planning with the Western Allies. This was a lack of communication that the Nazis would exploit to the fullest.

To be sure, France's entire war strategy was predicated on the defensive tactics that had proven so effective in the Great War. The nation had expended millions of francs, by far the majority of her military expenditures, to create the Maginot Line. This was an extensive network of pillboxes, trenches and many virtually impregnable fortresses that lined the entire border between Germany and France. The French felt, with some justification, that an enemy attack would have almost no chance of penetrating the Maginot Line.

The flaw in the plan, completely apparent to Germany, was that the Maginot Line only extended halfway to the English Channel. The French had not wanted to antagonise Belgium by fortifying that mutual border, so the northern half of the front would be defended by infantry, not defensive emplacements. The German General Staff knew they couldn't go through the Maginot Line, but by pushing through Belgium they could certainly go around it. The Western Allies intended to counter this threat by moving their troops into Belgium at the onset of hostilities, but, as stated, they had to make this plan without co-ordinating their intentions with the Belgians themselves.

The only significant land warfare occurring in Europe between October 1939 and April 1940 was a limited war in the far north – and it didn't even involve Germany. After the proud Finns refused Stalin's request for territorial concessions in the area of Leningrad, the Soviet Union invaded Finland in December 1939. In what appeared to be a colossal mismatch, the outnumbered, outgunned Finns literally skied circles around Soviet tank columns. The initial Red Army formations were repulsed with heavy losses; it wasn't until Stalin committed vast reserves to the assault that the Finns capitulated. They gave up some territory, including land adjacent to Leningrad and some key islands in the Gulf of Finland. What they took away from the 'Winter War' was a grudge against Russia that would come back to haunt the Soviets barely two years later.

The Soviets gained another benefit from the short, violent struggle in the northern forests. Stalin had executed many of his best officers during his paranoid purges of the 1930s, and the stunning defeat early in the campaign may well have alerted him to some key weaknesses in the Red Army command structure. Furthermore, the experience his troops gained in fighting a war under brutally cold winter conditions would become key to stopping Hitler's advance at the gates of Moscow in December 1941.

Hitler remained as audacious as ever, sending his forces into Denmark and Norway in a sudden onslaught in April 1940. Denmark, connected to Germany's north coast, was an easy target and fell after one day of fighting. Norway, theoretically, should have been a virtually unassailable target to the Third Reich, given the Royal Navy's vast superiority of strength, but German audacity, a surprise attack and some new tactics, including parachute attacks (see Chapter 5), allowed the Nazis to prevail there.

The real explosive power of the blitzkrieg was demonstrated for all the world when German forces, arranged in three massive army groups, attacked Holland, Belgium, Luxembourg and France on 10 May 1940. This campaign was one of the truly revolutionary convulsions in all of military history, changing the political landscape and the whole understanding of modern warfare, over the course of six bloody weeks.

Lost in the bloody memory of the First World War is the fact that, in the initial month of the war, Germany very nearly defeated France by launching a powerful invasion through the Low Countries and sweeping southward toward the great prize, Paris. Heroic French resistance at the Battle of the Marne (September 1914), notable for the fact that Paris taxicabs were mobilised to race troops to the very nearby front, halted the Germans outside the capital. Within another month both sides had entrenched, creating the muddy stalemate that would last until 1918.

In 1940, the German planners believed that armoured spearheads and close air support would give the attack enough extra punch to attain the glimmering city of Paris. However, after a flying officer – carrying the complete plans for the invasion – was forced off course and had to land in Belgium, the Nazis feared that their plan had been compromised. A daring young staff general, Erich von Manstein, conceived of a new plan, one he called *Sichelschnitt* (Sickle Slice). Instead of wheeling through the Low Countries and charging south, the Germans would slowly attack Belgium and Holland in an attempt to lure the Allied armies into those countries to defend the front. At the same time, the great concentration of the German panzer formations would sneak through the rugged Ardennes Forest of southern Belgium and Luxembourg – a section of the front expected to be lightly defended because of the hilly terrain and narrow, winding roads.

The sickle would then cut north, not south, striking all the way to the English Channel and cutting the Allied armies in two. The plan was adopted, and some 2.5 million German troops made ready to attack. They were organised into 104 infantry divisions and nineteen panzer and motorised divisions. They faced an enemy that, when Belgium and Holland's combined million men were added, actually outnumbered the attackers.

Furthermore, the French in particular had much larger and more powerful tanks than the Germans, and more of them. However, with the exception of one armoured division commanded by General Charles de Gaulle, all of the French armour was dispersed through the infantry formations. The defensively minded General Staff viewed their tanks more like partially mobile pillboxes than speedy weapons of attack. The Germans did have superiority in numbers of aircraft and in aircraft quality. The best Allied fighter plane was the British Spitfire, but the RAF was determined to keep most of those planes at home, for defence of Britain in the event such a battle became necessary.

The attack commenced on 10 May, only a few hours after Neville Chamberlain, realising he'd lost the confidence of his people and his government, had resigned, to be replaced as prime minister by Winston Churchill. In the pre-dawn hours of that day, the Germans repeated their by now typical pattern of complete surprise and sudden aerial attack against the enemy air force. The Western Allies reacted exactly as the Germans had anticipated, moving the British Expeditionary Force and a number of large, slow-moving French armies into Belgium. The Germans advanced against that Allied front slowly and gradually. Meanwhile, the panzers, under the command of soon-to-be-famous generals such as Heinz Guderian, Erwin Rommel and Paul von Kleist, slipped through the Ardennes, easily brushing aside the light French cavalry forces that were supposed to screen the region.

The German tanks crossed the key defensive barrier of the Meuse River at Sedan and Dinant almost before the Allies perceived the danger. French artillery positions were pounded by Stuka dive-bombers, the aircraft equipped with sirens as an additional terrorising element, and the panzers raced for the English Channel. De Gaulle's French tanks made one counter-attack, and a British armoured brigade tried to interrupt the advance with an attack at Arras, but the German tide was unstoppable. Within twelve days (on 22 May) the panzers reached the English Channel, and the vast Allied force in Belgium was cut off and surrounded.

Here Hitler displayed an uncharacteristic bit of hesitancy, ordering – over the objections of his field commanders – the panzers to halt and regroup. Hermann Göring promised that his Luftwaffe would destroy the British trapped in the pocket, but RAF fighters made this impossible. Even so, the French and Belgian armies had no escape from the trap. Belgium surrendered on 25 May, and the French were completely cut off from their homeland. However, the British used the lull to evacuate hundreds of thousands of their troops, as well as about 100,000 French, from the beach at Dunkirk. These men left all of their equipment behind, but they would form the backbone of an army that would come back against Germany, eager for revenge, a few years later.

Yet Dunkirk, which was in fact a desperate evacuation, was the only bright spot for the Allies in this campaign. With remarkable skill and efficiency the Wehrmacht pivoted about from north to south, commencing a drive on Paris by 5 June. The ever-opportunistic Mussolini brought Italy into the war, invading southern France on 10 June. The hapless Italians met a setback, as six French divisions obstinately repulsed an attack by thirty-two Italian divisions; but everywhere else the French army simply disintegrated. The government surrendered on 25 June, and agreed to turn over 60 per cent of French territory, including the entire Atlantic and English Channel coastline, to the conquering Germans.

The goal that Germany couldn't attain in the four-year bloodletting of the First World War had been reached in less than two months of 1940. The primacy of the blitzkrieg was there for the whole world to see.

My father bought a store right after the war started, so we moved from Prenzlauer Berg to the Wedding neighbourhood, just a little west of where we had been. It was more a blue-collar section of the city, not as nice as before but not too bad still. We thought of my father's shop as a 'soap store' but it really was more of a general store; he did sell soap, which was expensive and hard to find, but he also sold some things like stationery and other stuff like you might find in a hardware store.

There was our store in the bottom and apartments above and behind – actually, there were two businesses in the building, since there was a pub right next to my dad's store. Right behind our building was a tiny courtyard, and then another building beyond that. Each building was three or four stories high – and there were no elevators, just stairs going up and down.

My dad was not the best businessman. I remember once he got into an argument with a customer and kicked the guy out, and told him never to come back. I don't recall what the argument was about. There was another lady, in the neighbourhood, who would look in the store when she passed. If my dad was in there, she'd keep on walking, but if someone else (like my mom) was working there she'd come in and shop.

We had food stamps, for rationing, already when we moved there. You still needed money to buy food, but the stamps told you how much of certain things you were allowed to buy. I remember because my dad knew a guy in a bar further away, and we used to buy food from him on the black market

– meat, and bread, too. My dad was one of his best customers. What he was doing, that black marketeer, was dangerous, too. If the Nazis had found out they might have killed him, and at least they would have put him in a concentration camp.

But we also got food from regular stores, as much as the rations would allow. Every once in a while my mom would give me stamps to go to the bakery, and we would have a cake or something good. They also rationed soap – you could only buy a little bit of soap at a time. Since we sold that, we had enough to use, but it was so expensive that we had to be careful about using it, just like everyone else.

People didn't talk about the war much, and never to strangers. You had to know who you were talking to. By then they had big signs in the streets and on fences: '*Achtung*! *Achtung*! (Attention! Attention!) The enemy is listening – keep your mouth shut!' and stuff like that.

Sometimes you could talk to your neighbours about it, but even then you had to be careful. We had a neighbour who was put in a concentration camp for telling people that Germany was going to lose the war. He was an astrologist, wrote a column of that baloney for one of the papers. He said to some of us in the neighbourhood that the war would be lost because of where the stars were when Hitler was born. Somehow the Nazis found out about that, and they put him in a concentration camp for a while. When he got out, we used to ask him what was going on in those places, but he wouldn't say a word about it.

That was how it was with lots of people who were sent to the camps. Sometimes, if they decided you were German enough – or if they needed you to do a job – they might let you out again. They must have told them something, scared them pretty good, because none of them would ever talk about it.

Everyone says the German people should have known what was going on in the concentration camps, but we really didn't know. We thought of them like penitentiaries. Remember, the newspapers and magazines and radio broadcasts were all controlled – before anyone could publish an article, or go on the radio, they had to have permission from Goebbels and the Department of Propaganda.

– Helmut Jacobitz

Blitz to the East

Hitler's true objective had always lain to the east of Germany. The Ribbentrop/Molotov Pact of 1939 had been a cynical attempt to buy time, and it had worked. During the latter half of 1940 and the first months of 1941, the Wehrmacht and Luftwaffe had been shifting their focus to the greatest prize in Europe: the USSR. Beginning immediately after the fall of France, the Nazis began shifting their men and tanks to the Eastern Front, commencing a build-up that would last almost exactly a year.

For the rest of summer, 1940, the Luftwaffe would maintain powerful bases in France. From these they would attempt to destroy the RAF over England, paving the way for an amphibious invasion of that island. Hitler had expected the British to quit after the fall of France, and was surprised and frustrated when they did not. Göring told Hitler he would break Britain's back by air attack, but – as when he had promised that the Luftwaffe would destroy the British pocket at Dunkirk – the obese Reichsmarschall proved incapable of backing up his boasts. The tenacious defence of the British fighter pilots won the day, memorialised by Winston Churchill's elegant tribute: 'Never in the field of human conflict has so much been owed by so many to so few.' It was the first setback for German arms, and foreshadowed the rest of the war, where the elite tactical air force of the Luftwaffe would prove incapable of waging a strategic war.

Nevertheless, Britain had never been one of Hitler's true enemies – in fact, he felt that his Aryan people had a racial affinity for the Anglo-Saxons. Also, the loss in the Battle of Britain did nothing to dissuade him from his most pressing goal: the conquest of the Soviet Union. As he turned the energy of the Nazi state toward this exceptionally ambitious endeavour, moving troops, massing panzer formations, building airbases over the last half of 1940 and the first half of 1941, it seemed that only one person in the world remained totally blind to the Führer's intentions.

That person was Hitler's fellow dictator, Chairman of the Communist Party of the Soviet Union, Josef Stalin. Amazingly, one of the most paranoid and vengeful men ever to stomp across history's stage steadfastly refused to accept the fact that the Germans were preparing to attack his nation. When his own intelligence officers presented him with damning information about Nazi intentions, he imprisoned them. When diplomats from Britain and, eventually, the United States brought him reports of the German build-up, he ignored them. Even when German deserters came across the border in the weeks immediately preceding the attack, he disdained to heed the warning; usually such deserters were summarily executed. As German panzers were rumbling into their starting positions for the attack, and German guns were being sited for the initial artillery barrages, Soviet supply trains continued to rumble westward, carrying precious oil and other resources to the Nazis as per the treaty that Ribbentrop and Molotov had signed in 1939.

On 22 June 1941, the Wehrmacht launched Operation Barbarossa, the greatest military operation the world had ever seen. Some 3 million men, in 162 divisions, embarked on the surprise attack in true blitzkrieg style, beginning with pre-dawn air attacks backed up by artillery, with the panzer spearheads moving out at first light. In addition to German troops, some 200,000 men from the Nazi satellite states of Finland, Romania, Hungary and Bulgaria joined in the attack. The German General Staff planned for a campaign that was expected to last about four months.

The Soviets had a massive army of their own, poised close to the 2,000-mile border, a front extending from East Prussia on the Baltic Sea to Romania on the Black Sea. Initial German successes were spectacular: within a matter of weeks some half a million Soviet soldiers had been captured, and vast territorial gains had been achieved. The panzers raced eastward, encircling huge pockets of slow-moving Soviet troops, while the German infantry came up more gradually, squeezing and wiping out these encircled pockets. At Minsk, Smolensk, Kiev and Odessa, Nazi arms won great victories, and the Russians fell back farther.

The first vast territory to fall under the German occupation was the Ukraine where, at first, many of the citizens welcomed the Aryan attackers because they viewed them as liberators from their hated Russian masters. This euphoria didn't last long, as the SS units came along behind the front-line units and began to gather up Jews, Gypsies, communists and anyone else deemed unworthy of life in the Third Reich. Still the Wehrmacht spearheads plunged on, by late summer and autumn closing in on Leningrad, and as autumn cooled off the steppes, they even stretched almost as far as Moscow itself. It seemed the Soviets couldn't stop the Germans anywhere – all they could do was sacrifice great numbers of men and yield up huge swathes of land.

However, somewhere along the way, even under the rosy glow of all these victories, the German commanders began to take note of several pertinent facts: firstly, the Soviet Union was a massive country – the Russians could give up a lot of territory and still have huge stretches of land at their backs; secondly, there were an awful lot of Soviet soldiers available to replace the men killed and captured in the earlier battles, as Stalin began transferring reserves of Asian troops from Siberia to the front against the Germans; and thirdly, as autumn turned into winter, it was going to get very cold indeed.

The German offensive made it as far as the veritable gates of Moscow – some advance scouts actually spotted the towers of the Kremlin in the distance – but then the Russian resistance stiffened. The German troops suffered horribly from frostbite and hypothermia – they had not been provided with winter gear, since the campaign was expected to be finished by October. The water that cooled their machine gun barrels froze; the oil that lubricated their tank and aircraft engines turned to solid sludge; and the vast momentum of the offensive ground to a halt by the beginning of December.

Then the Russians, for the first time in the campaign, attacked. They swarmed across the snows, seemingly impervious to the chill, wearing white cloaks that camouflaged them against the wintery landscape. The lessons the Red Army had taken from the Winter War paid off a hundredfold, as the Soviet soldiers embraced the cold and used it almost like a crucial and irresistible weapon of war. The blitzkrieg, for the first time in history, had been stopped, and after the end of 1941 Moscow would never again be in danger from German arms.

For a short time after the war began I was a printer's apprentice, when I was about 15, 16 years old. The Nazis required all boys of my age to show up for training. I forgot what they called it, exactly, but it was a special corps and after the war started you had to go there once a week. They made us march and taught us how to shoot rifles, and some other stuff.

After not too long of a time, maybe three or six months, the leader said to me 'You already know this stuff, so you can sign the paper to show you completed the course.'

'I can't sign it,' I said. 'I have to get permission from my parents.' So I took the paper and got away from them – I guess I was the only one of my group who got away. Because when you signed that paper, saying you had completed the youth training, that meant you were signing up to be in the labour force that was a part of the army!

So I was working for a while, but of course they did find me and bring me an order to join the labour force. Hitler had started that all the way back in 1933, to get young people off the streets. That part of the Nazi plan actually worked – there was no unemployment, and lots of stuff got built. You lived in a camp, and he had those guys building the *Autobahn* and doing that kind of work.

The camp was called the *Arbeitsdienst*. It was only for boys; they had the girls doing other work, on farms and in households in the cities. For us, it started out as like a drill club, but it pretty quickly turned into military-type training.

Once I was in the labour force they tried to train us, and a lot of those kids could do nothing. They had been sitting at home or else working in an office, just reading and writing, so they didn't have any muscles. It was different for me, because I had been hanging signs with my father since I was about 13 years old. I'd had to carry a lot of heavy metal pieces pretty high up the ladders, and it was hard work, so I was in good shape.

Even so, when they got us out for training, they made us run on sand dunes and that was even harder work. You put one foot down as you try to climb up that sand and you sink right back down again! The guys who were in charge were called Commandos. One time I was running as fast as I could, and the

Commando called, 'Down!' You were supposed to fall over and do push-ups or something, but I didn't hear him and kept running right over the top of the dune.

I just kept going. That was in the afternoon, and when we got in line for our supper the Commando found me and gave me hell for not listening to him. He told me he would give me twenty minutes to eat, and then I had to be outside with full uniform, rifle, gear and my gas mask.

That was the worst part, the gas mask. You had this little canister that went over your mouth and you had to breathe through it. It was a filter, and it was hard to get enough air. Now this Commando was mad at me, and made me run around with the gas mask on. So this is what I did: I took a little match box and put it inside the seal of the gas mask, by my cheek where he couldn't see it. So at least I could breathe a little better, and not have to suck air just through that damned filter.

But he made me run for a really long time. It was on an exercise field that was flat, but it was still covered with really soft sand so that you sank in, and it was hard to run. I remember one guy, one of those office workers, who was training with the rest of us during the day, and he fell down and passed out. It made me glad that I was at least in kind of decent shape.

I figured out that guy, the Commando, hated Berliners, and especially Berliners from the Wedding. He used to scream at us, and call us all worthless communists. Of course, that neighbourhood had had a lot of communists living there before the Nazis came, but it didn't any more. You'd have to be a fool to call yourself a communist while Hitler was running the country!

I was still in the labour force when they sent us to Poland, to a camp near the city of Bromberg. This was a part of Poland where a lot of Germans lived. We were supposed to be building roads and bridges and stuff, and sometimes they'd send us into the forest to spend a whole day cutting down trees with axes.

But mostly we got drilled to get us ready for the military. They taught us how to dig foxholes and to build bunkers. We also had a lot of physical training, like running. They did some marching training too, but that wasn't a really big deal.

That was my first time being in a country that Germany had conquered. We always had a day off on Sunday and I used to go into a bar and have a beer. There were a lot of Poles who hated us, but they didn't dare say anything. But there were also a lot of Poles who had German blood, and they were happy to see us. So that bar would seem almost like I was in a bar back in Berlin.

– Helmut Jacobitz

I was still a really good student, but my mother treated me like a little girl. She had that temper, and she would still try to beat me or spank me when she was unhappy. I hated that damned *Seibenstream*! I guess I was 14 when she got mad at me and raised it to spank me. I reached out and took it away from her.

I said, 'You are never hitting me again!' And you know, she never did.

When I was 12 years old I finished six grades of elementary school, and needed to be accepted to a middle school. I wanted to go to one of the better middle schools, because you could learn foreign languages like French and English, which I wanted to do. You had to have good grades to get into those schools, and I had the grades, but you also had to belong to the *Bund Deutscher Mädel*, which was a government organization, like the *Hitlerjugend* (Hitler Youth) but for girls.

My mother didn't want me to join the BDM, because you had to swear an oath to the Nazis, but she let me try it. I went the first day, and this harsh-looking girl in a uniform told me that I couldn't wear my earrings – she made me take them off! So I left after that day, and told my mother that I was never going back. Of course, that meant that I had to go to seventh and eighth grades in my old elementary school, not one of the nice middle schools.

I think my mother was secretly pleased by my decision, even though I didn't know right away exactly what I was going to do from there. I knew they were drafting girls of my age, and making them load ammunition for the army and for the Luftwaffe, and I was pretty sure I didn't want to do that.

So I had to figure out something else to do.

– Charlotte Jacobitz

Stalingrad

After the setback at Moscow, the Wehrmacht barely survived the long, sunless Russian winter. The cold season spanning 1941–42 represented a turning of the war's tide in several ways. In December, following the Japanese attack on Pearl Harbor, the United States declared war on Japan. Although President Roosevelt certainly would eventually have found a way to bring the vast might of the USA to bear against Germany, Hitler rather insanely made Roosevelt's job that much easier when he immediately declared war on the US, to show his solidarity to his fellow fascists in Asia. (Japan had joined the Axis Powers, allying Germany and Italy as a full military partner by 1940.) The Second World War was truly, now, a world war – in 1942 conflicts raged in Europe, Asia, North America, Australia (briefly) and Africa; on sea navies shed blood in the Atlantic, Pacific and Indian Oceans and their surrounding seas.

Somehow the Wehrmacht's tattered remnants on the Russian Front managed to hang on until spring. German factories pumped out tanks and aircraft, and more young men were conscripted to fill depleted ranks. Then, with the warming weather, the crucial Red Army advantage waned.

Hitler, with his generals' increasingly hesitant advice, revised his plans for 1942. Instead of aiming for Moscow, the Führer turned toward the vast southern steppes of Russia, lands fertile with food-growing regions. Even more important for the survival of the Third Reich, those lands provided a route to one of the most prolific oil-producing regions in Europe, the Caucasus region between the Black and Caspian Seas. (For Germany and Japan, maintaining access to oil resources was already a crucial key to victory.)

When the weather warmed, the Wehrmacht moved out, and for a time it was like Barbarossa all over again as German panzers rushed forward, slicing through any Soviet formations that dared to stand in their path. The Don and Dnieper, great rivers of the USSR, had proven to be scant barriers in the face of the Nazi advance. Now, the greatest and very nearly the last of these lay just before them.

The River Volga is the longest river in Europe. Along its eastern bank, far from the German border, lay the city that is now known as Volgograd. When Stalin became dictator, he changed the city's name to his own and it would become a city, and a battlefield, that would prove to be the final resting place for many German soldiers.

It was a place then called Stalingrad.

Like most of Nazi Germany's grand strategic choices, the decision to commit an entire army to the capture of Stalingrad, and to hold that army there until it was annihilated, rests squarely on Adolf Hitler's stooped and corrupt shoulders. The vast movement into southern Russia commenced in the early summer of 1942, and carried the weight of all of Army Group South, with assistance from Army Group Centre. A key component, the strongest attacking element, of that force was General Paul von Kleist's First Panzer Army, a tank heavy force with great mobility and striking power.

Hitler first assigned Kleist to use his tanks to assist General von Paulus' Sixth Army in the capture of Stalingrad, but the Führer soon changed his mind and sent the armoured columns south in the overly ambitious drive into the Caucasus. The flanks of the Sixth Army were thus protected by unenthusiastic and poorly trained Romanian troops, instead of German panzers.

Von Paulus made it into the city of Stalingrad in September, but there he became bogged down against furious Soviet resistance. His troops battled their way toward the Volga River as, block by block, the city was reduced to rubble. German artillery pounded the Russian positions while Soviet guns, east of the river, returned the favour. A massive tractor factory, now used to produce T-34 tanks, was turned into a fortress even as it continued to function – tanks would roll off the assembly line, out the doors and right into the battle. Almost as if he had blinkers on, von Paulus introduced all of his reserves into a fight that the enemy was determined not to lose.

In November, Stalin and his best general, Field Marshal Georgy Zhukov, closed the trap. Powerful Soviet tank forces attacked north and south of the city, breaking through the Romanian-held flanks and quickly surrounding all of the Sixth Army. For three more months the battle raged, as von Paulus' men struggled to survive in a steadily shrinking pocket. Adding to their woes, the Russian winter closed in as the battle raged through December and January. Just before the final defeat, at the end of January, Hitler promoted von Paulus to the rank of field marshal, and pointedly reminded him that no German field marshal had ever surrendered to the enemy.

However, there was no hope. Some 100,000 Germans finally capitulated, and even more than that had perished in the battle. Of the captives, 90 per cent of them would perish in Soviet camps. Germany would never again win a great battle, and though her forces would fight on until ultimate annihilation, never could the nation replace the quarter of a million men who had fought their final battle at Stalingrad.

After my father kicked him out, my brother Karl was drafted. I don't really know the details of what happened to him, except that he fought on the Russian Front. He hated it, and he deserted the army. He talked to Hermann about it a little, but he never talked to me, so I don't know what he experienced there.

He tried to get to Switzerland, on the train, and he got all the way to the border. I don't know how he did it. It was quite something to travel on the train under cover, and pretty surprising to get that far, especially for a deserter. The Nazis had guys on all the trains, checking papers and orders and stuff. They used to check me all the time whenever I rode a train, because I was tall for my age – they wondered why I wasn't in the army, and I had to show them I was only 14 or 15 years old.

Anyway, Karl got to the Swiss border, but the guard on the Switzerland side made him go back. They wouldn't let him into the country. It was known at the time that if you could get into Switzerland, they wouldn't send you back. But he got stopped before he could cross.

He knew he couldn't go back to the army. They would kill him as a deserter – they would probably have hanged him. Karl still had his gun, and when the Swiss wouldn't let him in, he shot himself. He didn't shoot the Swiss guard who was stopping him – he turned the gun against himself. Just like that, right there at the border. I forgot the name of the city.

He was alive for a few days after that, in a hospital, with a bullet in his brain. My parents and I went to see him. The doctors were very nice, but they said he doesn't have a chance to live. One doctor pulled me aside and told me not to do anything foolish when it comes to me going into the army.

'Just serve,' he said.

– Helmut Jacobitz

5

Fallschirmjaeger

I had to do six practice jumps to qualify, the same as everybody else. When you had finished your six jumps, you got an eagle to wear, like a pin. It was a pretty high honour; we knew we were special soldiers.

– Helmut Jacobitz

The idea of the parachute goes all the way back to the Renaissance, where it was sketched out by no less of a luminary than Leonardo da Vinci, about 1485. The first actual use of the device dates to the late 1700s, when several (obviously brave) Frenchmen demonstrated working parachutes in jumps from tall towers and hot-air balloons. The word itself comes from the French, the combination of the words *para*, meaning 'to protect', and *chute*, which means 'to fall'. These early parachutes were linen sheets stretched over light wooden frames.

By the time of the First World War, parachutes had been developed for standard use by the spotters who observed enemy positions from tethered hydrogen balloons. These observation balloons were immobile, highly explosive bags of gas that made tempting targets for enemy fighter planes, and by the middle of the war the spotters had developed the tactic of jumping out of their baskets and parachuting to the ground upon the approach of an enemy aircraft. The bulky parachutes were suspended in bags below the observer's basket; they were not 100 per cent effective, but the spotters who jumped must have preferred their chances with the parachutes to the odds of surviving an enemy fighter-plane attack.

By the end of the war, the Germans had developed a parachute much like the modern version. This device was worn by the pilot and had a reasonable chance of deploying if the airman was forced to leap from his plane. (Of course, there were plenty of times when they didn't work, so the jump required a fairly high degree of desperation on the flier's part.) The American military aviation pioneer, General Billy Mitchell, suggested the use of parachutes to drop soldiers on to a battlefield before the end of the First World War. It was an intriguing and revolutionary idea, especially because at the time no nation possessed the number and size of transport aircraft necessary to make this wild idea a reality.

In the 1920s the Italians developed the idea of the static line, in which the parachute of each soldier in a transport aircraft is attached to the aeroplane with that line. The static line pulled the parachute out of its harness while the soldier was still very close to the aeroplane. It allowed for relatively low-altitude jumps, with the additional advantages that it kept the men of a single transport fairly closely bunched when they came down, as long as they jumped out the door in quick succession. The static line also helped make sure that the parachute deployed as desired. The Red Army of the Soviet Union was the first military formation to experiment with large-scale drops, employing 1,000 and then 2,500 men in exercises in 1935 and 1936. The Soviet attempts were primitive, requiring the men to climb out of a hatch on top of the fuselage, then line up on the wings so they could all jump together; but the technique was shown to have real potential.

The first of these exercises was observed by none other than Hermann Göring, the former First World War fighter pilot who was now the ambitious Nazi in charge of the fledgling Luftwaffe. He was determined to create a force of soldiers that could attack from the air for the Third Reich, and he devoted energy and resources toward the creation of the German airborne forces, men who would become known as the legendary *Fallschirmjaeger*.

By late 1936, a battalion of Luftwaffe troops was undergoing parachute training; by 1940 such men would number a full division. Göring's forces were additionally fortunate to have a dependable, fairly long-range transport aircraft available. The Junkers Ju 52 was a familiar tri-motor design that cut its teeth as an airliner in the early 1930s, even before the remilitarisation of Germany. It would prove to be a reliable Luftwaffe workhorse throughout the war years – at least until Allied air supremacy drove nearly all of the Third Reich's aircraft from the skies.

Contrary to popular belief, not all airborne troops were trained to parachute on to the battlefield. The typical tactic, perfected by the Germans, had a limited number of elite troops land in a drop zone with the objective of securing an airfield. Once they had a place for planes to land, more airborne troops would arrive on the battlefield via transport aircraft. These troops could bring in more equipment than parachutists, including heavy machine guns, light artillery, motorcycles and other small vehicles. Airborne formations of every nation, however, were trained to operate without the support of tanks, trucks and heavy artillery. They would always be at a disadvantage when facing enemy armour.

The first combat employment of the *Fallschirmjaeger* occurred during the invasions of Denmark and Norway (9–10 April 1940). Paratroopers seized a Danish airport in the northern part of the country; that field was quickly converted into a Luftwaffe base, allowing Me 109s and other short-ranged aircraft to reach targets in southern Norway. German paratroopers also seized several key bridges in Denmark, helping to ensure that small country's conquest in but a single day.

The next day the *Fallschirmjaeger* gave clear proof of their value in the battle for Oslo, the capital of Norway. Lacking any land connection to that Scandinavian country, all German assault forces had to be transported by sea and by air. Oslo was a key objective, the target of a large force of troops carried by naval transport and a much smaller regiment of airborne troops.

The Norwegians had a small army, but they fought valiantly. Especially effective was the defensive shore artillery at Oslo Harbour – these guns sank the German heavy cruiser *Blücher* and damaged many of the transport craft. The amphibious assault was thwarted, the ships veering away to land their troops on more remote stretches of the Norwegian coast beyond the reach of the capital's garrison.

The target of the airborne assault was the main airport to the north of the city. The installation was defended by a Norwegian anti-aircraft unit, but they were quickly overcome by the sudden attack of the German paratroopers. Norwegian fighter aircraft shot down five transports before German fighters, based on the field in northern Denmark captured only the previous day, drove them from the skies. The first parachuting *Fallschirmjaeger* secured the airport, and a steady stream of Ju 52 transports began landing, carrying planeload after planeload of reinforcements.

These elite troops wasted no time in moving out on foot, bicycle and motorcycle, as well as on commandeered Norwegian transport, as they advanced southward into the city proper. The Norwegian capital fell less than forty-eight hours after the start of the invasion, as the port batteries that had proved so effective against shipping were little use against foot soldiers attacking from the land. With the neutralisation of the big guns, ships could use the port to land more men, supplies and heavier equipment than could be brought in by aircraft.

The same fate as Oslo befell Stavanger, another key port in southern Norway, where the German paratroopers fought a pitched battle with Norwegian infantry, finally prevailing after suffering heavy casualties. Another large port was available, and the Kriegsmarine (German navy) wasted no time in taking advantage.

The campaign in Norway would continue for many weeks as troops of the Wehrmacht moved slowly north through the narrow, mountainous country. The paratroopers had been crucial in the first days, but now they were withdrawn as this had become an infantry battle. Hitler's eyes, meanwhile, had already turned to the west. As the plans for the invasion of France and the Low Countries solidified, airborne troops were given several key missions, important objectives that must be seized within the first hours of the attack.

By this time the *Fallschirmjaeger* had been organised into the 7th Air Division, under the command of General Karl Student. By 10 May 1940, he had some 4,500 parachute troops under his command, organised into six battalions. He had a further 12,000 men organised as an air-mobile light infantry division – men that could be transported by aircraft to captured airfields.

The plan called for Student to deploy five of his six parachute battalions against Holland. They were dropped at the very outbreak of the campaign on the morning of 10 May, landing on their targets with complete surprise. One of these units parachuted right into the Dutch capital, The Hague, where they were tasked with capturing the Dutch government. Their arrival caused confusion and panic, but in the end the Dutch army rallied enough to protect the seat of government and almost to wipe out the audacious paratroopers.

The other four *Fallschirmjaeger* units in the attack on Holland met with much greater success. Their objectives were a series of bridges across the massive channels of the Rhine River – bridges that, if destroyed, could seriously impair the German advance. These bridges were located in the cities of Rotterdam, Dordrecht and Moerdijk, as well as several more important river crossings in the countryside. The German paratroopers secured each objective within a matter of hours, though in one place they had to put out the lit fuse on a demolition charge that was moments away from destroying a key bridge. After seizing the bridges, the *Fallschirmjaeger* held them against persistent Dutch counter-attacks for several days, until the advancing infantry relieved them, crossed the bridges and brought the Dutch campaign to an abrupt, final conclusion (14 May).

The remaining parachute battalion was to be employed against Belgium, and it would attain what was arguably the most important objective of any small unit in this momentous campaign. Belgium had a large army – numbering some 600,000 men – and a well-developed network of defensive installations, all designed to capitalise on the country's several wide water barriers. The most important of these was the Albert Canal, which connected the Meuse River at Liege with the huge Scheldt estuary at Antwerp. The key to the defence of the Albert Canal was the huge, modern fortress of Eben-Emael. This vast concrete edifice was studded with heavy artillery positions, and the guns in those emplacements had clear lines of fire over the key bridges crossing the canal. The fort was garrisoned by more than a thousand men, including anti-aircraft gunners manning batteries on the roof.

Most of the paratroopers in the Belgian operation were tasked with seizing the bridges over the Albert Canal, much as their comrades had done in Holland. However, these bridges were exposed to lethal fire from Eben-Emael. To solve this problem, a small force – seventy-eight men – was to land by parachute and glider directly on the roof of the massive fortress. They attacked at the outset of the campaign, and in a brief fire-fight overcame the anti-aircraft troops and secured the roof of the fortress; they suffered six men killed.

Once in command of the roof, they dropped explosive charges into the ventilation shafts and gun emplacements of Eben-Emael, fending off counter-attacks by the garrison troops for a full day, until the first wave of advancing German infantry arrived on the scene. Every one of the bridges was secured, and the Wehrmacht poured into the heartland of Belgium, having breached a supposedly impregnable position on the very first day of the attack.

The proof was there for anyone who wanted to see: parachute shock troops had come of age.

So I was in the labour force in Poland, and our training was almost done. We still worked with the pick and shovel, digging and building, but we'd also trained a lot with rifles. It was more military than labour training by then.

One day I got an order to join a bunch of my comrades in a big meeting room. There were maybe 200 or 300 of us in there, and a speaker from the Wehrmacht came in. He showed us movies and pictures, and talked about how great it is to fight for the Wehrmacht. Finally he said, 'Okay, everyone, now you should sign up.'

But I said, 'I'm not signing up, I'm going home.' Which is what I did. Of course, they told me I had to go back the next day and I knew enough to do what I was told, so I went. On the second day there weren't so many of us – all the guys who'd signed up for the army were gone. So now a guy from the Luftwaffe came in and talked about how great it was to fight for the Führer, to fly aeroplanes. But again I didn't sign up, and I was sent out with the other guys who didn't sign.

The next day, same thing, only this speaker was from the Kriegsmarine. He showed us pictures of ships and U-boats, and talked about how they were going to do great things against the English and the Americans. Then he asked everyone to sign up – and of course I didn't sign anything.

The last guy, on day four, was from the SS, and he talked all about the Nazis. He showed pictures, and he had the shiny black uniform. He told everyone who had signed up for anything else to leave, and I stayed. But when he passed around the sheet to sign up for the SS, I didn't sign it. There were only a few of us who didn't sign, and he came up to us and started hammering on us, shouting and furious.

'How come you don't sign up?' he screamed at me.

'I already signed up for the Luftwaffe,' I smarted off to him.

'What the hell are you still doing here?' he shouted. 'Get out of here!'

I was the only one who got out of that room without joining the SS. Imagine that!

But I wasn't ready to go into the air force yet, either. I decided to go home, and take a little vacation. My old boss had lots of work making signs, and he pestered me to come back and work for him. But I decided I would rather go and build aircraft. My brother had been doing that at the Heinkel Werkes for years, since before the war, and I wanted to do that too. He had worked himself up in the company, was pretty important and necessary, so he couldn't be drafted. I thought I would go there and, like him, be exempt.

But I was only there about three weeks when I got an order that was stamped 'Air Force' and I was told that they were putting me in the Luftwaffe. So they gave me a train ticket and told me to report. I was supposed to be there at 10 a.m., but I met a girl at the train station. I asked her which way to go and she showed me, but we were having such a nice time talking that I stayed around there for a couple of hours.

When I finally showed up for the air force, I was pretty late, and the guy there started screaming at me. 'Do you know what you're here for?' he shouted.

'*Ja*, to be in the air force,' I said. I was thinking that I was going to be one of those guys who takes care of the aeroplanes – we used to called them *Paupscheiner*, which means 'clean the pot'. I knew a lot about sheet metal from all that sign-making work, and of course there's lots of sheet metal in an aircraft, so it made sense. Plus I was reporting to this guy in a hangar, so I thought they wanted me to do maintenance work on aircraft.

'You're going to be a paratrooper!' that guy told me.

Well, I almost pooped my pants. But that's the way it was; and I couldn't do anything about it.

– Helmut Jacobitz

Pyrrhic Victory

Airborne operations had proven capable of yielding dramatic results in the campaigns of 1940, so much so that before the end of the year the US army took steps to form its own paratrooper force. Great Britain also began to train and organise airborne troops. In both Allied nations, the idea remained controversial, because of the aviation resources required, and also because there was a strong belief in the officer corps that the best soldiers should be scattered through the regular formations of the army, instead of being sectioned off into small, elite formations.

Lost in the debate was another key factor, which is that airborne operations had already proven to be exceptionally dangerous for the soldiers who were vertically inserted on to a battlefield. Almost by definition they would begin a battle already surrounded, behind enemy lines. Furthermore, because of the limits inherent in their transport, they would lack not just tanks and heavy artillery, but effective anti-tank weapons to defend themselves against counter-attacking enemy armour. Supplies, notably ammunition – which got used quickly in a fierce fire-fight – had to be carried in by the tenuous aerial supply line.

As 1940 moved into 1941, however, stark demonstrations of these lessons still lay in the future. The German *Fallschirmjaeger* still had one key campaign to fight, one great victory to win. By spring 1941, Hitler's plan for the invasion of the Soviet Union – the campaign that would for all intents and purposes determine who won the war – was well under way. However, the Führer had to deal with a vexing situation in the Balkans, on the southern front of his intended campaign, that demanded German attention.

For all of his pomp and speechmaking, his stylish uniforms and his early leadership of the fascist movement, Benito Mussolini's Italy was proving to be a rather inept ally when compared to the mighty Nazi war machine. The Italians had been routed by the British in Egypt and Libya. In early 1941 that situation had been stabilised when Hitler dispatched General Erwin Rommel, soon to be known as the Desert Fox, and a division of German tanks to Libya. By May, Rommel's Afrika Korps of German panzers and Italian infantry was restoring Axis primacy and driving the British back toward Alexandria and Cairo.

However, Mussolini had further aggravated Hitler by starting a war with Greece, a war that pitted the relatively modern Italian army and air force against a much smaller Greek force equipped with obsolete equipment. It should have been a short, sharp war with Italy triumphant, but over the winter of 1940/41, the stubborn Greeks refused to follow the script. By spring, not only had they kicked the Italians out of Greece, but they were now advancing into the Italian territory of Albania, the base of Mussolini's Balkan operations. Without German assistance, it began to look as though Il Duce's men would suffer a catastrophe.

The independent and thus far neutral nation of Yugoslavia stood between Germany and Greece, but Hitler wasn't one to let a detail like that slow him down. He decided that he needed to secure his southern flank before the invasion of Russia, so he authorised the invasion and conquest of Yugoslavia to be followed by the swift overrunning of Greece. The campaign was quick and successful, bearing all the hallmarks of the now perfected blitzkrieg concept. Large and mountainous Yugoslavia was attacked by surprise, as usual, and occupied in eleven days (6–17 April). Greece held out another ten days, only long enough for Churchill to rush British troops from Africa to Athens, where many were captured and the others had to be immediately evacuated.

Most of the evacuated troops, British and Greek together, were moved to the large island of Crete, perhaps a hundred miles south of the mainland. There they presented a powerful base for naval and air operations, a bastion in the eastern Mediterranean Sea that posed a clear threat to Rommel's operations and to Italian control of that great body of water. Hitler wanted that threat removed.

Like Norway, Crete presented a military objective that the Wehrmacht could not reach via overland attack. Axis naval operations in the Mediterranean were the province of the Italian navy, the most modern of Mussolini's three branches of service. Of course, the Luftwaffe, flying from newly captured bases in Greece, could project air cover as far as the island. Consequently, the Germans drew up an assault plan calling for an airborne attack on the island to be coupled with an amphibious landing of German troops transported by the Italian navy.

The combined British/Greek force on Crete consisted of about 40,000 men under the command of New Zealand Major General Bernard Freyberg. A squadron of RAF fighters on the island was forced to withdraw under tremendous pressure from the Luftwaffe, but in late April and early May the Allied troops worked frenziedly to prepare Crete's defences, expecting attack both from the sea and the air.

General Karl Student remained in command of the *Fallschirmjaeger*, which had been expanded to become the XI Airborne Korps. The lead formation remained the 7th Parachute Division, which had achieved such fame against Holland and Belgium. The assault began on 20 May, with parachute attacks against the three main airfields on the island. All three attacks suffered heavy casualties, and failed to attain their objectives against the alert defenders.

However, at one airfield, Maleme, the *Fallschirmjaeger* managed to establish a perimeter near the installation, and the next day Student brought in the rest of the 7th Division for a parachute drop. The landing troops suffered heavy casualties but enough troops survived to gain control of part of the airfield. Student sent in his next reinforcements, the air-mobile 5th Mountain Division, in a desperate attempt to hold the position. Many transports were shot down on the approach, and the rest landed under intense enemy fire, often crashing on to the field.

In the meantime, an attempt to deliver reinforcements by sea was utterly destroyed by the Royal Navy, as an Italian convoy met interception by British ships, resulting in the loss of some 5,000 German troops. Braving intense air attacks, the British ships maintained control of the waters around Crete, preventing any Axis troops or supplies from reaching the island by sea.

However, the *Fallschirmjaeger* around Maleme were aided by relentless ground attacks by the Luftwaffe, and slowly Freyberg's troops were pushed back. With the airfield finally secured, more supplies and men came in by air, though the Luftwaffe's force of transport aircraft had been savagely depleted during the campaign. Many of Freyberg's men were finally evacuated to Africa (28–31 May), though some 12,000 men were taken as prisoners by the Germans. The 7th Parachute Division lost about 6,000 men, something like half of its strength, in the fight.

The capture of Crete was the first purely airborne offensive operation in history. Though it ended in success, the extent of the losses was so extreme that even Adolf Hitler – never one to care excessively about the welfare of his men – was too shocked ever to authorise another airborne attack again. From here until the end of the war, the *Fallschirmjaeger* would be used as well-trained, highly motivated infantry.

So I found myself in the paratroops. At first I had a few months of training with the rifle and other weapons. This was in early 1944, so I had just turned 18. But I also had to learn how to jump out of aeroplanes, even though we knew we didn't have any aeroplanes left, at least, not enough to send a bunch of paratroopers anywhere. Most of our training included marching. They'd make you carry your pack and your rifle and everything, and then train by marching sometimes as much as 50 kilometres, like 35 miles, in one day!

But they taught us how to hook up our parachutes to a static line, which is like a D-ring attached to a cable inside the aeroplane. It's also attached to your parachute, so when you jump out the door, the line pulls out your parachute, which is the one that keeps you from breaking your neck.

The worst part is you are jumping from a plane up there, and down below there are guys shooting at you. You can't hide! So you'd have to fly as low as possible, which for us was about 80 metres (250 feet). You have just a few seconds in the air – by the time your 'chute opens you're like 20 or 30 metres above the ground.

They spent a lot of time teaching us how to land, too. You were supposed to stay on your feet and take a couple of steps, forward or backward, when you landed. If you fell you had to get right up. They were always working on that – you had to keep your feet together. If they get too far apart, maybe one hits a rock or something, and then you fall and break your leg. You could roll backward, or forward, or sideways. But you had to get right up. The only time you stayed lying there was if you broke your leg. And that didn't happen very much.

After you got up they wanted you to run around your parachute in a circle to flatten it down – if it was windy, and your 'chute fills up with wind, it can pull you pretty hard, knock you down and drag you somewhere you really don't want to go. If you were just a little unlucky, you'd never get up.

I had to do six practice jumps to qualify, the same as everybody else. When you had finished your six jumps, you got an eagle to wear, like a pin. It was a pretty high honour; we knew we were special soldiers.

It turned out that I was pretty lucky when we were done with that training. It was, I don't know, about March or April of 1944. There was the Russian Front, of course, where most of the German army was. That was terrible, especially in the winter. It was really far from Germany, but we knew the Russians were coming closer. The Russians and the Germans, they really hated each other, and if you were captured they would probably kill you instead of put you in a camp.

Also there was fighting in Italy. That had been going on for about a year, since the Germans had been pushed out of Africa by the English and Americans. Italy had quit the war, changed sides actually to join the Allies. The Italian people caught Mussolini and his wife, or maybe his mistress, I'm not sure. But they hung them upside down and burned them to death. Anyway, the German army took over the war in Italy, and they were holding back the English and Americans pretty well. After a year, they hadn't even made it to Rome, which is only about halfway up the Italian boot.

But by then we were also expecting the English and the Americans to come ashore somewhere in France, and we were pretty sure this was going to be a huge attack, like the start of a whole new war. We had that whole coastline to defend, and didn't know where they were going to come, but we knew it would be somewhere. So I was sent to join a parachute battalion near Brest, in the very far west of France. That's in the province of Brittany, the part of France that sticks out into the ocean on the north-west corner of the country.

Rommel, the Desert Fox, was the commander of all our troops in France, and General Student, who had always been the airborne commander, was still in charge of the *Fallschirmjaeger*. We knew that we would fight as infantry, then, though some of the old-timers (there weren't many of them left) talked about the earlier battles where they had jumped out of aeroplanes. That was back when the war was going well for Germany.

The French coastline was pretty well built up, but it was a very long coastline, including the whole English Channel and even down the west coast, on the Bay of Biscay. There were lots of pillboxes and dugouts with machine gun nests, and a lot of German troops all over the country. But it was hard to prepare, because we had no idea where they were going to land.

And we kept up our training, and waited for the invasion to come. Being in France was sort of like being in Poland – the people didn't want us there, but they didn't really say anything. Actually, if any Frenchman opened his mouth to complain, they arrested them right away – the Gestapo or the SS would.

Of course, the Nazis were really mean to everyone. People were careful not to do anything around those guys. I know that they had an underground in France, but from what I saw it wasn't much. The Nazis, like the Gestapo, were watching everything and everyone.

So most French people acted kind of neutral. I tried to learn a little of the language, but I wasn't there very long and didn't have a chance to learn much. I do remember one guy, in a village where I was staying, he knew some German and he talked to me. It was in a pub. He said that he thought the German soldiers were mostly decent. I agreed with him, said they were mostly decent, but you always have creeps no matter where you go.

But it was true that we were ordered to behave humanely, like civilised people. If you did anything wrong to the French people the army would put you in jail. That guy agreed that we Germans were behaving okay. Of course, he was fairly friendly to me while we were talking, but inside who knows what he was really feeling?

– Helmut Jacobitz

6

Bull's Eye on Berlin

Two Jehovah's Witnesses came to my house a couple of years ago, and they wanted to preach to me. I told them I knew all about it. And they said, 'No, you don't!' They tried to scare me with stories of Armageddon. And I said those stories wouldn't scare me any more. 'I've seen Armageddon,' I told them. 'I've been there.'

– Charlotte Jacobitz

Even before the start of the Second World War there were generally understood to be three important combat missions for a military air force. The first of these was to establish air superiority – that is, to have an active and dangerous force of high-performance fighters or pursuit planes that could shoot down enemy planes and eventually drive the enemy air force from the skies. The second mission was tactical ground support, during which aircraft attack enemy ground troops in support of friendly ground operations. The third is strategic bombing, attacks that seek to weaken an enemy's ability to make war by undermining national infrastructure, industry and civilian morale. (Two other missions, aerial observation and air transport of troops and supplies, were also performed by brave fliers in military aircraft, but they are not considered 'combat missions' for purposes of this analysis.)

The first mission had been developed and refined during the First World War. Both the Allies and the Germans had built many types of fighter planes during the Great War, and the aerial duels waged by the brave fliers of these rattletrap machines created perhaps the only quasi-romantic images of that dire conflict. Flying aces such as Baron Manfred von Richthofen (the Red Baron) and the USA's dashing Eddie Rickenbacker became national heroes.

In the period between the wars every nation sought to build higher-performance fighters with the understanding that this mission would continue to be important in the foreseeable future. Biplanes made of wood, with open cockpits and skins of fabric, evolved into sleek metal monoplanes, with glass canopies to protect the pilot from the elements. At the start of the Second World War, Germany's Me 109 and the British Spitfire were generally regarded as the best fighters in the world. The front-line fighter of the USAAF at the time was the Curtiss P-40 Tomahawk, which was considerably slower and less manoeuvrable than the most modern European types. In 1941 Britain and the United States would learn, to their dismay, that the Japanese Zero was another high-performance fighter belonging in the first rank of the world's pursuit aircraft.

The tactical ground-support mission was attempted with only limited success in the First World War. Both sides had used aircraft to shoot at and bomb enemy troops on the ground, but limitations on munitions and aircraft performance prevented these early efforts from yielding any dramatic results. Still, these missions had the worthy objective of supporting land operations, and because their potential was recognised they became at least a part of every major nation's aerial strategy as the Second World War approached. These missions were initially tasked to single-engine dive-bombers and twin-engine medium bombers, though eventually many fighter planes were also rigged to carry small bombs for this purpose.

The third mission was recognised by a few visionaries, and neglected by many others. This was the strategic-bombing task, which required heavy, long-range bombers capable of carrying a lot of high explosive or incendiary ordnance. Strategic bombing, for the first time, allowed a nation's military to strike at an enemy's industrial heart and civilian population without resorting to the indirect pressure of a blockade, or the often unattainable necessity of a physical invasion. The Germans made the first tentative steps toward strategic bombing in the Great War, employing both lighter-than-air Zeppelins and twin-engined biplane bombers to fly to Britain and attempt to disrupt port facilities and other industrial centres. These efforts were too small and scatter-shot to do much damage, but they seriously terrorised the civilian population of Britain; and in light of this experience, 'terror-bombing' became a part of every air force's doctrine.

As the Third Reich rearmed during the 1930s, the Luftwaffe took shape under the leadership of Hermann Göring, a modestly accomplished fighter pilot in the First World War. The Germans put great emphasis on the first two missions, designing and building high-performance fighters and fast tactical bombers, but neglected to create a long-range force of heavy bombers.

The air forces of Great Britain and the United States were established and developed with different fundamental objectives than the Luftwaffe. The Germans viewed their aircraft as an important adjunct to the army. The western democracies, under the leadership of bombing advocates including Air Vice Marshal Harris in Britain and General Carl Spaatz of the United States, placed a lot of emphasis on the strategic bombing mission. Of course, they also developed high-performance fighters as well, but they were much slower than the Germans when it came to co-ordinating the use of tactical air forces with the activities of army units on the ground.

The stunning success of the Luftwaffe in the early stages of the war should be evident by now. However, during the Battle of Britain, in August and September 1940, German fliers suffered their first major setback of the war. This was, in great part, because Göring was trying to use a tactical air force for a strategic mission – the destruction of the RAF within its own country. The Battle of Britain was decided basically as a battle of fighter forces for air superiority; the main purpose of the German bombers was to serve as bait to draw the British fighters into battle, since they lacked the size and bomb capacity to seriously disrupt factories and major infrastructure. Each fighter force fought valiantly, to the utter limits of its men and machines, but eventually Fighter Command of the RAF prevailed.

Of course, there are a number of advantages inherent to an air force flying over its homeland: downed pilots that parachute to safety can fly new aeroplanes instead of become prisoners of war; aeroplanes can fly more and longer missions because they don't need to account for the time and fuel needed to reach distant objectives; machines that crash-land can possibly be repaired or at least cannibalised for spare parts; and the developing science of radar, introduced by Britain in 1940 but used extensively by Germany afterwards, allowed a nation to recognise when an enemy air raid approached and gave it the opportunity to allow its fighters to challenge (or avoid) it as necessary.

Each of these factors helped the British in 1940. Later, the same advantages would transfer to the Luftwaffe as, from 1942–45, it fought a valiant but ultimately losing struggle to control the skies over Germany. By that time, it was the Allied air forces that were taking the war to the enemy homeland. It would be a long and bloody campaign, costing the lives of countless fliers – and impacting the lives of virtually everyone living in a German city.

Britain, isolated on her island, had no means of striking against the German homeland by naval or ground forces. However, under the guidance of Air Marshal 'Bomber' Harris, the United Kingdom was committed to raining destruction on the German homeland to the maximum extent possible. Very quickly, the British learned that unescorted bombers were easy prey for enemy fighters, if those fighters could see their targets, so the British adopted the tactic of night raids, a plan they would carry throughout the rest of the war. As early as May 1942, Harris amassed a force of 1,000 heavy bombers, and sent them on a raid against the massive railroad yards at Cologne. This attack did serious damage, significantly disrupting German supply and manoeuvre.

The Americans, in the meantime, had joined the war in Europe by the start of 1942, but took most of that year to build up their bomber strength. Operating from an increasing number of huge bases in England, the US 8th Air Force cut its teeth on raids against German-controlled ports in France, Belgium and Holland, as well as other nearby targets. Unlike the British, the Americans had designed their heavy bombers with a great deal of armour protection; planes like the B-17 Flying Fortress and the B-24 Liberator also bristled with lots of machine guns. Factors like these enhanced the bombers' air-to-air combat capability, but meant that US bombers could carry significantly less weight in bombs than their British counterparts. Still, American doctrine called for daylight bombing raids, when specific targets were easier to identify and hit.

Originally it was intended that these planes would fight their way to a target during broad daylight, relying on armour and armament to fend off enemy attack while they employed advanced bombsights to make precise attacks. Throughout 1943, the Americans gradually built up to large-scale raids, but they lacked fighters with long enough range to accompany the bomber, and found that the guns and armour defence of even the heaviest bombers were insufficient to protect the planes from enemy fighters. Not only did the Luftwaffe still have great numbers of the old standby, the Me 109, but it introduced new, even higher-performance aircraft. Notable among these was the Focke-Wulf Fw 190; upon its introduction in mid-1943, it surpassed the Me 109, the British Spitfire and American types such as the P-38 Lightning and P-47 Thunderbolt in performance. Despite US efforts to focus its raids against aircraft factories, German industry continued to churn out fighters faster than the Allies could shoot them down, and the Messerschmitts and Focke-Wulfs made life in the skies over Germany very dangerous for any planes daring to fly there during daylight.

A long-range raid against the Romanian oil fields at Ploesti (1 August 1943) resulted in more than 60 of 178 attacking planes being lost; and a daylight raid that smashed an important ball-bearing factory at Schweinfurt (14 October 1943) resulted in 60 lost bombers and 140 damaged out of 288 planes taking place in the attack. These efforts were not sustainable – it was clear that the American air forces needed a high-quality fighter with long enough range to accompany the bombers on their missions, or they would be restricted to nearby targets or, like British Bomber Command, night-time raids.

Even as early as 1942, bombers would sometimes come to Berlin at night and drop bombs. My Aunt Dora had six children, and her apartment got destroyed in one of the very first raids on Berlin. She lived in the Wedding neighbourhood, the same area we lived. The government gave her money and a new apartment to replace what had been bombed out. Of course, they had to stop doing that after the bombing kept getting worse and worse. They didn't have the money or the goods to replace people's losses, and they ran out of empty apartments to put them in, too.

Sometimes, I had just hardly gone to bed and then the sirens would sound. We had to run down four flights of stairs to the cellar, and then wait for a long time. You never dared to undress, because you never knew when you were going to have to go running down there with everyone else in the building.

At first, the bombs were rarely close to where we lived. They didn't come that often, and it was only at night. It was more of a nuisance than a dangerous threat – at least, that's how it seemed.

Since I wasn't willing to go to the *Bund Deutscher Mädel* – the 'Hitler Youth for girls' school – I was sent to trade school. That was called the *Berufschule*, and it didn't have the academic classes, like the foreign languages, that were available in the BDM. Even so, my first teacher recognised that I had some potential because she encouraged me to sign up for an apprenticeship as a bookkeeper.

When I was 15, which was 1942, I started at the *Berufschule*. I was ready to take that apprenticeship, so I did that right away, which meant that I had to take bookkeeping classes both before and after school, as well as go to school all day. But I learned quickly, and found that I had a natural talent to handle columns of numbers, and before the year was out I was able to get hired as a bookkeeping apprentice at the Deutsche Bank, which was the central bank of Germany.

But right after I was hired I was drafted. The Nazis had women do things like carry ammunition to anti-aircraft guns, and they made me report to a draft centre. I stood in a long line to have my health checked. I was scared stiff, because I didn't want to carry ammunition, I wanted to work in the bank. A girl in line told me, 'Don't say you can't walk. Too many people say that to get out of it, and it just makes them mad.' But when I got to the front of the line, the doctor kept dropping hints to say I had trouble walking. Finally, I caught on, and told him I couldn't walk well, so he exempted me from service. I got back to the bank and my boss smiled at me and said, 'Oh, you were exempted? I had a feeling you would be.'

I worked at the main office on Mauerstrasse, which was a famous old building, a real landmark. It was a pretty eye-opening experience for a girl from Wedding, since it was right in the heart of the city. The Tiergarten Park was nearby, and the big avenue of Unter Den Linden went past not so far away either. A couple of blocks away was the Hotel Adlon, one of the great old hotels of Berlin, and the Brandenburg Gate.

At first, we didn't have to worry about bombers coming all the way to Berlin in the daytime, since the city was so far away from England, where they came from. But as the war progressed, they kept getting closer and closer. Finally they were bombing Berlin all the time.

I had been working there for a few months, in early 1943, when I got really sick in the stomach. It turned out I had appendicitis. They rushed me to the Virchow Krankenhaus (Virchow Hospital) which was named for the doctor who was the first man to open up a human chest while the patient was still alive. The beds were all full because so many people were being injured by the bombing, so I was operated on in the cellar. They didn't have any beds for me to recover there, and I was still pretty sick, so they put me on a lorry with some other sick people – it wasn't very clean, and it smelled like horse manure!

From there I went to the train station, where they said they'd send me to a hospital in Saxony to recover. It was a twenty-four-hour train ride. Mostly the hospital was full of wounded soldiers, so I was put in a ward with a few other civilians.

I was there for four weeks, and it was kind of a scary place. There was a lady who talked to herself, and was knitting all the time. She had a pair of men's boots next to her, and sometimes she would talk to the boots. Another woman just lay on her bed and laughed now and then. I remember at one point a man came in and took the boots away. The lady on the bed laughed out loud, and said, 'They're going to gas the boots!' At the time, I didn't have any idea what she meant by that, but the words stuck with me.

Finally I was well enough to take a regular train back to Berlin, and I went back to work at the bank. I was 16 years old, and trying to learn how to fit in to the working, adult world. In Germany, you used to say *Guten Tag* ('good day') or *Guten Morgen* ('good morning') when you greeted someone. Now, in the bank the official greeting was supposed to be *Heil Hitler*. But sometimes you could get away with *Mit Deutschem Grusse*, which means 'With German greetings'. That was the one I preferred to use.

The Deutsche Bank was an old building, as I said, and it was very large. They had elevators for clients and managers to go between the floors, but for us workers to go up and down they had this device called a paternoster. It was a series of little platforms, like small closets, that continually moved up one shaft and down another on a pulley system. Half of them would be going up and the other half coming down at any one time. They were always moving – they didn't stop at the different floors like elevators. You just stepped on and stepped off while it was still moving. It was scary!

You had to be smart about how you got on and off. You watched it really carefully, and you had to step just at the right time. When I had just started working there and I tried to use it, I usually missed it the first time and had to wait for the next platform so that I could try again.

When the bombing raids started to come to the city during the daytime, which was more like 1944, we had lots of alarms. Air-raid sirens would go, and people would head to shelters and bunkers. At the bank, they wanted us to take our typewriters down to the shelters with us. They were big, and heavy, too, those old office machines. So the men would take a table, and put like three or four typewriters on it, and then take the whole table down in the elevator. And we would ride the paternoster down to the street level.

But they wouldn't let us take shelter in our own building, I guess because it wasn't really a bunker. It was only half underground, and still had windows opening up out into the street. They would keep all the machines in there, but we had to go find shelter somewhere else. We were not even allowed to stay in the bank during an air raid.

The first place we ran was the Hotel Adlon, which was a huge building, and very sturdy and old. It was near the chancellory, where Hitler was a lot of the time. I heard that Hitler didn't like the Hotel Adlon for some reason; when he was in a hotel he always stayed at the Kaiserhof. Anyway, the Hotel Adlon had a basement, though it wasn't deep or secure, and on one of the early raids my girlfriend and I tried to get there in time, but it was already full. As more and more raids happened it always filled up before we could get there. They wouldn't let any more people in.

So next we ran to the train station, the subway. But that was so open. When you are in the station, down by the tracks, you can still see up to the sky. We could hear them shooting up there – it scared the heck out of us! We needed to find a safer place to take shelter.

The next time this other girl from the bank and I were running for a shelter. We were hurrying along when we heard these planes flying low, right over us, and we were the only people in the street. We stayed together against the wall, crouching down low, while these planes zoomed past. I still have nightmares about that!

And then the air raid was over, and we were about the last people to hear that it was all clear; people started come out of all these shelters. And we had to walk back to the bank and get all our stuff from the cellar to take it back up to where we worked. It was a bank, of course, so they wanted to make sure that everything was secure.

There was a Swiss man working there, at the bank. He had brought his family to Berlin with him, his wife and daughter. He could have stayed in Switzerland, but the bank paid him really well, so he came to work at the Deutsche Bank. Actually, there were a lot of people who came from Switzerland working there. Swiss bankers, I guess, really knew their business.

One day he didn't come to work, and he missed two more days before he finally came in. He said that he couldn't work – he was looking for his family. His apartment was bombed during the daytime, when he was working and he wasn't home. When he saw it, his family was gone, and nobody knew anything about them. He finally found the head – just the head – of his daughter; she had been 18 years old. He never found his wife. That was a terrible thing; I felt so bad for him.

– Charlotte Jacobitz

Raids with Range

Although the bombers themselves were clearly crucial to the bombing campaign waged against Germany from 1943–45, one could argue that the single most important aircraft type of the strategic-bombing campaign was the North American P-51 Mustang, a fighter. This splendid aircraft was a high-performance machine that, in manoeuvrability, speed, weaponry and other aspects, was the equal of the best-performing German piston-engine fighter, the Focke-Wulf Fw 190.

In addition to its exceptional performance in air-to-air combat, the Mustang could be equipped with disposable, wing-mounted fuel tanks. These provided the P-51 with a very long range, and by 1944 they were able to accompany the daylight bombing raids to targets as far from Britain as Berlin, and even beyond. Coupled with the vast manufacturing capabilities of the United States, fighters and bombers in almost inconceivable numbers arrived in Britain and formed massive aerial armadas carrying the war against German industries and cities.

By the beginning of 1944, 1,000-plane raids had become commonplace. In a brutal week of aerial battle during February, the Americans by day and British by night carried out devastating attacks against Leipzig, Regensburg, Augsburg, Fürth and Stuttgart. The Luftwaffe battled these raids ferociously; over the course of the week-long battle the Allies lost 244 heavy bombers and 33 fighters. However, the Germans lost nearly 700 planes in the air, with many more destroyed on the ground. Exerting further pressure on the Third Reich, the bombing attacks were again directed against German aircraft manufacturing-plants, drastically curtailing the production of new machines.

From March through to May, the Luftwaffe lost nearly 4,000 fighters. Though industry, under the tireless efforts of Minister of Armaments Albert Speer, somehow managed to keep up aircraft production under this rain of destruction, the loss of skilled pilots created a drain on the German air force that could never be replaced.

The strategic-bombing campaign experienced a brief hiatus between late May and July 1944, as the heavy bombers were diverted to supporting the massive invasion of Normandy, Operation Overlord (see Chapter 7). During the second half of the year, however, the aerial offensive built to a thunderous crescendo. Targets were shifted from the shattered aircraft factories to the oil industry and, later, the railroad network.

Of course, even daylight 'precision' bombing was very imprecise, and a terrible number of bombs fell upon residential areas and other non-military objectives. As for the British, their night raids could not be aimed very carefully at all, and Bomber Command was for the most part limited to striking crude and destructive blows against the general mass of German cities.

By 1945, only a few cities in the Third Reich had been spared these brutal raids. One of them, Dresden, was a historic and beautiful city in eastern Germany that possessed only limited military significance, but harboured numerous structures of great historical significance; in mid-February it was destroyed over two days of relentless day and night raids by both British and American bombers. At least 100,000 people perished in what remains to be the most destructive bombing attack in human history – a scale of destruction greater even than that inflicted by the atomic attacks against Hiroshima and Nagasaki later that year.

Germany, of course, was not giving up without a fight. During the last months of the war a new invention by the erstwhile aircraft designer, Willy Messerschmitt, arrived on the scene with the potential to change completely the balance of the air war. The Messerschmitt Me 262 was the first jet-powered fighter in the history of the world, capable of flying at speeds 200 miles per hour faster than the Mustang. If these jets had arrived sooner, in greater numbers, they could have wreaked havoc on the 8th Air Force and Bomber Command. As it was, they were too few, too short-ranged and too new – they suffered numerous teething troubles as pilots tried to master the new machines under combat conditions – to influence the outcome of the war.

One day we got only a little notice for the air raid. The sirens went off and we hurried downstairs and over to a nearby bunker we had found. This bunker had been built as an air-raid shelter, and it was two stories down. The bombs were already exploding by the time we got down there.

The whole building was shaking like a ship in the storm. There was this huge crash, and we knew a bomb had come down practically on top of us. It was right next door, but it didn't explode. At least, not right away; it was a time bomb.

Then it exploded and blew up the whole elevator. The bunker filled with smoke, and we had to put wet clothes over our faces just so we could breathe. You held the cloth right up to your mouth and closed your eyes, and even then you could barely breathe. So much smoke – I thought for sure we were going to die from it!

But someone found an emergency tunnel that went under the bank, and we stumbled along that and came out into the street. Only we didn't recognise it – the buildings were gone, and the street was covered in a bunch of boulders, the pieces of the buildings that had been knocked down.

We learned that the bomb had exploded in a public bunker, right next to our shelter. That one wasn't as well made as ours, it was only one storey down. They told us that 150 people died in there when that bomb exploded. And as far as I could see it was only smoke and ruins, and fire – there were lots of fires.

So I was afraid, of course. What happened to my mother? To our house? I went to the train station I used every day to go home, and it was completely gone. There was just a big crater in the ground.

I walked home, I think. I must have, but I can't remember how I got home. And as I went west, toward our neighbourhood, it got even worse. I couldn't tell the streets from where the houses had been, but I guess I knew which way to go.

When I got home, I found that in the front of my apartment building the whole street was on fire. They had used those fire bombs, and they were still burning even on the stone and the pavement. I learned later how those worked: they're a bunch of little bombs inside of a large container, and the container breaks open and scatters the fire bombs. When they hit, they explode into flames, and scatter around this gooey stuff [napalm] that burns everything it touches.

I couldn't come in or even reach the house that way. I went around to the back, and there were these huge horses closed up in our backyard, running around in a panic. I finally ducked past the horses and made it into the cellar, which was the bomb shelter for the building.

I found my mother and brother were okay, but my mother was really upset. She and my brother had gone to the house shelter when the bombers came, and they were trapped because of the fire in the front and these huge horses in our back yard. She didn't dare come out of there! It was a bizarre scene; the local dairyman had penned up his big draft horses in the yard, and they were terrified by the bombing and fire, ready to stomp on anyone who came near.

The Deutsche Bank had been destroyed in that raid, so when I went back to work there wasn't any place to go. A few days later they had several of us employees go over to the Reichsbank; the Reichsbank gave us some space to work, and we had offices there as 'guests'.

That lasted for only a little while, though. I guess it was about the start of 1945 when I tried to go to work one morning, and they wouldn't let anyone in. They said the Reichsbank had been bombed this time, even though it looked okay on the outside it was wrecked inside, so we didn't have a place to work.

There were houses and high rises, four or five stories, around that bank, and I remember that an aeroplane had crashed into one of the highest ones. It was still hanging there, up above the city. Maybe he was the one who had bombed it; I don't know. The whole house was broken, with the walls knocked down, but in this one corner there was a shrine for Jesus – they must have been Catholic – and it was still standing. People were looking at this picture of Jesus that hadn't been even damaged.

So I didn't have work any more. I know that was early in 1945, come to think of it, because my neighbour in our apartment building had a little baby boy on 1 January 1945. And we all had to run down four flights of stairs to the bunker in the cellar, and that baby was screaming his head off – you know, he was scared. And she had two little toddlers, and this baby, and everybody else was mad at her for having this screaming baby. So one day I took the baby and as soon as I held him, he was quiet.

After that, I would take the baby whenever there was an air raid. I had our bags, with clothes and stuff, and a gas mask, and that baby, and I would run down to the cellar. We took shelter like that for the rest of the war, until the Russians came, while the city kept getting pounded to pieces around us.

Two Jehovah's Witnesses came by my house (in Los Angeles) a couple of years ago, and they wanted to preach to me. I told them I knew all about it. And they said, 'No, you don't!' They tried to scare me with stories of Armageddon. And I said those stories wouldn't scare me any more. 'I've seen Armageddon,' I told them. 'I've been there.'

–Charlotte Jacobitz

7

The Normandy Campaign

I was laying down and hugging the dirt, and one shell hit the road right there and exploded maybe 20 feet away. It was a hell of a blast! The guy in front of me got hit on the head. So I went over there and patched him up, using my first-aid kit – each of us carried one of them. He was bleeding pretty bad, because he hadn't been wearing his steel helmet.

– Helmut Jacobitz

If Stalingrad was the battle that determined whether the Soviet Union or Nazi Germany would still stand after the dust of the Second World War settled, the Normandy invasion was the event that ensured that the Soviets would not be the sole masters of Europe when hostilities finally concluded. The largest amphibious invasion in history, the landings that occurred on the coast of France on 6 June 1944 represent an amazingly audacious attack and an Allied victory that was very far from a sure thing. If the invasion had been repulsed, it is possible that the USSR would have been master of the whole of the European mainland by the end of the war.

Operation Overlord was the codename of the invasion, which was under the overall command of US army General Dwight Eisenhower ('Ike'), who would be known to history as the commander of the Supreme Headquarters, Allied Expeditionary Forces (SHAEF). The invasion had been in the planning stages for years, with the overly optimistic Americans originally hoping to accomplish it in 1943 and the British sensibly fighting to delay it until the early summer of 1944. By June of that year, with the Russians rolling toward Germany and the French coastal defences growing steadily stronger, there was no possibility of further delay.

More than 2 million US servicemen had been deployed to Britain for the coming campaign, with more crossing the ocean all the time. About half of these were combat troops, while the other half were support personnel. A further million sailors would man the ships and landing craft carrying the invasion troops across the English Channel. Some 7,000 fighter and ground-attack aircraft would support the mission, and Eisenhower was further given direct control of the 2,500 heavy bombers of the 8th Air Force for the weeks preceding and following the invasion.

Much thought went into the precise location of the invasion. The first choice and most likely area, the Pas-de-Calais, was the bulge of the French coast near the Belgian border where the continental mainland and England were closest together – on a clear day, a person could see the white cliffs of Dover from the French shore. Also recommending Calais was the fact that it was almost 200 miles closer to the German border than the beaches at Normandy. Precisely because it looked and seemed like such an obvious destination, however, Calais was rejected in favour of the long, mostly gentle beaches of Normandy.

Although the Channel was wider at Normandy than at Calais, it was still narrow enough to allow the crossing vessels to make the voyage in a single night, and for short-range Allied aircraft to cover the beaches easily from their bases in southern England. A number of huge British ports, including Dartmouth, Portland, Southampton and Portsmouth, lined the island's southern coast within easy reach of Normandy. With the exception of a rugged section of bluff in the middle of the landing zone, the Normandy beaches were generally wide and flat.

Also of significance, the Allies had enough intelligence about Hitler's fears and German plans to realise that the attack was anticipated at Calais, and they knew better than to strike directly into the heart of the enemy's defence. In fact, Eisenhower exploited Hitler's fixation on Calais by creating a phantom army, under the command of his most famous tank general, George S. Patton, and basing this imaginary force in south-eastern England. A steady stream of radio chatter gave the Germans the impression that huge numbers of troops were waiting to cross from Dover to Calais. Hitler fell for this sham hook, line and sinker, and even for weeks after the invasion troops had landed he refused to allow his field commanders to move any of the troops garrison-ing the Calais area over to the real battlefield. Through most of the summer Hitler continued to insist that Normandy was just a diversion.

However, the German defences along the Normandy shore were indeed formidable. The commander of the Western Front since early in 1944 was

Field Marshal Erwin Rommel, the Desert Fox of African fame. Even before he had taken command, the entire coast of Europe, from Holland to the Brittany peninsula, and southward to the border with Spain, had been fortified with gun emplacements, pillboxes and garrisons of German troops. Hitler termed this *Festung Europa*, or Fortress Europe.

The so-called 'Atlantic Wall' had been stiffened with massive guns removed from the French emplacements of the Maginot Line, and the defences left no stretch of the coastline undefended. Under Rommel's leadership, the defensive positions had been further enhanced. Stakes had been placed across broad fields that might have made attractive landing zones for Allied gliders – the Americans referred to these stakes as 'Rommel's Asparagus'. The approaches to most of the beaches had been lined with steel girders, planted firmly in the seabed and jutting sharply upward, to serve both as anti-tank obstacles and hazards that could tear the bottoms out of landing craft.

In France Rommel had fifteen good infantry divisions (including several *Fallschirmjaeger* units, now serving as foot soldiers) and ten panzer divisions, in addition to more than thirty divisions of lower-quality training and coastal defence troops. However, the gifted tank commander had his hands tied to a certain extent by his Führer – Hitler refused to allow Rommel to move his panzer division without specific permission from Berlin.

The invasion was slated for the pre-dawn hours of 5 June, but a savage spring storm raged in from the Atlantic, tossing the waters of the Channel and barring the fleet's departure from England on 4 June. In one of the more influential uses of the new science of meteorology, Eisenhower relied upon reports from his weather forecasters, who analysed storms in the North Atlantic and suggested enough improvement of the weather on 6 June that the supreme commander dared to authorise the invasion. In the event, the Allies derived an extra benefit from this gamble, since the weather was so bad that Rommel, who had been in Germany visiting his wife, decided he didn't have to worry about the invasion on 6 June and ended up staying home for another day – he spent the day of the landings hurrying back to his headquarters instead of commanding his troops.

The actual landings would be made by three airborne divisions (two US, one British) landing by parachute and glider, and five infantry divisions rolling ashore on the five beaches that had been designated as landing zones. The two westernmost beaches, Utah and Omaha, were targeted by American troops. Utah was dangerously removed from the other beaches, but it was ruled important because its capture would put the invading troops within striking distance of a desperately needed port, Cherbourg. The next beach, Omaha, presented the toughest physical obstacles, including a steep bluff offering the defenders a commanding field of fire over the entire landing zone. US army rangers would be tasked with scaling this cliff and seizing the heights there. The British beaches, Gold, Juno and Sword, fronted upon the major city of Caen, and would anchor the left flank of the offensive while the Americans hopefully made headway on the right.

Inspired and emboldened by the example of the German *Fallschirmjaeger* earlier in the war, the British and Americans had made great strides in developing airborne tactics and training troops to augment their own armies. They had used battalion-sized paratroop units in Operation Torch, the invasion of North Africa, in late 1942, and regimental attacks against Sicily in the summer of 1943. The airborne component of Overlord would constitute the largest airborne attack in military history to date.

As the two American beaches were isolated from each other, and from the main punch of the British, each was provided with a full division of airborne troops to support the infantry. The soon to be famous 82nd ('All-American') and 101st ('Screaming Eagle') Airborne Divisions were charged with seizing inland obstacles, impeding German manoeuvres and holding some key bridges and causeways necessary for the landing troops to move inland, off the beaches. The British 6th Airborne Division would land east of all the beaches, attempt to secure a key bridge across the Orne River outside of Caen and also serve as flank protection for the British beaches.

The weather and the moonless night combined to give the landings complete tactical surprise. The paratroopers landed behind the beaches, suffering heavy casualties but sowing confusion and delay in the German response. The amphibious troops stormed ashore on all five beaches, plunging inland at four of them. Only at Omaha beach, under the shadow of those daunting bluffs, did the invasion falter. Until the very end of the first day, the survival of the initial wave of troops was very much in doubt. Fortunately for the fate of the free world, the absence of Rommel and Hitler's orders freezing his panzer divisions in place both served to delay a counter-attack that quite possibly could have shattered the landings and driven the Allied forces back into the sea.

After heavy losses, the rangers finally seized the top of the cliffs, and Omaha was the last beach to be secured. By nightfall on D-Day, all five beaches were in Allied hands. The Germans were mustering additional troops to the defence, and the rugged Normandy terrain – the bocage – presented daunting obstacles to the attackers, but the Western Allies had come ashore on the Continent, and they were there to stay.

I was still with my unit in Brittany, near Brest, when we got word that the invasion had come ashore in Normandy. We were under the command of General

Student, who was a pretty famous officer – he'd been commanding German paratroopers through the whole war. My company was just part of that division, of course – we had about 100 men.

We got orders to march to Normandy, which was maybe 200 miles away. We would march for about twelve hours every day. Each day we would hire or confiscate a large wagon from a farmer, and would put our heavy equipment, sleeping kits and all that stuff, on the wagon. So each soldier only had to carry his small stuff. That farmer would come with us for one march, and then he would go home and we'd get a different farmer from that local area to haul our stuff the next day.

Actually it was mostly during the night that we marched, because we were worried about the bombers that were flying all over the place during the day. The little planes, one and two engine, we called *Jabos*, and we really hated them. If they saw you moving on a road, they'd fly down and shoot their machine guns. That's why we hid out during the day and waited for evening before we started to march.

So when we finally finished the night's march, it would be really late. Sometimes we'd have to just sleep in the ditch right there by the road, but if we were lucky we'd find a barn. I don't remember the exact time it took, but I think we'd walk maybe 20 miles each night. That part of France is pretty flat, so it wasn't too hard to march.

Sometimes we were pretty hungry. I remember once we didn't have any food, and I went up to this farmer and asked him for some eggs. He gave me some spotted ones – but I thought maybe the eggs had the measles. So I got some different ones from him. If I had time I'd fry them up in this little frying pan I had. But if I couldn't cook them, I would put holes in the shells and suck the eggs out. I liked to eat those raw eggs – they tasted pretty good.

Some guys dropped their mess kits because they didn't want to carry them, but I always kept mine. It had a metal lid that folded down, so you could carry stuff inside of it, and cook things like stew or soup in there. I always kept my knife and spoon there too. Later on, when we were in combat, other guys dropped all that stuff when they were running around. But I kept mine with me the whole time! I also kept my water bottle, so I was the guy everyone asked to share water, because we got pretty thirsty.

After maybe eight or ten days we started getting closer to Normandy. That was the first time I was near any fighting – and what a battle it was!

We were approaching the front, and I remember we had to spread out so that we weren't marching in column formation any more. Each man was 10 to 15 feet apart from the other guys. So the English or Americans would soon see us marching down the street and start firing their big guns, the cannons, at us. The shells would explode nearby and we would all dive for cover. You wouldn't hear the shells coming through the air, but often you would hear the guns that were shooting them. It made you pretty nervous, even when they were not aimed right at you. So we would lay down flat, but there wasn't much of a ditch and we still felt really exposed.

I was lying down and hugging the dirt, and one shell hit the road right there and exploded maybe 20 feet away. It was a hell of a blast! The guy in front of me got hit on the head. So I went over there and patched him up, using my first aid kit – each of us carried one of them. He was bleeding pretty bad, because he hadn't been wearing his steel helmet. We hated to put them on; we all wore them on our belts while we were marching. I guess that fellow got out, evacuated because of that wound.

After the barrage stopped we started marching again, and I think everyone was wearing his helmet this time. We moved right up behind the front line of the battle, and there we deployed for the fight. We always had two lines, a front line and a second line. If the front line broke down the second line took over, still moving forward. There was some fighting there, and we were right at the front line and they started shelling us again. So we dug our holes fairly deep because we knew we would be sleeping in there.

I was there for a few weeks, rotating back and forth. You had to stay a couple days right on the front and then you would get a couple of days behind, because on the front you couldn't sleep. You'd be awake twenty-four hours a day, no way you could sleep.

We had our rifles, of course, everyone carried one of those. We also carried hand grenades. We had two kinds of those, the big ones with a stick and a knob at one end – the ones the Americans called 'potato mashers'; and smaller, round grenades that were maybe the size of a large orange. We called those 'eggs'. They could do a lot of damage. Of course, there was a light machine gun in our company too. And we had some portable rocket launchers for shooting at Allied tanks. I didn't carry one of those, but I learned how to use it – that came in handy later!

We split up when we reached the fighting and half of us went right into the front, where we had to dig holes. The guys in the second line stayed maybe 2 kilometres (a little over a mile) back from the front. All the time we were wondering how come we had this big fight here in Normandy. The Americans and English should have been stopped right on the beaches, not after they got into the farms and fields.

It was a stupid thing from Hitler, because he said 'let them land first' and then we'll see where they land, and we'll trap them and kill them. Like we did the first time, where was that? The raid on Dieppe, I think, which is a small French port. They let them land and killed most of the English and the rest got on to a few boats they took back to England. But that was just a little attack, a raid, not an invasion.

So in Normandy Hitler ordered that we let them land, because he was certain we'd surround them and kill them. The generals told him not to let them land, because once they land they'll stay. But you know how Hitler was. Nobody could argue with him. So as soon as the Americans and English landed and got off the beaches, they built trenches and brought ashore so much material that we knew they weren't going away.

We were going backwards all the time. We'd fight and hold on for as long as we could, and we were pretty good at shooting at the American soldiers when we saw them. They weren't crazy about getting shot at, which is natural enough, so they'd lie down and dig their own holes. But then they'd open up on us with their big guns, and we'd just dig down deeper and hope to be lucky enough to stay alive.

I should mention that, where I was on the front line, every field had a hedgerow around it. Each field was little, and was surrounded by this big hedge that you couldn't crawl through or see over. Those hedgerows were all over in Normandy. What the farmers do, and have been doing practically forever, is they pick up the rocks and they put them around the field so they could plough the dirt. All these little fields, maybe an acre or two, are surrounded by rock walls, and then they plant bushes on top of them. That keeps the wind off, because it gets fairly windy in Normandy. So you have all these little fields, and each was like its own courtyard or something, surrounded by a wall.

You can still see them if you're in a plane going over from England to France. Look out sometime, and you can see those fields all around Normandy. It looks like a chequerboard from above. Those things the French called the bocage, but they were thick, tangled hedgerows. You couldn't really go through one; you had to find an opening.

One night I was laying on the front line right by one of those hedgerows, and there was an opening. Each field had one or two of those. It was a dirt road, not much more than a path, and it dipped down through a gap in the hedge. I was laying there for a long time and I got up and I had my rifle in my hand. And I walked a little bit here, to look in the opening, and all of a sudden there was an American guy, with his rifle. He aimed at me and I pointed my rifle at him. We both started shooting at the same time, but we both missed and quickly ducked away. I ran behind the bushes on my side of the hedge, and he ran around the bushes there.

I thought, by gosh, what now? He's trying to kill me, that I know. So I took a hand grenade – one of the egg kind – out and I armed it, which you do by pulling a cap that's attached to a sturdy string. That starts a little timer going, and you have to get rid of it fast. I tossed it over the hedge and heard it explode in the other field. I still didn't know where he was. So I went all the way up to the far end of the field. There was a little opening again, and I looked around it, and there he was laying. So the hand grenade had got him in his butt or somewhere.

I went over to him and helped him up and took him back over to my side. He was bleeding, but he could walk. He didn't have his gun any more so he was my prisoner. Only then did I find a German machine gun nest, all covered up so nobody could see it. I didn't see it before, or know it was there.

They said, 'Did you throw that hand grenade?'

I said, '*Ja.*'

They told me they were just getting ready to fire, and they would have killed him. The machine gun was only 50 yards or so away from where we had our little gunfight. I saved that guy's life by throwing my grenade at him!

So I took him then and patched him up with his own first-aid kit from his own backpack. And then someone took him back as a POW.

– Helmut Jacobitz

Battle in the Bocage

The terrain in Normandy proved exceptionally disadvantageous for the attacker. Each field, with its virtually impenetrable wall of rocks and tangled hedges, became a miniature fortress in its own right. As such, each field had to be taken in ferocious combat, and that accomplishment simply led to the discovery of another, essentially identical, mini-fortress just beyond.

The defenders took advantage of every nuance of terrain, even as the Allies continued to bring more men, guns, tanks and trucks over the beaches. The day after the invasion the Allies installed two 'mulberries', giant artificial harbours created by sinking old ships to use as breakwaters. One of these, on Omaha beach, was destroyed in a storm on 19 June, but the other served as a useful terminal for supplies throughout the campaign.

The Americans fought their way north toward the port of Cherbourg, desperately needing a place where they could dock ships carrying supplies and reinforcements across the Channel. They cleared the key crossroads city of Carentan by 17 June, after tough fighting against an SS panzer division and several regiments of *Fallschirmjaeger*. Even without a port, the relentless build-up continued, with nearly all the new equipment and reinforcing troops coming ashore through the British mulberry on Gold beach.

Some of Germany's best troops were holding the line south of the Allied beachhead. These included the SS *Hitlerjugend* (Hitler Youth) panzer division, fanatical Nazi soldiers equipped with some of the Third Reich's best tanks; as well as the 1st and 2nd SS panzer divisions, all facing the British in the

1 Charlotte looked after her younger brother Paul, throughout their childhood and the war years.

2 Charlotte was photographed at age 4 or 5 with her brother Gerhard, but her father cut Gerhard out of the picture after the boy's tragic death in 1933.

3 & 4 Charlotte mailed this picture, labelled, 'To remember your daughter, Charlotta, Berlin, 8.10.41', to her father when he was in the military; he kept it even through his years in the French POW camp and brought it home after the war.

5 A young teenager, Charlotte stands with her mother and her brother Paul in about 1941.

6 Charlotte was very devoted to her father, Paul, who wore his uniform on a visit home on leave.

7 Paul Wolff lost his legs because of gangrene contracted as a POW. He adored his children and grandsons, and is shown here with the infant Helgo Jacobitz in 1954.

8 Karl Jacobitz, Helmut's next-older brother, committed suicide rather than return to military service on the Russian Front.

9 This old photo, recorded on tin, shows Helmut, his sister Gretel, his mother Anna and his father, Hermann Sr.

10 This early school photo includes both Helmut, top row, far right, and his sister Gretel, top row, far left.

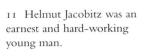
11 Helmut Jacobitz was an earnest and hard-working young man.

12 Hermann Jacobitz posed with his wife, Anna, and children Helmut, Gretel and Karl outside his *Seifenladen*, or 'soap store', which also sold hardware, glass, lamp oil, dishes, flower pots, brooms, cleaning supplies and other general goods. This is the last picture taken of Karl before his death.

13 This page from Helmut's *Soldbuch* – his military field journal and ID pamphlet – is discoloured from the blood shed when the young paratrooper was wounded in Normandy.

14 Helmut did a favour for a small-town police chief, who then issued him this falsified ID that allowed him to carry food from the countryside into Berlin without fear of confiscation.

15 Food ration cards, such as this one, were issued to all Germans by the Nazi government during the war.

16 Helmut's company made signs for many other businesses, including a large account with Schultheiss Beer and the Salamander Shoe Company.

17 Helmut's brother and father joined the couple on their wedding day, shortly before a legal spat estranged the family.

18 Charlotte and Helmut were married on 26 November 1949.

19 The wedding was a simple affair, with a ceremony at the city hall, and a dinner at Charlotte's parents' apartment.

20 After 1961 the Jacobitz family embraced life in the United States, travelling around the country extensively, including this trip to the Grand Canyon during the middle of that decade.

21 The Reichstag building, like much of the rest of Berlin, was reduced to a ruin by the bombing campaign and the final battle in the city.

22 The Nazis frequently organised massive rallies, such as this one at the Lustgarten, Berlin, during the mid-1930s.

23 Adolf Hitler would become known as the face of evil to most of the world during the twelve-year tenure of his 'Thousand Year Reich'.

24 Premier Josef Stalin ruled the Soviet Union with an iron fist, and committed perhaps as many atrocities as his Nazi counterpart.

25 Hitler and his cronies, Reichsmarschall Hemann Göring, Italian Dictator Benito 'Il Duce' Mussolini and Italian Foreign Minister Galeazzo Graf Ciano, emerge from a meeting.

26 Reichsmarchsall Josef Goebbels, the Nazi Propaganda Minister, ordered the deaths of his own wife and children at the fall of the Third Reich.

27 American B-17 Flying Fortresses of the 8th Air Force flew many daylight bombing raids over Berlin and other German cities.

28 The high-performance North American P-51 Mustang was the first fighter with enough range to reach Berlin from bases in England.

29 American and Canadian transport aircraft unload provisions during the Berlin Airlift at Tempelhof airport, in 1948.

30 The bocage countryside of Normandy rendered every field into a small fortress, enhancing the German defence and greatly prolonging the battle there.

31 Americans of the 1st Infantry Division storm on to Omaha beach on D-Day, with the daunting cliffs looming above.

32 President Kennedy discarded his prepared speech and spoke to Berliners extemporaneously after he observed the bleakness of East Berlin.

33 This section of the Berlin Wall, in the shadow of the Brandenburg Gate, was dismantled by both East and West Berliners in the weeks after the November 1989 revolution.

struggle for Caen. That city was supposed to have been captured within a day or two of D-Day, but it still held out nearly a month later.

To the west, the Americans of the 29th Division – one of the units to come ashore on D-Day – and the 2nd Division battled their way toward the key crossroads town of Saint Lo. They were resisted every step of the way by the stubborn defence of General Karl Student's II Parachute Corps, including the 3rd Parachute Division and the 6th Parachute Regiment. The advance was painfully slow, but eventually the crushing American artillery superiority began to dominate the battlefield. Tanks couldn't move through the bocage, but cannons could fire over it, and with the canopy of these barrages the men of the US army finally pushed into the road junction of Saint Lo by the third week of July.

There was more bocage in front of them, and the Germans had a stout line defended by some of the best soldiers in the world, but beyond lay open terrain, the perfect tank country of northern France.

One guy depended on the other guy. We were close together, but I had no real 'buddy buddy' guy. A comrade is someone you have to be with, whether you like it or not. And once we were in that Normandy battle, we were losing guys every day, wounded or killed. It didn't make sense to be too friendly with someone.

But there's always somebody you like better than somebody else. There was one fellow, a *Gruppe* leader, who was a farmer, a shepherd, and he acted like he was so much smarter than everyone else. He made a big deal of it, like he was almost a doctor. Because when the sheep are sick you have to butcher them and eat them. I still remember that guy, how he was always bragging about it; I didn't care for him too much.

One time a lieutenant got a bunch of us together, and lined us up and told us to get ready to attack. He said, 'Assemble for counter-attack.'

At that time, the Americans were just one field away from us. We knew they had a lot of guys over there, and tanks, mortars and machine guns.

I thought, 'Oh my gosh, what an idiot. Attack if you want, but don't drag me along!'

But he was a big-mouth loud guy, and he was yelling at all of us – and then there was a loud *BANG*, and his arm was hanging down just by a shred. There was an American tank over there, behind the hedge, and it fired at him and there was just some meat hanging down where his arm had been. Somebody put a tourniquet on it, and he took a knife himself and cut off what was left of his arm. And that was the end of the counter-attack.

We were mostly two days or maybe three days on the front line, and you couldn't get much sleep at all because you had to watch for enemy soldiers moving around. Maybe you would doze off for one or two hours during the night, but then you woke up and had to watch again.

Then we got to go back for a couple of days on the second line and then you could sleep all day, sometimes twenty-four hours and had some decent meals. Of course, they did bring you food on the front line, even hot food when they could, but they could only do that in the dark, and you'd still be eating down in a hole in the ground, worried about getting shot or bombed. It was definitely a relief to get back from the front, even if it was only 2 kilometres, for a couple of days.

At one time I was at a place where there was a little stream right in front of me. We were right next to it and we were waiting for the Americans to come; we expected them to attack at any time. It was dark and you couldn't see more than a few feet. I could just make out a little reflection of the water, but everything else was shadows. And then we heard splashing, like people going in the water, and I said to myself, 'Oh God, here they come!'

You can't see anything! It was really confusing, because you just have your rifle there and you're all by yourself and you wonder: 'What's going on?' We opened up with our guns even though we didn't have any targets, and blazed away for maybe a minute or two. But when we stopped shooting, there was no one there.

It must have been just rats or something, because the Americans never came. It turned out they were not really crazy about fighting at night. But in your mind it's different than reality, and you can think it's guys coming, especially at night. Sometimes they attacked us and sometimes they didn't. That's part of what made it so stressful being on the front line.

I still remember we had to dig down all the time for our shelters. What do you call those pits? Foxholes, I think. And we were sleeping in there and living in there the whole time we were on the front.

One day the Americans started shooting with the little cannons, the mortars, which were really nasty. We really hated those! Mortars are not really accurate and they don't shoot far, like cannons, but they are easy to carry around and to set up. A couple of guys can bring one into position and set it up in a minute. Then one guy drops the shell down the barrel and it shoots high up in the air, and comes down on top of the enemy.

The mortar shells just had to touch a bit of grass from the lawn or something to set off the blast. Sometimes even before it hits the ground it explodes already, maybe a few feet above the ground. We were in the foxholes so a lot of the time the blast didn't do anything. But they sure made us keep our heads down.

When we went to the front line, on one day, there was a small street that was paved, and at the side they had a little ditch where water ran. We were running along the street, trying to get to the foxholes on the front line, but there was an opening and the Americans and English could see us. They started shooting those mortars, and they must have zeroed in on the road pretty carefully because the barrage was really accurate. We lost quite a few guys there, before the rest of us reached the holes.

– Helmut Jacobitz

A Bomb at the Wolf's Lair

Things continued to get worse for Hitler as the hot summer month of July 1944 passed. The situation in Normandy gradually slipped from German control. Although the Allies had lost some 125,000 men in the campaign so far, those losses were being more than replaced by fresh troops arriving daily from Britain and the USA. German casualties numbered about 115,000, including more than 40,000 soldiers captured as POWs, but these were men the Third Reich could no longer replace.

Hitler's forces were being pushed back on every front. In Russia, the largest force under German arms, Army Group Centre, was all but annihilated by the Soviet summer offensive. In Italy, Rome had fallen to the victorious Allies, as the British and Americans, operating side by side, continued to advance steadily up the peninsula. In Normandy, the position of the defenders had been stretched to breaking point with the loss of the key crossroads of Saint Lo. Now the American armoured divisions were piling up behind the front line, waiting for the chance to stage an epic breakout.

In Germany itself, even Hitler's own officers were finally ready to turn against him. The mastermind of the plot was Colonel Count Claus von Stauffenberg, a genuine war hero of the Third Reich. He had been badly wounded in action in Tunisia, losing one hand and several fingers from the other. His mind remained sharp, and so he had been transferred to General Staff duty in Berlin. He carefully gathered a small, tight-knit group of co-conspirators, men of experience and influence who believed that Hitler was leading Germany to complete and utter ruin. Some of his fellow plotters were of general rank, but in this matter Colonel von Stauffenberg was the leader of them all.

This scion of proud Prussian aristocrats quietly organised an assassination attempt. Obtaining a time bomb from British agents, he concealed that bomb in a briefcase, and carried it to the wooded compound known as the Wolf's Lair, deep in the forests of East Prussia. The bomb was not a ticking clock, but a chemical fuse that would ignite a powerful charge several minutes after the bomb was armed. Von Stuaffenberg carried the bomb into the bunker where he was to brief Hitler on the status of reserve troops. Another plotter commanded the switchboard at the East Prussian installation, and would put out word as soon as Hitler was confirmed dead; still others were in charge of seizing key points in the capital, taking control of the army and neutralising Reichsmarschall Himmler and other key Nazis.

The plan was sound, but the planners were unlucky. The briefing attended by Stauffenberg occurred on 20 July 1944. It was supposed to take place in a concrete-walled, underground bunker – a hardened location that would have magnified the lethality of the blast. Instead, repairs were being made on the sheltered bunker, so the meeting was held in an above-ground barracks, a wooden shell of a building.

Still, Stauffenberg got very close to Hitler, started the fuse, and left the briefcase on the floor under the briefing table, right next to the Führer. The colonel then left to catch a flight back to Berlin, and another officer, nervously preparing to brief his master, pushed the briefcase farther under the table so that he could stand closer. This placed a heavy cement table support between the bomb and Hitler.

The bomb exploded with dramatic effect, destroying the conference room, killing the officer who had inadvertently moved the briefcase, and burning, deafening and infuriating Hitler. Immediately the SS and Gestapo moved into action. Stauffenberg's role had been discovered by the time his plane landed in Berlin, and he and all of the plotters were arrested, tortured and killed within a matter of days. Hitler survived to lead Germany to ruin, and the only result of the assassination attempt was to make him even more of a paranoid lunatic than he had been before.

One weapon we did have that worked pretty good was a rocket launcher used to shoot at tanks. We used to call it a 'smoke pipe'. I guess the real name was *Ofenrohr* or *Panzerschreck*. The Americans had it too [a bazooka] but theirs was lousy, much smaller than ours. The *Panzerschreck* was a tube, and you put a rocket in, aimed it, and shot. Ours was fairly big in diameter, like the chimney pipe from a stove, and the rockets were big, too. They were real good up to 100 or 150 metres, so we didn't have to go too close. They were fairly deadly: if they hit the tank they wrecked it.

One time I could see several American tanks coming at us. We had been pushed out of our line of foxholes and were going backward, kind of running away. The guy beside me dropped his *Panzerschreck*. I picked it up and shot at the closest tank and the rocket exploded right on top of it. I could tell that the tank wasn't destroyed, but whoever was in there got frightened by the blast and jumped out of the tank and ran away. A guy who worked for me after the war had been a tank driver, and he said the noise when something like that happened was just awful, which is probably why the Americans ran away.

Anyway, we went into the tank and found chocolate and some other good stuff. The tank was still working, so some guys from my company even drove it around a little, and thought about fighting from an American tank. I didn't want to do that, but I was pretty happy about the chocolate!

We had other anti-tank weapons too, one that was very short. You had to be real close, and I didn't use one of those. It had only a very short range, maybe 20 or 30 metres, so you had to get right next to the tank to do any damage to it. The missiles attached themselves to the tank and started a really hot fire.

That's why you see all kinds of stuff now around those modern tanks. Soldiers put sand bags, chain link fence, all kinds of wire and even spare tyres around them because once these hot burning missiles hit the tank they melted right in and then exploded. That's the way they used to work.

The Americans were kind of new to the war, so they fought different from German tactics. When somebody was shooting at them they took cover; usually we could stop the infantry from attacking that way. They wouldn't go in unless everything was finished on our side because they had all the firepower.

Compared to us, it was frustrating, because we didn't have anything any more. They had lots more big guns, and lots more mortars, than we did. We had better tanks than the Americans, but they had a lot more tanks, too. So they would just plaster the German lines with lots of high explosives. Sometimes they would use aeroplanes to drop bombs on us, too.

Only when they decided that almost everything was gone on our side would they come on the attack. Mostly, though, they had such firepower, they would destroy our men and our camps with artillery. They killed a lot of my comrades that way.

– Helmut Jacobitz

8

Million Dollar Wound

It was the worst thing I have ever seen in my life. Those guys with no legs were crying out, trying to crawl away from the burning train, dragging themselves along the ground with their hands while bombs exploded and machine gun bullets hit the ground all around.

– Helmut Jacobitz

The steady advance of the Americans on the Normandy right flank was aided by a crushing superiority in artillery, and the complete mastery of the air that had been attained by the tactical air forces. In addition, more men, supplies, tanks and ammunition were pouring over the beaches every day, while Allied air power created huge problems during daylight for any German movement by rail or road. All of these factors combined to make it only a matter of time before the German line would have to crack.

British forces on the Allied left still struggled mightily to enter the city of Caen, which had been stoutly held by Germans since they had resisted the first push on D-Day itself. On 26 June, General Montgomery ordered Operation Epsom, a strong effort to push through the Odon River valley south-west of the city. After two days of hard fighting, British troops and tanks seized a hill commanding the south bank of the river, a position that threatened to cut off Caen from the German line to the west. However, Rommel brought up powerful reinforcements, including several panzer and SS panzer divisions, the latter of which had Germany's best tanks and most fanatical soldiers; and Montgomery was obliged to pull his men back.

The Caen sector would be a thorn in the Allied lines until the end of the Normandy campaign. Straddling an estuary, the city blocked British advances to the east and to the south. During the battle the Germans consistently posted their heaviest armour formations here. On 8 July Montgomery's men tried a direct assault against Caen, Operation Charnwood, but after hard fighting only controlled part of the city. A few weeks later, in Operation Goodwood, the field marshal sent 1,000 or more tanks against entrenched Germans on slightly elevated ground to the south-east of the city. The attack ground to a halt with the loss of some 400 British tanks, and was called off on 20 July – the same day some of Hitler's officers tried to blow him up in the Wolf's Lair.

While the British wrestled with Caen, the Americans on the right flank of the invasion gradually pushed their way across the Cotetin peninsula and closed in on Cherbourg. The latter city was to be the first French port cleared by the invading troops – and port facilities, such as docks, cranes and a road network were desperately needed as the Allies continued to cram more men and material into the beachhead that was still hemmed in by tenacious German resistance. Cherbourg was taken just before the end of June, after savage fighting, but the Wehrmacht had been so efficient at destroying the harbour facilities, such as docks and cranes, that it would be the end of summer before the Allies could begin offloading supplies and men there.

Lacking a port, all that personnel and equipment still had to come in over the beaches, which inherently limited the pace of the build-up. Though the Americans had manufactured an amazing array of ships and landing craft capable of shallow water and beaching operations, they remained subject to the winds, tides and storms that have always plagued the English Channel. However, the influx of forces over the beachhead continued doggedly, while the United States sent tens of thousands more men, as well as tanks and heavy guns, across the Atlantic. For now, these reinforcements piled up at depots in Britain, waiting for an opportunity to land and to find space to advance into the crowded battlefield.

British and American fliers had complete command of the air over Normandy and the rest of northern France. Fighters and fighter-bombers roamed in constant patrols, shooting up trains, vehicles, soldiers and fortified positions in support of the ground troops. Copying the tactic originated by the Germans, aircraft target spotters now accompanied the ground troops, and could call in exceptionally powerful and accurate air strikes against small, but tough, targets. The heavy bombers, meanwhile, gradually shifted back to the strategic-bombing campaign against the German homeland, and nearly all of the Luftwaffe's fighters were employed in resisting that effort, leaving the skies over France the free hunting ground for the Allied air forces.

The lethality of that air superiority was clearly demonstrated on 17 July 1944, when the staff car carrying Field Marshal Rommel along a French road behind the front was strafed, leaving the German battlefield commander critically wounded. He would survive this attack, but barely, and the wounds would spell the end of the remarkable career of the Desert Fox.

By autumn, Rommel would be implicated, almost certainly falsely, in the 20 July plot against Hitler. The Gestapo would come to his home in Saxony and give him the option of being executed as a traitor, with all the attendant punishment such a doom would bring upon his wife and son, or of committing suicide and being buried as a national hero who had 'died of his battle wounds'. Ever thoughtful and considerate, the agents of the Gestapo even brought him the poison pill he would use to take his own life.

In my memory I had only been on the front a few weeks before I got wounded, but in my battle diary I see that it was more like 20 August, so I guess I had been there for more than two months. We were still doing the same thing, fighting for two or three days, constantly, then pulling back from the front to sleep for a day or two. All too soon we'd be sent back to the front.

Already my company had gone from about 100 men when we arrived in Normandy down to about twenty a few weeks later, because of casualties. We then got reinforced back up to 100, and but after more fighting we were again down to near twenty. Most of those casualties were caused by artillery and mortars; not too many guys had gotten shot by bullets, or by tanks.

By then the Americans seemed like they had tanks everywhere. They'd started putting these big girders on the front of the tank hulls – metal shafts that stuck out like the tines of a fork. They would drive the tanks right into the hedgerows. Most of the time they'd get stuck, or have to back up again, but every once in a while they'd break through the hedge, making an opening where more tanks and men could charge through. That was always a nasty surprise!

In all this fighting, we didn't really have a sense of what was going on beyond our fields and foxholes, our little part of the front. I know that we were pretty much at the breaking point, but we'd fight as long as we could, and then get back again. Each day you were in the foxhole, all you wanted to do was to stay alive for another day.

I learned later that by 1 August the Americans had broken through our lines near the western end. General Patton was in charge then, and his tanks were racing all across France. Some of them went into Brittany, where my unit had been stationed before the invasion, and others went south and east, toward and even past Paris.

But we just kept on fighting, trying to give up only one field at a time.

– Helmut Jacobitz

Cobra

The Normandy campaign changed in dramatic fashion just before General Patton arrived on the scene to command the newly created American Third Army. The famously aggressive, bellicose Patton was to be given command of a very tank-heavy force, under the direct operational control of General Omar Bradley, who was promoted to command of the Twelfth Army Group, which would include both Patton's Third and Hodges' First Armies operating side by side. However, the tanks still needed an opening to exploit their mobility.

To set the stage for Patton's unleashing, General Bradley conceived of Operation Cobra. This creative plan was viewed as a means of breaking the terrible stalemate in the bocage, and Patton would be just the commander to put that plan into action. The plan entailed a massive effort along the entire Normandy Front, with the British at Caen attempting – very successfully, it turned out – to convince the Germans that the main effort at a breakthrough would come to the east, in Montgomery's front. In the meantime, Hodges' men would batter at the left end of the German line, just north of the city of Avranches. When that line cracked, Patton would be ready with huge columns of fresh armoured divisions, poised to break out of the hedgerows and race across France.

Operation Cobra commenced on 25 July. To kick off the attack, Eisenhower once again pulled the heavy bombers of the 8th Air Force away from their strategic mission, employing more than 2,000 of them in an unprecedented effort to pulverise a short section of the German Front. These bombers did their job and then some, killing thousands of German troops and rendering many square miles of the French countryside a virtual moonscape. The bombardment was so thorough that dust and smoke obscured the target to the point where many of the bombers ended up dropping their ordnance on American troops. Nearly 500 GIs, including General Leslie McNair – the highest ranking US army officer to die in the Second World War, who had been visiting from Washington to observe the operation – died under the impact of these bombs that fell 'short'.

However, the line had been breached, and American tanks rolled through the shattered bombing zone and into the open countryside beyond. On 1 August, Patton and the Third Army were activated, and 'Old Blood and Guts' commenced one of the most spectacular mobile campaigns of this or any other war. As Montgomery's British troops finally broke out of Caen and started moving eastward along the coast, Patton's tanks dashed in a spreading wave of liberation almost as fast as their drivers could push.

I was part of a platoon defending a house next to one of those bocage fields, and I was lying down, taking shelter from the mortar rounds. They were always showering down on us, those damned things! One of them exploded very close to me, and I got a bunch of shrapnel hits, mostly on my shoulder and my upper arm. One was a big one, but there were lots of smaller holes, too.

I could walk, but I was bleeding pretty badly and I couldn't use my arm, so as soon as the mortar rounds stopped landing I got up and went to my officer.

'I'm wounded,' I told him. 'I'm going back to headquarters so they can patch me up.'

Well, he could see I was bleeding, so of course he let me go. In those field headquarters, even with the companies, they had first aid stations and medics, guys who wore red crosses and they could put bandages on to stop the bleeding. They did that, but told me to walk a little way back to the field hospital.

If you were a little more badly hurt they would send you to one of these field hospitals, which might be anywhere, like in a barn or a school – but still close to the battlefield, and a temporary setup. It's small and primitive, not like a real hospital, but they have morphine and can give you stitches and stuff. I went there, and got the big hole and some of the little ones stitched up. Then they sent me back to the main hospital, which was bigger still, and farther from the front lines. For that I got to ride in a wagon, and it was still a military hospital, but better than the one in the schoolhouse.

So with my shoulder all patched up I was still going to be out of action for a while, so they put me on a train with a bunch of other wounded guys. It was not a Red Cross train, just a regular freight train. But I think they painted the red crosses on the top and the sides, which meant that train was not supposed to be attacked. Sometimes, though, I know we used those trains to transport German troops back to the front, which we weren't supposed to do.

They had the cars lined with straw, and men were just lying on that straw. A lot of them were hurt worse than me. There were guys who had lost both of their legs in the car with me. The train started moving, to take us all the way back to Germany where we would get treated in a real hospital.

– Helmut Jacobitz

The Falaise Pocket

Montgomery finally achieved his breakthrough at Caen, as the entire German line in Normandy collapsed. With British troops augmented by many Canadians, and even an armoured division of exiled Polish soldiers, Montgomery's Twenty-First Army Group began advancing up the Channel coast, liberating the ports of Le Havre and Dieppe along the way. Never speedy, but always doughty and persistent, the British field marshal advanced steadily against very light opposition.

To the south, Patton's Third Army, with its armoured spearheads, swung through a wide hook, while Hodges' First Army cleared Brittany and the west coast of France. The port of Saint-Nazaire fell quickly, but the Germans fortified and defended the key harbours at Lorient and Brest; these would not fall for several months. The real progress was made in the open French countryside, where Patton's tanks seemed unstoppable and German resistance was non-existent. Very swiftly they had circled around and advanced farther to the east than the British armies moving along the coast.

In between the two Allied thrusts were two mostly intact German armies, the Seventh Army and the Fifth Panzer Army. These were the troops that had been holding the line in Normandy. Now they tried to fall back, but they lacked the vehicles of the Allies – and even though the ubiquitous M4 Sherman tank was no match in battle for the German Panther and Tiger tanks, the Shermans were reliable, and very, very fast. Also, the Wehrmacht remained continually hampered by attack from the air; it was almost impossible for German troops to travel by road during the daylight hours.

The retreating Germans congregated around the large town of Falaise, a key rail and road centre. Recognising the opportunity, Bradley ordered several of his divisions to charge north, to the east of Falaise; while Montgomery sent a Canadian and the Polish armoured division south. When the two pincers met, they would close shut on a trap containing about as many German troops as had been lost at Stalingrad.

Fearing an accidental clash between the Twenty-First Army Group and the Americans, Bradley called a halt to the closure of the pocket. Some Germans managed to escape from the death trap, but the Allies sent in waves of aircraft to pound seemingly every square mile of the Falaise pocket. Rommel's replacement, Field Marshal von Kluge, was killed by one of these airstrikes, and the *Jabos* ranged free, pouncing on anything that moved.

Meanwhile, Free French forces attached to Bradley, but under the direct orders of General Charles de Gaulle, entered Paris to frenzied celebrations on 25 August. The enclosing spearheads at Falaise advanced slowly and cautiously, but the German escape route had, for all intents and purposes, been closed.

I was happy to be heading back to Germany, even though I was wounded. I think everyone was in pretty good spirits when that train pulled out of the station.

But we hadn't gotten very far from Normandy when we were attacked by *Jabos*. These were American planes, twin-engine Lightnings I think, and some single-engine planes too. Maybe Mustangs or Thunderbolts? There weren't a lot of planes, but enough to stop the train. They were firing their machine guns and shooting up the train, and they were dropping bombs too. The train had to stop – I don't know if they blew up the engine or destroyed the tracks – but everyone got out and tried to run for shelter.

It was the worst thing I have ever seen in my life. Those guys with no legs were crying out, trying to crawl away from the burning train, dragging themselves along the ground with their hands while bombs exploded and machine gun bullets hit the ground all around.

There was a haystack right in front of me and I tried to crawl under it with some other guys. It was a warm day, so I was carrying my jacket, holding it in front of me, and another Lightning came down and dropped a bomb really close to it. It exploded and I got a chunk of shrapnel in my knee – it hurt like hell.

But somehow I got up from that haystack and ran, or limped, over to the farmhouse. I pushed into the house and sat down with a bunch of other guys. Most of us had already been wounded, and now we were pretty stunned and shaken up.

I looked at my jacket, and it was all messed up, completely ripped apart. It had one really huge hole in it, made by a big piece of metal from that bomb that came flying through from one side to the other when I was running, crouched over, holding my jacket in front of me. If it had come one foot closer to me it would have killed me.

When the attack was over the train was wrecked, and parts of it were burning. Lots of guys had been killed, and others, like me, had been wounded again on top of whatever wounds had put us on the hospital train in the first place. We just waited there, exhausted and frightened, not knowing what was going to happen.

Finally they sent buses to pick us up from that farmhouse, and from wherever else wounded men who escaped from the train had found shelter. Those buses took us back to a hospital, a real one. From there we had to ride another freight train back to Germany, but that one at least made it all the way.

– Helmut Jacobitz

Patton's (Fuel) Tanks Run Dry

The collapse of the Falaise pocket effectively finished organised German resistance in France. In the south of the country, an amphibious landing (Operation Dragoon) had landed Allied troops around Marseille. These advanced swiftly up the Rhone River valley, and in early September they linked up with Bradley's troops. Montgomery's men continued to move up the Channel coast, though the Germans fortified and held on to several key ports, including Calais, Boulogne and Dunkirk.

Patton's men continued to roar eastward, penetrating into Belgium and Luxembourg. In this effort they were supplied by the 'Red Ball Express', a series of truck convoys, often driven by African-American soldiers in the still-segregated US army, who hauled as much fuel, ammunition and other supplies as their vehicles could carry to the forward combat units.

In fact, the war might have been over in a few more weeks except that, by then, still restricted by a lack of port and supply-loading facilities, Patton's advance came to a halt for the simple reason that his tanks ran out of fuel. There was simply not enough port capacity to bring the necessary supplies in over the beaches, and through the small, damaged harbours thus far captured.

The true prize in the fight for supply capacity was the massive Belgian port of Antwerp, with its deep-water harbour and vast network of wharves, warehouses and shipping facilities. Surprisingly, the Germans were unable to hold on to this important city in any strength, nor did they sabotage the docks the way they had done at many smaller ports; by early September Antwerp was in the hands of Montgomery's men. The vainglorious field marshal missed a chance to cement this accomplishment, however, when he failed to order his men to clear the Germans out of the islands of the Scheldt estuary which, at the time, were very lightly garrisoned.

These islands controlled the water approaches to Antwerp, and in enemy hands they rendered the port unusable. The Wehrmacht swiftly moved in reinforcements and fortified the islands, and it would not be until November that the islands were cleared and the port opened. The battles to take these key islands cost Montgomery many, mostly Canadian, casualties, and proved to be a key mistake in the field marshal's usually meticulous and careful approach.

So it was that, by the middle of September, the Allied advance had essentially ground to a halt along a line running from the English Channel to Switzerland. It was not enemy resistance, but lack of fuel that had stopped the armoured spearheads. But the Germans were not beaten, and they would take very good advantage of the respite provided by the Allied supply crunch. When the attack resumed, it would smash against the so-called Siegfried Line, or Westwall, an extensive line of border fortifications that would take more than half a year to breach.

Once we got away from the battlefield we were put aboard a real hospital train, a nice one, with clean beds that were all prepared for wounded men. That one took us all the way to the Rhine, which might have been the first time I saw that river. It was the first time I remember it, anyway. The train ran down the French side, the west bank in the valley, and you could look across and see those grand castles up on the bluff on the German side.

We crossed the Rhine and went all the way into Austria, to a nice hospital. In Austria, too, we didn't have any American or British bombers coming over.

In the hospital in Austria I had a pretty nice time. It was good to be away from the war! My arm was already infected, from my time on the front line, but the doctor healed that infection. He told me I was supposed to exercise the arm, which was still pretty hurt. I couldn't lift it above my shoulder.

I could mostly do whatever I wanted while I was in Austria, but I did keep exercising because my arm was so stiff, and I didn't want to be a cripple. My knee was a little stiff, too; I limped when I walked, but that wasn't too bad.

Only then, after maybe two or three months, I noticed that my arm was getting pretty good. That doctor used to come and check on everybody, and he told lots of guys, 'Okay, you're better, you can go back to the army.'

I didn't want to go back to the army, I have to admit. So I stopped moving my arm higher. Finally, the doctor decided to let me go home to Berlin for a while, since he wanted that bed for someone else. There was another guy there from the east, and his home had already been overrun by the Russians so he didn't have any place to go. I said he could go to Berlin with me, and the doctor gave me an extra month of leave because I took that guy with me.

On another occasion I remember that I got a chance to visit Berlin because I was escorting a [German] prisoner to a military prison in Potsdam, which is a suburb of the capital. I had that guy handcuffed to me for the whole ride from Austria to Potsdam. But after I delivered him, I had a few days free to go to Berlin and visit my family.

– Helmut Jacobitz

Seasons of Stalemate

In the west, Eisenhower's heady days of rapid advances had come to a painful halt in Belgium, and at the borders of Holland and Germany. The Allies had outrun their supply lines, which were still restricted by the lack of adequate port facilities on the coast of the English Channel; the Wehrmacht, now defending practically at the gates of Germany herself, had regrouped and dug in with Teutonic tenacity. Lacking the fuel and supplies to continue with his 'broad front' attack, Eisenhower yielded to the persuasions of Field Marshal Montgomery, and agreed to launch a daring airborne attack in Holland.

In September 1944, the Allies launched the greatest airborne assault in history, Operation Market Garden, in an attempt to seize three key bridges in Holland with parachute and glider troops, paving the way for an armoured thrust all the way across the Rhine. In Cornelius Ryan's memorable title, quoted from a British military planner, the assault extended itself 'a bridge too far'. The British 1st Airborne Division, at Arnhem, was surrounded and annihilated by two German SS panzer divisions – troops that were supposed to be refitting far from the front, but turned up in a place none of the attacking planners expected them to be. Market Garden was the last time, probably even extending to future military history, in which airborne troops would be employed on such an ambitious mission.

As winter set in offensive operations necessarily slowed to a crawl in the snow and the mud. In December 1944, Hitler's madness was displayed more vividly than ever, when he gathered his remaining armoured formations for one last powerful offensive. He did not deliver this thrust against the lethal menace of the huge Red Army; instead, he stripped tanks and men from the Russian Front and sent them west, launching Operation *Wacht am Rhein* (Watch on the Rhine). More commonly known to the Allies as the Battle of the Bulge, this huge struggle would last for more than a month, from mid-December 1944 until late January 1945. In the end, in terms of extent, casualties and scope, it would be the greatest battle ever fought by the US army, and it would end in a crushing German defeat, forever shattering the ability of the Wehrmacht to launch powerful attacks. Its main effect was to delay significantly the Western Allied advance, ensuring that it would be March before the British and American troops fought their way across the Rhine and into the heartland of Germany.

I got two or three months of time to be in Berlin, and it was good to be home. But it was different, too. By then there were bombing raids on Berlin, and they were bad. I was still at a hospital for recovery, kind of an asylum I guess, and they had the radio on all the time. The first warning of an air raid would come on the radio, and it would be the sound of a cuckoo, like on a cuckoo clock.

That meant there was the chance of an air raid. Then if it seemed like the bombers were going to come to Berlin, they'd sound the sirens, and everyone would head to the bomb shelter. There was a bunker in the basement of the asylum where I would go. My parents had a shelter in the cellar of the apartment building, where lots of people would go. But that wasn't enough for my mother – she would go mostly to the real bomb shelter, which wasn't too far away.

Then, finally, when they decided I was as much better as I was going to get, they sent me back to the front. But now that the Germans were out of France, my paratroop unit was in Holland, far in the western part of the country. There wasn't any fighting there, because the Americans and British were crossing the Rhine farther to the south. They were attacking toward Germany, and we were off to the side of the war.

I remember that they were putting all kinds of guys into the army, by then. In Holland I was talking to these old-timers, mostly pretty old men who had worked in coal mines. Some of those guys could hardly walk any more, but they gave them weapons and told them to fight for the Führer.

I guess they were drafted because the mine was not important, the last few months of the war. Trains weren't running much, so they couldn't take the coal to the factories, and a lot of the factories had been bombed anyway. But there were a lot of those guys who still thought we were going to win the war!

We did have some new weapons, some long-range rockets, at the end of the war. They were firing them over to London, like that was going to make the English stop fighting the war. But these old guys had heard so much propaganda that they were basically brainwashed, and believed everything they heard over the radio.

Of course, I didn't believe in that stuff, because of how I had been raised. But a lot of people, smart people, fell for it.

– Helmut Jacobitz

9

Battle for Berlin

We called those Nazis 'werewolves'. They would shoot any Germans who weren't fighting the Russians. When people, regular citizens, would go out, they would wear a white cloth to show the Russians that they weren't soldiers, and those werewolves started shooting Germans who had the white cloths on, shooting their own people! They'd shoot no matter who it was, kids or whatever. They were crazy guys, real fanatics.

– Charlotte Jacobitz

Hitler's desperate gamble, the invasion of the Soviet Union, had stalled at the gates of Moscow in 1941. He decided to put all of his chips on the table in 1942, with the massive drive across the southern steppes; a move that resulted in the catastrophic defeat at Stalingrad, the epic battle fought through the autumn of 1942 until February 1943. By 1944, the Red Army had turned the tide against the Third Reich, sweeping like a force of nature toward Germany, devouring every obstacle – including Army Group Centre – standing in its path.

In 1945 that tide washed up on the shore of the German heartland. As bleak, violent winter turned to spring, the Soviets occupied all of East Prussia, driving hordes of refugees before them. Poland, Romania and Bulgaria's Nazi masters had been replaced by the military men and political commissars of Josef Stalin's USSR. Already puppet communist governments had been established in those states, offering a glimpse of the fate awaiting Hungary,

Czechoslovakia and however much of Germany would end up under the Soviet boot.

And the Russians rolled on. The pressure in the Balkans continued relentlessly as the Red Army stood at the gates of Budapest by the beginning of 1945. That great city was the key to the whole of Hungary, and it was clear that it would not be able to hold out for long. Here, once again, Hitler demonstrated his increasingly tenuous grasp of reality, when he ordered his few remaining reserves on the Eastern Front sent south, for the battle in Hungary. This move, furiously protested by the new Army Chief of Staff Colonel General Heinz Guderian, had the effect of leaving Berlin defended only by a thin shell of second-rate troops.

By the last months of the war, Hitler's madness was consuming him in a way that was obvious to everyone who had daily contact with him. The assassination attempt of the previous summer had driven his paranoia to frenetic levels, causing him to distrust nearly everything that was told to him by his knowledgeable and experienced military advisers. He was profoundly medicated, taking many drugs to control his moods and a variety of physical ailments. At the same time his megalomania was fully unleashed, demonstrated in his belief that he was infallible, and that everyone around him was a fool. He devoted massive amounts of time to the most minute of tactical decisions – matters that should have been left to colonels, even captains – and ignored the reality of ultimate national destruction that was becoming more evident every day.

In studying Hitler's behaviour at the end of the war, it becomes clear that he really didn't care if any of the German people, any cities or farms or industries, survived the war that he had brought upon them with his own fanatic, racist ambition. He declared that the people had failed him, that they all deserved to die, and his actions specifically forbade his exceptionally capable military leaders from taking steps to improve Germany's position at the end of the war.

Already stories had come from East Prussia of mass rapes of German women by the Soviet hordes, of massacres and butchery, of enslavement, wherein men and women were hauled off to the east by the trainload, children left behind to starve. While Goebbels' propaganda machine continued to churn out the usual pablum, declaring that Germany was winning the war, that her enemies were desperate and would soon be at each other's throats, it was clear to nearly every German except Hitler that the war was going very badly indeed. The great and historic cities of the German homeland had been shattered, one by one, by the strategic-bombing campaign. The front lines that had once been so distant – southern France, central Russia, Egypt – were now at the borders of the Third Reich. In the case of East Prussia, in fact, territory that had been Germanic for centuries was now inundated by the Slavic wave.

As these dark truths sank in, another fact became clear to nearly every German: if they were going to lose, if soldiers were going to be captured, homes and farms occupied by the invader, it was far better if those invaders were British and American than if they were Russian communists. Nevertheless, this was a matter that lay far outside the control of most ordinary Germans. In fact, by late winter 1945, the mathematical truths were visible to anyone who could read a map. And those truths were dire.

The greatest military prize of Germany, the national capital, and the symbolic location most meaningful to all the Allies and, indeed, the rest of the world, was the city of Berlin. By February 1945, the Soviets in the east had swept through all of Poland and penetrated into Germany territory as far as the Oder River, a north–south barrier that twists through mostly flat countryside no more than 35 or 40 miles east of Berlin. Three massive military 'fronts' (the Soviet version of a German or Western Allied 'army group') were poised at the Oder, momentarily exhausted but quickly absorbing supplies, replacements and reinforcements. These fronts were commanded by Stalin's most accomplished generals: Rokossovsky, Zhukov and Konev. Each was a proud, ruthless commander, eager to seize the final prize.

Meanwhile, in the west, the British and Americans had yet to cross the mighty strategic barrier of the Rhine. Then, even when they crossed that river – which they would do in March – their spearheads would stand hundreds of miles from the objective of Berlin, with the whole of the German heartland standing in their path. It was a race that the Soviets could not help but win.

By the time that the Russians were getting close, the Nazis had built huge bunkers in Berlin, several of them. They were very tall, with lots of cannons on them, anti-aircraft guns for shooting at bombers. But each was also a bomb shelter. They were so large that, at the bottom, they brought trains in – each was like its own train station.

You were safe from bombs in there, but boy was it an awful place to be. I went in there once to hide from an air raid, but never went back. There were so many people in there, thousands and thousands in each one, people that had nowhere else to go. Each hallway was lined with beds, one, two, three on this side, three on the other side. It was so full of people that the smell was unbelievable.

You couldn't get any air. It was so hot, too. I felt like a little mouse in there, and I really had to get out. I knew if something bad happened, if a bomb broke through, I would never get out. I couldn't even move.

They tried to bomb it because of all those guns on the top, and they hit it, but they didn't destroy it. I guess it was just too big, and too strong, to be blown up. They were still standing after the war, though some of them had been damaged. People used to joke, after the war, that the Americans couldn't blow them up.

Strange to say, there were still some things that were going along just like normal. I remember early in January 1945, a new movie had come out that I desperately wanted to see. It was called *Die Goldene Stadt*. I can place the date pretty exactly, because you had to be 18 years old to see it, and it was just short of my eighteenth birthday, which was the end of that January.

The Sprengels were still our neighbours. Herr Sprengel, Max, still believed in Hitler, and didn't seem too worried about how the war was going. My mother and his wife remained good friends. Anyway, he knew that I wanted to see that movie, and as some kind of party official he decided he could take me, so we went to that movie together and sat down. The lights dimmed, and then before they even started the credits an usher came, shining a flashlight in my eyes. He told me to get out – that I was too young to see that film! Max left with me, and I could tell he was really embarrassed that he hadn't been able to get me to see the movie.

And all the time the bombers were coming over, and more of the city was being destroyed. We had a man, a civilian, called an *Opmann*, on our block; every city block had one of them. They were in charge of keeping track of who lived there for ration cards, and so forth. Food was really limited, I think it was down to 800 calories per day. I used to volunteer to the *Opmann* to serve on a bucket brigade, if we ever needed to fight fires. If you were on the bucket brigade, that added 100 calories per day to your food ration coupons.

Often our electricity would go off, sometimes for two or three days at a time. We knew that the Germans were retreating all the time, but Goebbels would still come on the radio and tell everyone that we were winning.

Did I mention that I saw him, Goebbels, once? He was finance minister as well as being in charge of propaganda, and I worked in the Reichsbank when he came through. Oh, God, he looked so pitiful! He had a club foot, and one shoe that was a high heel because his foot was so bad.

But boy could he talk. He talked and talked, and lots of people believed him. But my mother still listened to the BBC, when everything was quiet. It was like two in the morning, and she would have the radio on and listen to the German language news from England. And they would tell us what was really going on. We knew we were losing the war.

That radio seemed really loud, too! You know how old radios were, with the whistling and screeching while you try to tune them in? I used to say, 'Why do you do that? Why do you listen? You know it's against the law!'

I was scared. I was just a teenager, and I knew they could get her for that. But because she listened, when Goebbels said, 'We are winning! We are winning!' we knew that he was lying.

– Charlotte Jacobitz

The Jaws Close

At SHAEF, General Eisenhower was known to be a careful planner, and the advance across the Rhine River was a meticulously planned operation; not as complicated and daring as Overlord, to be sure, but even more massive in the scope of men, material and geography. Eisenhower wanted the main thrust against Germany to be made in the north, by British Field Marshal Montgomery's Twenty-First Army Group. Montgomery's troops faced the next key objective, the German industrial heartland of the Ruhr valley, and also had the shortest route to Berlin.

To the south, the American soldiers and officers were not content to let their British rival steal the glory. On 1 March, a small detachment of soldiers from General Hodges' First Army managed to snatch a massive bridge across the great river at Remagen, defusing the demolition charges minutes before the Germans could destroy the span. Appropriately enough, this prize was called the Ludendorff Bridge, named in honour of one of the military leaders of the First World War, who had led Germany so close to disaster thirty years before. Hodges, still part of Omar Bradley's Twelfth Army Group, immediately began pushing men and tanks across the captured bridge, and established a perimeter on the east bank before the Germans could drive him back.

South of Hodges, the always aggressive General Patton had brought his Third Army up to the river as well. As Montgomery's men gathered supplies and resources, supported by what would be, yet again, the largest airborne assault in history, with more troops to be ferried by landing craft and boats across the river on a wide front, Patton ordered his men to cross in rubber rafts, while his engineers cobbled together ferries out of rafts and river boats, and threw together temporary bridges so that American tanks could cross. Like Hodges, Patton's men crossed the Rhine ahead of Montgomery, albeit only by a day in the case of Third Army.

Over the night of 22/23 March, Montgomery's British, Canadian and American soldiers crossed the great river barrier in Operation Plunder. Four full airborne divisions dropped on the east side of the river, though, unlike during Market Garden, they landed close to the advancing ground troops, and were swiftly absorbed into the onrushing assault wave. For once, the airborne troops suffered relatively light casualties.

Now the race to occupy Germany was on in earnest. Leading Allied officers, from Montgomery and Bradley to army commanders like Patton, to field officers and men in the trenches, all hoped to get to Berlin before the Soviets. They didn't know that a decision had already been taken at the highest headquarters: Eisenhower had been told that the capital city of Germany was to be a Russian, not a Western Allied, prize.

Operation Eclipse was the name of the grand strategic plan for the occupation and partition of Germany. It had been approved at the highest levels at the Yalta Conference, in February 1945, by Soviet Chairman Josef Stalin, British Prime Minister Winston Churchill and US President Franklin Delano Roosevelt. Eisenhower knew about the plan, but many of his subordinate commanders did not.

Eclipse was obviously a practical plan. The Soviets, with their massive army, were approaching Germany from the east; therefore, they would take control of the eastern part of the country. The Western Allies came from the west, with the British on the left (north) flank and the Americans to the right, on the south. The Western Allied occupation zones were essentially determined by the organisation of the D-Day landings of 6 June 1944. When Eisenhower's forces hit the beaches, the British were on the left flank, the Americans on the right. It would have been a logistical nightmare to alter this deployment as the campaign progressed, so when the Allies turned toward Germany the British, on the left, moved into northern Germany, while the Americans, on the right flank, entered the south.

So the occupation zones of the British and Americans were likewise determined by practicality – each nation would occupy the territory held by its troops at the end of the war. Additional provisions were made for a small French zone of occupation, since liberated France was beginning to contribute more and more troops to the final push. (Even Stalin agreed to a French zone, as long as it came out of the already agreed upon Western Allies section.)

After the war, it would become popular for some prognosticators from the western democracies to claim that Eisenhower 'let' the Russians have Berlin. Notable authorities, including even General Patton, suggested at least privately that the British and Americans should have gone to war with the Russians right away, using the Allied Expeditionary Forces to drive the Red Army back to the original borders of the Soviet Union. This argument ignores obvious realities of the war: no matter how magnificent the accomplishments of the British and American troops during the war in Europe – and they were magnificent – it is simple fact that the war on the Eastern Front was an order of magnitude larger than the war in the west. The Soviets had a much, much larger army in the field than the Western Allies. They had greater numbers of men, more (and better) tanks, more aircraft (albeit lower quality) and a vast industrial base right behind their lines. Any notion that the Western Allies could have defeated the Red Army in direct combat is nothing more than a fantastic pipe dream.

The fact is that Berlin, by April 1945, lay directly in the path of the implacable armies of the Soviet Union. By this time in the war, the Red Army was a thoroughly experienced, well-equipped and massive fighting force. The front-line soldiers were generally well disciplined; however, the rear echelon troops, many of whom came from the Asian steppes of Siberia and Mongolia, were regarded even by their own commanders as exceptionally brutal. These were the men who had indulged in the orgies of rape and murder as the Soviet forces had swept closer and closer to the German heartland.

It must be remembered that the war between Nazi Germany and Soviet Russia was one of extreme cruelty on both sides. Under the auspices of the SS, the Nazis had practised genocide, extermination and enslavement on a never before seen scale as they had swept eastward through the Ukraine, the Russian heartland, the steppes of Georgia. Now the Russians were coming west, and they were coming not just for victory, but for revenge.

Finally the Russians were right outside the city. Now again Goebbels came on the radio, this time to say we should take shovels and sticks, whatever we could get our hands on, and use them to fight the Russians when they came in the city. He told us that the Führer was disappointed in us, that we should have done a better job of fighting.

That idiot, Goebbels! He got what was coming to him: like Hitler, he killed himself. But did you know that, before he died, he poisoned his wife and his six kids? They were really cute kids, little ones, and he killed them before he killed himself.

But I didn't find out about that until later. We could start to hear the battle already; it was coming that close to the city. We had been hoping it would be the Americans coming to Berlin, but it was the Russians. We thought about going to one of those big bunkers, but my family decided to take shelter in the cellar of our apartment, which was a five-storey building. There were a lot of people down there.

It was getting pretty terrible there at the end. I remember dead horses in the street, killed by bombs, I think. People would come up to them and slice meat off their bodies right there. They'd go away with these backpacks that just had blood dripping out of them.

The army had built barricades across all the streets, so that tanks couldn't get through. They called them *Panzer Sperre*. It was a huge wall across the street, right in front of our building. They built those things all over, mainly to stop tanks. The whole city was fortified.

The Russians kept getting closer and closer, and we knew the end was coming. It was Hitler's birthday, 20 April, that my mother, my brother and I packed up satchels with some clothes, and got ready to head down to the cellar. We planned to stay in the apartment building's shelter until the battle was over.

Max Sprengel came out of his apartment and saw us in the hall, getting ready to go down the stairs. He still had his little Hitler moustache and his silly uniform.

'Where are you going?' he said.

'We're taking shelter before the battle!' my mother told him. 'The Russians will be here any day! Can't you hear the cannons?'

And she was right, you could hear the gunfire outside of the city. But Max shook his head. 'Those are fireworks! They're celebrating the Führer's birthday! The Russians are a long way away!'

I think he was serious, but he was wrong. So we went downstairs, and joined most of the people from our building in the bomb shelter in the cellar. And before long they were fighting right on our street, shooting and exploding things all over the place.

Two boys came down there, like 15 or 16 years old. They were wearing soldiers' uniforms, but they were crying, they were so scared. One of them had lived in our building – his mother was down there in the shelter with us. We could have gotten in a lot of trouble, from either Germans or Russians, for hiding deserters in there, but of course we let them stay. Some men put up a barricade, like a big sheet of wood over a cubby, and they went inside there so that they couldn't be seen if any soldiers came down into the cellar.

We knocked holes in the walls inside the cellars, so we could go from one building to the next without going outside. So we were all hiding down in the basements of these buildings. The electricity went off, and for three days we didn't have any power, and we had run out of food by then, too. Over the last few days we moved a bit, through those holes in the walls, and we ended up in a building down the street, around the corner from our own apartment.

'I still have a few potatoes at home,' my mother said.

So she went through the cellars, and through the holes in the walls, all the way to our apartment. There she climbed up the stairs. We had to leave the door of the apartment open when we left – everybody did, so the German soldiers could get in and out if they ended up fighting in there. It was actually more than a block, a couple of blocks away. She went up the stairs, with all the doors open, and found in our apartment that the German soldiers had put boards across all the windows, leaving just a little hole that they could shoot out of. But there weren't any soldiers there at the time.

She said she took the planks out because she was afraid that if the Russians saw them they would just burn down the building. Then she went to the box where she had kept the potatoes, but the box was empty. She went to the neighbour – a different neighbour from the Sprengels – who was still there in his apartment, and asked if they ate the potatoes.

'We were starving!' he said. 'And we thought you were all dead. So yeah, we ate them.'

He thought my mother, my brother and me were all dead! So my mother asked him where her pail was, because she at least wanted to bring some water back. But they said they didn't know, that someone must have taken it.

So my mother came back to the bunker after all of that and she didn't have any food, and she couldn't bring any water. We were getting really hungry and thirsty. I think it was two more days we stayed there, with nothing to eat or drink. Finally, it got really quiet outside – for once there was no shooting, no fighting near where we were.

'Come on, let's go across the street,' my mother said to me. 'That's a factory where they used to pickle herrings. Maybe we can find something to eat there.'

This was a big company, where they put the herrings in oil and salt, stuff like that. She thought there must be something to eat there. But we were too late, just too late. Lots of other people had been there, and they had taken all the fish, the oil, the salt, anything that might have been good to eat.

My mother found these boxes, without labels. They had some white powder in there, and she didn't know what it was. But she thought maybe we could eat it, because it came from a food factory, so she said, 'Let's take one of these back with us.'

So we came back on to the street, and now we could see the Russians at one end, and we knew there were German soldiers hiding at the other end. We started to cross the street, and all of sudden this voice starts shouting, in German but speaking with a Russian accent.

'Leave the street! We are going to start shooting again!' he called.

We raced across the street and back into the shelter. I remember thinking that was awfully nice of them. They didn't shoot while we were out there. They probably knew we were just trying to run for food and water.

Actually, those Russians were nicer than some of the Germans. We called those Nazis 'werewolves'. They would shoot any Germans who weren't fighting the Russians. When people, regular citizens, would go out, they would wear a white piece of cloth to show the Russians that they weren't soldiers, and those werewolves started shooting Germans who had the white cloths on, shooting their own people! They'd shoot no matter who it was, kids or whatever. They were crazy guys, real fanatics.

So anyway, we took that powder from the box and mixed it with a little water – I don't remember where the water came from, but it was all we had. My mother hoped it would thicken into kind of a paste or something, but it didn't. We didn't know if it was poison, or what.

'If we die, we all die together,' she said. We were starving, and we needed to put something in our stomachs, so we ate it. We didn't die, but it was strange, we couldn't go to sleep, any of us, for maybe twenty-four hours after we ate it.

And it was really hot and stuffy in there. The next morning, I think it was about 5 a.m., I decided I needed some air. It was really quiet outside, no bombs, no shooting, and I thought it was safe to go and get some air.

I went up the stairs out of the cellar but before I even stepped out of the building two Russians soldiers were there, and each of them grabbed one of my arms. They were drunk – I could see that for sure, and I think they were looking to grab a girl. They were Mongols, too, I'm pretty sure; they looked like they came from Asia.

The funny thing is, I wasn't even scared. My head was blank, except I was thinking of the two young men who were hiding in the cellar with us. I thought if they found those two guys, who were German soldiers who had deserted, they would have burned the whole building down.

These men started to drag me out of the doorway, but at that moment a Russian officer came down the stairs from inside the building. He gave an order to the two men, in Russian so I couldn't understand what he was saying. But one of the men let me go and the other didn't. So the officer gave another order, and the one who had let me go hit the other one over the head with his rifle butt and knocked him right down. Then he put him over his shoulder and carried him off.

Then the officer sat down and talked to me. He told me that I looked exactly like his sister, back in Russia, that I could have been her doppelganger. This other girl, Ingrid, also came up from the cellar. She was my age, and had been in my class in elementary school. Later, though, she had gone to the BDM, so I hadn't seen her much.

The Russian officer spoke German very well, and he seemed like a nice man.

'The war is over,' he told us.

'But there are still werewolves out there!' I replied.

'No, they're not there any more. The war is almost over everywhere, and it is over right here.'

He also told us that the fighting troops were fairly decent men, but he warned us about the ones who followed the fighting troops. 'You have to beware of them,' he said.

And it was true. A lot of them were looters, and they did rape a lot of women and girls. He told us to stay on the upper floors of the building, since those

Siberian soldiers, who'd mostly never been in cities, wouldn't go above the second floor.

We took his advice after I told my mother what he'd said, so for a little while we hid in our apartment on the fourth floor, and stayed away from the windows. And he was right about that, too: sometimes Russians came into the building, but they didn't like going up the stairs. Twice, though, my mother hid me in a wash basin under the bed, when we heard Russians tramping around below.

Remember my good friend was Vera? She was the one who had just adored Hitler before the war, at least until the Kristallnacht. She told me the story of what happened to her. She was grabbed by one of those guys and carried up to an empty apartment, just one where the people were gone down to the bunker. He threw her down on a bed and took off his gun belt and put it down. As soon as he did she grabbed the gun and threw it out the window – and he took off running! I guess he didn't want to be there without his gun, so he just ran away.

Another girlfriend of mine was a year younger than me, maybe 16 or 17. She got pregnant from being raped. They took the baby a few weeks later, aborted it, because there was nothing else anybody could do. So Vera and I were very lucky. But still, I remember those other Russians shouting at us to clear the street before they started shooting. Not all the Russians were bad men. Still, my mother didn't let me go out by myself for a long time, not until way after the war.

Finally it was really quiet, and we really started to believe that the war actually was over. We were sitting in our apartment then, still with no food, which was bad enough, but we also didn't have any water. You know, you can be hungry for a while, but you need to have water or you'll die.

But we heard from some other people, I don't know how the news got around, that in the back of a building a few blocks away was an old pump, one that had been there for probably hundreds of years. So we took a washtub, you know one of those big buckets with two handles, that needs two people to carry it. My mother and I went, after first leaving my brother behind down in the bunker.

So we found that pump and filled the tub with water. It was really heavy, but we started to carry it back to the shelter – and then shooting started up again! Each of us was more scared than the other, and whenever one of us stumbled more water would spill out. By the time we got back there was just a little left, and we made sure everyone knew it was for drinking, not for washing.

But we got some water to drink, and we were able to stay there a few more days, until the war was really over.

The last thing I remember about the war was our neighbour, that Nazi, Max Sprengel. I don't know when he and his wife went to the bunker, because it was after my family took shelter on 20 April. But eventually the Sprengels went to one of those big government bunkers, with the anti-aircraft guns on top. Probably because they were party officials, they had it a little better than the rest of us, in that shelter.

But after it was over, he came to our apartment, and he brought a loaf of bread and, I can't remember for sure, maybe some potatoes. It was food that they had saved up in there, and he shared it with us. He was glad we were okay, and we were glad he and Frau Sprengel were okay, also. I still remember what he said, as he gave my mother that food.

'I want you to know,' he told her. 'That I never turned you in.'

– Charlotte Jacobitz

10

War's End and Home

For us to blow up the dykes after the war would have been crazy. The Dutch would have killed us! But the threat worked, and the British gave us permission to go home as a group. There was no restriction on our weapons.

– Helmut Jacobitz

The end of the war in Europe, when it came, was sudden, complete and cataclysmic. Soviet troops had reached Berlin on 22 April 1945, and surrounded the city by 25 April. That same day, American spearheads of General Omar Bradley's Twelfth Army Group made contact with units of Marshal Konev's First Ukrainian Front at Torgau, on the Elbe River. Further south, Patton's Third Army had driven through Austria and plunged into Czechoslovakia, while British units finally broke through in northern Italy to make contact with Tito's partisan army in northern Yugoslavia.

The Battle of Berlin finally came to an end on 3 May 1945. Following Hitler's suicide on 30 April, Admiral Dönitz, commander of the Kriegsmarine, ascended to overall command of the Third Reich. The Führer's hand-picked replacement, Dönitz spoke to his people over the radio and, without apparent irony, announced, 'German men and women ... our Führer, Adolf Hitler, is dead. He died a hero's death in the capital of the German Reich, after having led an unmistakably straight and steady life.'

Following this last bit of propaganda, Dönitz hastily arranged an end to the war in Europe. The formal surrender of German forces occurred on 8 May.

The 'Thousand Year Reich' that the Nazis had birthed in 1933 had lasted for just over twelve years. In its wake, the regime left an entire continent scorched and devastated, with a great many populations seeking vengeance against the German people.

In most places, the troops of the Wehrmacht, the SS and the Luftwaffe had already been overrun by the advancing tide of Allied armies, with surviving German soldiers being captured as prisoners of war. France, Belgium, Poland, the Balkans and all of the German homeland were in the hands of either Eisenhower's Western Allied forces or of Stalin's Red Army. In a few places, however, including Denmark, Norway and the north-western coastline of Holland, the war ended without the German garrisons having been overcome in direct battle.

As for the people of Holland, their experience during the war had been brutal, and had lasted for five long years. Invaded by Germany on 10 May 1940, the Dutch had been swiftly overwhelmed by German tanks, infantry and air power. On 13 May of that year, the Queen of Holland and her government departed The Hague by ship, destined for exile in England. The next day, even as the remaining Dutch leaders tried to negotiate a surrender, Rotterdam became one of the first large cities to experience terror bombing. The Luftwaffe plastered the business district of that thriving commercial metropolis with a brutal and punitive air raid, and threatened to visit that punishment upon every other Dutch city if the nation did not immediately capitulate.

On 15 May 1940 Holland surrendered to Germany, beginning an occupation that was to last until the same month in 1945. During that time, the Gestapo and a fascist puppet government controlled from Berlin exerted ruthless control over the population. The methodical Dutch had maintained excellent and detailed civic records, which made it easy for the Germans to locate Holland's Jews. They and other 'undesirables' were taken away in great numbers – including, eventually, Anne Frank of Amsterdam, whose diary was to become a profound and lasting testament to Nazi barbarity. In the end, Holland would suffer the highest proportion of deaths – more than 2.3 per cent – of any country occupied by the Nazis during the Second World War.

In the waning weeks of the Second World War, it had been Canadian troops of Field Marshal Montgomery's Twenty-First Army Group that finally liberated most of Holland. Montgomery's men entered the country from the east, since much of Holland had been bypassed as the Allied armies advanced to the Rhine and beyond in their headlong rush to defeat the Germans. In only a few places, mostly in the very low coastal regions in the far north and west of Holland, did some German troops still remain undefeated when the orders to surrender finally reached them.

We *Fallschirmjaeger* were lucky, in that we were posted in far western Holland, and the Americans and British simply went around our part of the country on their way to the Rhine. I didn't arrive in Holland until after the big parachute attack when the Allies tried to capture three bridges at Eindhoven, Nijmegen and Arnhem. They got the first two, but General Student's First Parachute Army chewed them up pretty good at Arnhem. *That* was a bloody fight. Afterward, the Allies decided to cross the Rhine farther to the south. It took the whole winter, and some bloody battles, but eventually they made it into Germany.

So there was no fighting where I was. We kept listening to the radio, with Goebbels telling us that the war was going well. Meanwhile the Allied broadcasts, in German, reported that Eisenhower's armies had crossed the Rhine in March 1945 and the Russians were closing in on Berlin. When even Goebbels announced that the final battle for the Reich was beginning, we knew the war was nearly over.

Finally Admiral Dönitz came on and told us that Hitler was dead. Later we learned that the Führer had killed himself in his bunker. First he killed his dog – he used the dog to test whether a cyanide capsule was really poisonous. Then his wife, Eva Braun, whom he had married just the day before, took one of those cyanide pills and died. Hitler shot himself in the head.

They told us that Adolf Hitler gave his life fighting for Germany, and that Dönitz was the new Führer. He was ready to give up everything, so the war was over a few days after that. Even before the end of the war (on 8 May) the last of the troops in Holland, including my regiment, arranged to surrender on 5 May.

Of course we wanted to go home, and we were pretty worried about the Dutch people – they were very bitter against Germans right then. I was also lucky, because the unit I was in, the paratroopers, was one of the few that was still together when the war ended. We said that we wanted to go home together, but the English wanted us to turn over our weapons and surrender. That would have meant being in the middle of the angry Dutch, with not even our rifles to protect ourselves.

We were in a part of Holland that's below sea level, where there are a lot of dykes. Our commander decided to use that as leverage: instead of giving up our weapons and turning ourselves over to the British, we threatened to keep fighting and to blow up all the dykes in the country. We knew – and the Dutch knew even better – that if you blow up the dykes, half of Holland would be flooded. In fact, the Dutch thought about destroying their own dykes when the Germans invaded in 1940, but they decided it would have been suicidal. They would have killed lots of their own people, and even after the dykes were repaired and the water pumped out, it would have messed up the country for ten or twenty years because the salt water in the fields would make them infertile.

Of course, for us to blow up the dykes after the war would have been crazy. The Dutch would have killed us! But the threat worked, and the British gave us permission to go home as a group. There was no restriction on our weapons.

Still, we had to turn everything else over to the English soldiers. I had won an award for being wounded, what the Americans call a Purple Heart. But a soldier took it from me when I was captured, and now he's going around showing everyone that he won a Purple Heart! They took everything we had, even my pictures, before I was sent home. They took our backpacks, underwear, socks, uniforms, all the medals, any other insignia that we had. We knew they would take everything. Before I went to the control I decided to bury one of my medals and my knife by a tree, and then go back and get it. But I never got back there, and now I don't know where it is – except in Holland someplace.

Still, the war was over, and I had survived, and I knew I would be going back to Germany. When many of the soldiers (from other units) were marching home, without their weapons, the Dutch people would spit on them and kick them and throw rocks at them, because they knew the Germans had no weapons. But we had our rifles, so they didn't dare try that on the paratroopers. They just watched, some of them jeering a little while others were kind of sullen, while the men of my unit marched back to Germany. It was not a long march – even though we were in western Holland, it's a small enough country that the men could get back to our own homeland in just a few days.

Although for me, I heard about that part later, since I didn't have to march home from Holland. I had that shrapnel in my knee, from the attack by the *Jabo*, and that made it hard for me to march. Even when I was posted in Holland I didn't have to march, I just stood on the side, because of that knee. After we surrendered, in the same camp where we had to give up all our stuff, an English doctor checked me out and agreed I was not able to march. So I was able to get a ride on a small ship, one of the few German minesweepers that had survived the war. That ship took me and other wounded soldiers through the North Sea, back to Germany.

– Helmut Jacobitz

POW or DEF

The Geneva Convention of 1929 spelled out very specific requirements for the treatment of enemy Prisoners of War (POWs). These included the necessity of feeding the prisoners the same level of basic nutrition as a nation fed its own soldiers. The Geneva Convention may have seemed almost quaint in light of the brutality of the Second World War – and certainly the Germans made little or no attempt at honouring its provisions regarding POWs, while the Soviets and Japanese had never signed it to begin with. Still, the Western Allies made a conscientious effort to adhere to the pact's requirements. (Perhaps it is worth noting, also, that another of the convention's prohibitions, that against using poison gas on the battlefield, was honoured by all participants in the Second World War.)

With the collapse of Nazi Germany, however, the number of surrendered German soldiers quite simply overwhelmed the ability of the Americans and British to feed them. The Western Allies had prepared for about 3 million German prisoners, but found themselves having to care for more than 7.5 million in Germany, and another 1.5 million in Italy. Up to a million of the Wehrmacht soldiers captured by the Western Allies had been fleeing westward to avoid being taken by the Russians.

The problem was further compounded by the fact that there were some 10 million displaced persons in Germany – most of them slave labourers brought there from conquered countries during the war, though some were the survivors of concentration camps. The majority of both groups were emaciated to the point of starvation, and the Allies gave nourishment of these unfortunates a higher priority than they did to surrendered German soldiers. Food supplies were additionally stressed immediately after the war, when many people of German ancestry were forced out of their homes in Poland, Czechoslovakia and other countries, returning to their ancestral homeland as refugees.

Best estimates are that the average sustenance of a German citizen in the summer of 1945 was just around 1,000 calories, and as low as 840 calories in the Ruhr valley. Much of this was due to the state of Germany itself. For two years fertiliser (other than compost) had been virtually unavailable to farmers, since the country's stocks of nitrogen and phosphate had been directed to weapons production. This alone had dropped agriculture production by some 25 per cent. Additionally, it was difficult to get the food from the farms to the markets. The Allied bombing campaign had devastated Germany's railway network, eliminating more than half of the nation's locomotives, rolling stock, bridges, terminals and track. Food-processing centres, like every other industry, had been hammered, while manufacturing of machinery had been devoted to tanks and aeroplanes, not tractors, for many years.

A final factor impacting food supply and distribution in Germany was the partition of the country. Many of the food-growing regions, especially in the areas of the Oder and Neisse Rivers, were in the Russian zone of occupation, and Chairman Stalin was in no mood to export any of his hard-won booty to his former enemies. In Western Allied occupation zones, the Red Cross tried to intervene, but General Eisenhower's Supreme

Headquarters (SHAEF) forbade the organisation from feeding their former foes. Eisenhower later argued that this was to hold stockpiles in reserve in the event of a winter famine, but as a result vast quantities of donated food supplies spoiled in railway carriages or were kept indefinitely in storage because of SHAEF's decree.

Given the vast and insurmountable problem of feeding all of these people, General Eisenhower proclaimed that German soldiers who had surrendered at war's end would not be considered prisoners of war. Instead, they would be classified as Disarmed Enemy Forces (DEFs). This classification put the onus of feeding those Germans upon the people of that defeated country, rather than the occupying forces.

In the end, the defeated soldiers of Germany, like their non-combatant countrymen and women, were left to fend for themselves.

Think of what the map of Germany looks like. When the minesweeper brought me home, I was taken to that little section on the coast of the North Sea, between the Rhine River and Bremen. It's the short stretch of coastline between Holland and Denmark. When we got there we were kind of like prisoners of war, only we didn't have anybody guarding us. We were free. They had us sleeping in a barn – there was no barracks any more. There was no fence around us, or anything.

We were lucky, too. Some of the guys from the army got placed in detention camps, by the English, the French and the Americans too. They were treated really lousy. The Allies would give them hardly anything to eat. They had nothing to wear, nothing to cover themselves up for shelter. At least we were sleeping in the farmer's barn, on hay up there in the loft. We didn't have to work, or march, or anything.

Some of the men who lived in Western Germany just left, went home. The Allies didn't try to stop them. Lots of guys from Eastern Germany, or, like me, from Berlin, couldn't go home yet, because the Russians weren't letting anyone into their zone. So we had nothing to do except wait.

But I'm a guy who always has to be doing something. So while we were staying in this barn, I saw the farmer taking care of his field. Just the way I am, I got involved and I started helping him right away.

Actually, it's kind of funny to remember it now. The first time, it didn't work out so well. The farmer needed help getting his potatoes out of the ground. Now, in most of Germany you use a rake to get the potatoes. It was like a claw, and you rake up through the green stuff and get the potatoes. But there in Friesland [extreme north-west Germany, next to Holland] you use a small spade.

The farmer was pretty bossy about it. He said, 'Here, go and get the potatoes!'

He had a small potato field for his personal use, mainly, behind his house. He gave me a bucket and a spade and I started digging down into the ground. He came around after half an hour and said: 'Aren't you done already?'

'I'm down three feet and I can't find any potatoes,' I said. I was using the spade like a shovel, and digging!

He got pretty annoyed. 'You're a stupid city dweller!' he told me, and he pushed me aside and dug them himself.

But I soon met another farmer, and I helped him all the time. And by doing that, I used to eat with the farmer and his family, not with the soldiers. He had fairly good food for that time, when most of the public had barely anything to eat.

– Helmut Jacobitz

A Fatherland Divided

Following the war, Germany was partitioned into occupation zones. Much of the rationale as to which country controlled what territory was simply a matter of military operations and geography. The Soviets, of course, occupied the eastern part of the country – the zone that would later become East Germany – because that was the part of the nation held by the Red Army.

Eventually western Germany would be divided into a large British zone, in the north-west; a large American zone in the southern and west-central part of the country; and two smaller French zones adjacent to the borders of *la belle France*. (By the end of the war, France had contributed a number of divisions to the Allied war effort and her new leader, General de Gaulle, felt very strongly that she deserved a share of the prize.) The city of Berlin was in the Soviet zone, but it was divided separately into East Berlin, communist-controlled, and West Berlin, which was shared by the three victorious Western Allies. East Prussia and parts of Pomerania and other provinces were torn away from Germany and added to Russia, Lithuania, Poland and Czechoslovakia (see Map 2).

The plan for the partition of Germany was called Operation Eclipse, and had been codified by the Allies during a series of meetings at the highest levels. The Allied heads of state known as the 'Big Three' – President Franklin Roosevelt, Prime Minister Winston Churchill and Communist Party Chairman Josef Stalin – met first in Tehran (November 1943), and later at the Crimean resort town of Yalta (February 1945) to discuss the strategy for ending the war and occupying Germany. All three were determined to make sure that Germany was not able to rise from the ashes of this war to menace Europe again. The leaders also agreed, most notably at Yalta, that nations liberated from Nazi rule would be allowed to democratically establish free and independent governments.

Even before the fall of Berlin, Stalin revealed his true intentions. After the Russians drove the Germans out of Poland, they ruthlessly purged any anti-communist members of the Polish resistance. The Polish government-in-exile, based in London, was branded reactionary by the communists and forbidden from playing any role in the restoration of Polish 'sovereignty'. This exclusion had been foreshadowed by a horrible crime immediately after the fall of Poland in 1939. Most of the highly patriotic and dedicated officer corps of the Polish army had been massacred in cold blood by the NKVD (the Soviet secret police, forerunners of the KGB). In reality, the new government was a mere puppet for the Kremlin. Similar fates befell Romania, Bulgaria and Hungary while the war still raged. In the Balkans, only Yugoslavia retained a vestige of independence, primarily because that nation's powerful partisan forces – united under the charismatic and influential Marshal Tito – had liberated the country almost without outside aid. While his nation would be part of the Communist Bloc, Tito's forceful presence allowed Yugoslavia to retain a measure of independence unique among the 'socialist republics'.

With the end of the war, similar fates befell the people of Czechoslovakia and eastern Austria (including Vienna). Like the rest of Eastern Europe, the new governments in these territories were all versions of the Soviet Socialist Republics (SSR) installed by Moscow. After several years as occupied territory, East Germany would eventually follow suit.

While there was agreement among all the Allies that Russia needed some insurance against another devastating invasion, the extent of Soviet control over the liberated territories came as a rude shock. As late as March 1945 President Roosevelt still thought that Stalin could be treated as a reasonable man, an opinion not shared by Winston Churchill or Roosevelt's own ambassador to Moscow, Averell Harriman. By the time the US President recognised the truth, it was too late. Roosevelt's health had been failing even at Yalta, and when he died of a brain haemorrhage on 12 April 1945, Stalin became new President Harry S. Truman's problem.

The Soviet occupation was marked everywhere by ruthless purging, show trials portraying anti-communists as agents of fascism and mass deportations of people to Soviet gulags in Siberia and other remote regions. Stalin hand-picked the rulers of his satellite countries, in effect creating a barrier of communist countries many hundreds of miles wide to guard Russia's western border.

Despite the intentions and desires of the Western Allies, there was nothing they could do to prevent Stalin's iron hand taking control. In any event, the British, Americans and French faced many challenges in their own occupation zones. Nazis were purged from positions of authority, but there were few trained administrators to take their places. In fact, General Patton created some controversy by allowing a few Nazi bureaucrats to remain in place. He argued that they were the only people who could do the necessary jobs.

The occupying powers struggled to feed the vast populations of displaced people in their respective zones, while restoring some semblance of normal life to a shattered country. Germany's cities had almost all suffered great damage from bombing, and basic aspects of infrastructure – water supplies, sewers, electricity, public transport – all needed major repairs. In the American zone, Frankfurt, Nuremberg, Munich and Cologne all became important centres for recovery. The British faced similar problems in the great port and industrial cities of Bremen, Hamburg, the Ruhr valley and Hanover.

They were looking for tradesmen in those days, and my trade was making signs. In the German language, *Buchstaben Klempner*, 'sign-making', is very similar to the word for 'plumber' [*Klempner*], though of course I knew nothing about plumbing. But when they read the name of my trade, they said, 'Oh, he's a plumber.' For that reason, I got sent to Hanover.

In Hanover we were in a barracks across the street from an English barracks. There was no fence around us or anything, so we were free to go into town, to watch movies, to go out with girls. Of course, I didn't go to town! But others could if they wanted to.

We Germans were supposed to take care of all the maintenance work in the English barracks. Remember, they thought I was a plumber. So I did a little work for them, just as little as I could get away with. Mostly I just refused to work. They paid very little, like a dollar or a mark a day. For that you couldn't do much – it was about enough to pay for admission to one movie. I thought, 'If they're not going to pay me a decent wage, why should I work?'

But we didn't have it that bad in the city. I told you how other soldiers in other camps were treated really lousy. The French were especially bad: they wouldn't feed their German prisoners, and they asked them to sign up for the French Foreign Legion. They were really cruel about it, and set it up so that lots of men just signed up out of desperation.

They did it like this: they had a camp for the Foreign Legion, and a camp for the prisoners of war [Disarmed Enemy Forces] right next to it. The legion already had Germans serving in it, as well as French and people from all over. In their camp they were playing football, eating and drinking. You had a hell of a life there. But in the prison camp you had nothing, not even a tent! You dug holes in the ground and lived in those holes, and it was freezing when the weather got cold. And they all wanted to get out of there. My future father-in-law was in one of those camps, and he came home starving.

So meanwhile I was spending time in that British army barracks. After a little while even the Englishmen didn't really believe I was a plumber. But I was still supposed to help take care of the barracks, which was not so bad. They made some of the German POWs from a regular camp go in the compound and clean it up. Some of those English were mean. They smoked their cigarettes and then they dropped them, big pieces, right in front of the Germans and they smashed them with their boot heels.

Those POWs would scrape them together to try and make cigarettes out of the scraps. Plus, they didn't get any food. They used to go in the trash cans and get food out of there. I was embarrassed about it, but at least I had food, and they didn't. As a matter of fact, I was eating with the English mostly, and they had a lot of good food. I didn't even touch the German food anymore, except maybe for a bit of sausage.

But, a funny deal, I found myself with a lot of money. I maybe shouldn't even mention it, but I will. It happened in that English barracks. Like I said, they wanted us to work there, but I didn't want to work for only one mark a day. So I did a little bit of work, but mostly I just walked around there all day. One day I went up in the attic of that barracks, and this was maybe kind of stupid, but I looked all through there.

I found this backpack, from an Englishman, that was hidden up there. It had lots of personal items in it like socks and underwear, and a lot of German postage stamps. When I first found it I took some of the socks, because I didn't have any – at that time we were all wrapping pieces of cloth around our feet. None of the German POWs had socks any more.

That evening I told the guys in my barracks about the postage stamps, and asked if they could have any value. One fellow goes, 'Oh *ja, ja*. Those postage stamps can have lots of value, hundreds of marks worth.'

I said to myself, 'Oh my God!'

This is what I think happened: While the war was going on, when the battles came close to their houses German civilians would go and take shelter in the bunkers. But they would leave their houses unlocked, because if there was a fire in there the firemen had to be able to get in to fight it, to put the fire out.

So the English came in to the unlocked houses, and this guy found those stamps and took them. That's looting, isn't that what you call it? So he stole the stamps from a German house. Then later I guess that someone else, probably a German prisoner, stole that backpack from an English soldier, took what he wanted and then left it there, with the stamps still in it. Then I found the stolen backpack just by accident and the stamps were still in it.

So the next day I went back to the backpack and got all the stamps. I took them around to the stamp dealers in Hanover and asked them what those stamps were worth. Everyone had a different idea about that. One guy said he'd give me so much money, another one would give a different amount. One said he needed a couple days to evaluate each stamp, but I said, 'My God, no!' After I went to three or four guys, I went back to the one who offered me the most. He paid me 2,000 marks for the stamps! Now remember, I made 30 marks a month, so I'd have to work years to own that much. So I was a rich man, all of a sudden.

Then one day, a fire-fighting company from the Berlin fire department came by our barracks and slept there overnight. They were from Berlin, but had been working in Hamburg, which had been bombed even more than Berlin, which was much farther inland than Hamburg. A funny deal was, this was our fire department, the one right on the corner where we used to live in Berlin!

So I knew they were going back to Berlin, and I wrote a letter to my parents to tell them I was in Hanover. At the time, they didn't know I was there, or even that I was alive. I gave the fireman that little note and he took it back to Berlin and gave it to my parents and told them, 'Here, your son is still alive.'

My parents told my older brother Hermann that I was in Hanover. He had been working in the aircraft industry during the war, which was an important enough job that he hadn't been drafted. He had an apartment, or a room, in a town called Vienburg. That town was right on the border of where the Russians came at the end of the war. The Russians actually came right into Vienburg and occupied it, but because of the peace agreement between the Russians, the British and Americans, Vienburg became part of West Germany when the country was divided, and the Russians went back.

Anyway, Hanover wasn't too far from Vienburg. As soon as Hermann learned where I was, he came to see me, which was a really nice surprise. He told me everything was okay at home, and also that if I wanted to go home, I could do it. He could tell me how, but he warned me I had to be careful if I was going to try.

We went out to have a beer, and it was starting to seem like life might be normal again. I told him about Holland, and the English barracks.

He said, 'I have a story, too.'

And then he started to tell me what had happened to him. When the war was over, Hermann tried to get back to Berlin, to see what was in his apartment and also to see about our parents. But he went on the train, which had to pass through the Russian zone.

He shook his head, like he really couldn't believe it had happened. 'The train had just started moving very slowly, when these Russians came through the car. There was an officer and three soldiers, with machine guns. They grabbed me by the collar and told me I was under arrest.'

'What for?' I asked him.

He shrugged. 'They don't need a reason, except that I was a man. Over there, in the east, they're taking any German males, from age 14 to 60, and arresting them. Rumour is that they're all being sent to Russia and forced to work in camps. I guess Stalin wants Germans to clean up and rebuild Russia.'

'How did you get here, then?' I asked.

'Well, that's my story,' he replied. 'They took me and a bunch of other Germans in a train, going east. After a couple of days we got off and were put in a camp on the way to Russia. I learned we were still in Germany, but somewhere near the Polish border.

'In that camp they shaved all my hair, right down to the skin. They did that to all the prisoners – it made it really easy for them to identify us. So I'm thinking, 'How in hell do I get out of here?'

'I didn't know how I'd do it, but I decided to escape. I was by the camp depot, where the supplies were brought in, and I saw a Russian truck nearby, with the engine running. No one was looking, so I dropped to the ground and climbed underneath, between the rear wheels. There was some space there, so I pulled myself up on the axle, on to the part that didn't move, the differential, I think it's called.

'The drive shaft was right next to me, and when a driver got in and started going that metal shaft was spinning, inches from my hands. It moved when the truck moved, and stopped when the truck stopped at the gate of the camp.

'And right there a Russian soldier came right up to the truck. I could see his dirty boots just a few feet from my head. I'm sitting there holding on to the differential and the soldier started talking, in Russian. I didn't understand what he was saying, but he sounded angry and I thought, "Oh my God, he got me."

'I was afraid they'd beat me up, maybe even shoot me for trying to escape. But just before I gave up and started to climb out, the soldier started kicking the tyres. It turned out he wasn't talking about me – he was talking about the tyres!

'So I held on and the truck took off and went out of the camp. It kind of lurched around a corner and I almost fell off, but I didn't want to take a chance on getting run over. Finally it had to slow down over a rough stretch of road. That's when I let go of the differential and dropped to the ground. The truck rolled on and I hopped to my feet, free and out of the camp.'

'But you were still a long way from home, right?' I asked.

He smiled. '*Ja*, but the Russians didn't have me any more.'

We had another beer and he told me the rest of his story. The first thing he had to do was get a hat, since his shaved head made him look like an escaped prisoner. But he was able to steal a cap right away, so that covered his bald head. Then he just started walking. It took him a couple of weeks, but it wasn't unusual for someone to be walking along the roads then – all kinds of people were doing that. He just made sure to avoid Russians, and by the time he made it back to Berlin, his hair had kind of grown down and he didn't look like an escaped prisoner any more. He made it home, my parents told him about the note from the fireman, and that's how he came to find me in Hanover.

– Helmut Jacobitz

11

Aftermath

Food, our dinner, was usually one potato. I'd come home and my mother was grating that potato and putting it in water. Maybe sometimes we also had a carrot or something to put in there, but usually it was just potato and water. Just one potato for the whole family, then with maybe one slice of bread, nothing on it, to go with it.

– Charlotte Jacobitz

It is not too much of a stretch to say that the central personal conflict of the Second World War was the struggle between Adolf Hitler and Josef Stalin. Both men were utterly ruthless dictators who were absolute masters of their respective, and very powerful, nations. Each was responsible for the deaths of millions of his country's own citizens, people whose only 'crime' had been to be born in a place or of an ethnicity that was displeasing to their national leader.

Hitler's crimes are too numerous to recount, but the Holocaust certainly ranks highest among them. An atrocity somewhat less well known, though equally well documented, is Stalin's scheme to wipe out individual peasant farmers during the 1930s through the creation of massive, government-controlled collective farms. Realistic estimates suggest significantly more than 10 million Soviet citizens perished during these forced migrations, people who were expelled from their land and left to starve. If those estimates are accurate (and they tend to be fairly well accepted), Stalin's collectivism famines might have actually killed more people than the Holocaust.

Equally ruthless was Stalin's treatment of his own military. Much has been made of the poor performance of Soviet arms in the early campaigns of the Second World War, including the invasion of Finland in 1939 and the utter destruction of Russian front-line units following the Nazi invasion, Operation Barbarossa, in the summer of 1941. To a great extent, these disasters were of Stalin's own making, since during the 1930s he had ruthlessly purged the Red Army's officer corps of many of its most capable leaders. As often as not, these career soldiers were guilty of nothing other than being the target of Stalin's mistrust.

Whereas Hitler had the Gestapo and the SS to keep his own people in line, Stalin had the equally cruel and ruthless NKVD – which, in the post-war years, would evolve into the KGB. Both leaders were paranoid, but Stalin's paranoia was on another plane to anyone else's. History will never know how many people were tortured, executed or sent to the gulags for no other reason than that Josef Stalin distrusted them.

Stalin was also a skilled puppet master, brilliantly playing on the fears and insecurities of his underlings, working them against each other, commanding unquestioning obedience at every turn. The Battle of Berlin provided a classic example, when he offered the great prize of the Nazi capital to his two greatest front commanders, Zhukov and Konev. Each, he knew, would drive his men ruthlessly and accept tremendous casualties, for no other reason than that he wanted to outperform his rival.

One other fact of Stalin's life bears some reflection and, in fact, marks him as an incredibly successful – albeit monstrously brutal – dictator. Unlike all of the other mad, power hungry dictators of the Second World War, Stalin lived a good many years after the war.

In addition, his crimes did not conclude with the cessation of hostilities.

I wanted to go home; I didn't want to stay in that camp. They were releasing people who lived in western Germany, in the Allied occupation zones. But they still wouldn't let us who lived in the east, or in Berlin, go home, because they were afraid the Russians would take us. It was a known fact that people who tried to go home to territory under Soviet control would get arrested by the Russians and sent to Russia, which is what happened to my brother – at least, it would have if he hadn't been able to escape. But I talked to my brother, and he told me how to get across the border and on to the train to Berlin.

I knew that things were bad in Berlin, that they didn't have much food. At that time I had friends, Germans, some who were cooks in the kitchen of the English barracks, others who cooked in the German kitchen. So I went to them and told them I was going to Berlin. From the German kitchen I got bread and stuff when I told them I was going to leave. Then I went to my friend who worked in the English kitchen and he gave me a big piece of meat, the kind of thing that was really scarce in Berlin.

So I got a big backpack and filled it up with all this food, and then I came out of the barracks – which, as I said, had no fence around it. A funny deal was, an English driver was waiting there in his truck, and he saw me with my heavy backpack. He said, 'Where are you going? To the railroad?' When I told him I was, he said I should hop in, and he drove me right where I wanted to go. That's the way I ran away from the POW camp – the English driver took me right to the train station!

The train stopped at the border of the Russian zone, and I got off. This is where my brother had told me how to get across. There was a Russian guard-house right in the middle of the street, and they stopped all traffic from west to east. But my brother knew right where the Russian soldiers were standing, and he told me, and explained how I could get around it.

I went on the *chaussée*, which I guess you'd describe as a paved highway out in the country. It was a pretty main road, with ditches on each side, and it went through rural country, where there were farm fields and small groves of woods. When I got close to the Russians, I ducked off the road and cut through the fields, behind trees and hedges so they couldn't see me. Once I was safely past, I came out of the field, crossed the ditch, and I strolled on to the street on the other side of the guard post.

From there I went right to the train station in the Russian zone, and I bought a ticket and took the train back to Berlin for the first time after the war. And soon I was there, right back at my parents' apartment. They were very happy when I came home with all that food, because they didn't have much at all.

But there was a guy in Berlin called a street *Opmann*, a civilian officer who was in charge of everyone in the neighbourhood. He arranged for the official food to be rationed out. He gave out the ration cards, and you needed a ration card to get food. He asked me about my discharge papers from the army, which of course I didn't have, and he told me I'd need those papers before I could get a ration card. If I didn't have the papers, he couldn't get any food stamps for me.

So, since I couldn't stay in Berlin without food stamps, I ended up going back to the POW camp. I just reversed my path around the Soviet guard post; the British weren't trying to keep people out or arrest them. The mail was going through slowly, and when I got back to the barracks I got a letter that my mother wrote me, saying that my food stamps had come through. The policy had changed, and the people who distributed them were able to do it now without my discharge papers. There was no problem; it was just the way it worked: first you need the papers, then, over maybe a couple of months of time, they changed the procedure and you didn't need them.

I took all my stuff and started back to Berlin, where they already had my food stamps waiting for me. Once again I stopped at the English kitchen before I left, and they gave me all kinds of food, but especially meat. The English mostly ate sheep – they would go crazy for lamb and mutton. I guess they got that meat from Australia, typically, because the English themselves didn't have much meat in their diet either.

That's the way it started in Berlin. I was supposed to work in the city to get my food stamps, but I said, 'I'm not going to work, not for lousy food stamps!' They gave you 800 calories a day in food stamps, and I wasn't going to work anyplace for that little bit.

My dad had his store, which sold soap, and hardware, and other odds and ends, and I started working in the store. The way I worked was that he would give me the name of a guy going around getting merchandise that my dad could put in the store to sell. I would get the merchandise, and it was mostly legitimate – hardly anything came from the black market. But I did learn that there was a black market, and that was where more products were available.

I started to do more of that, both with farmers in the Soviet zone and farther west. At that time they didn't really check you when you left West Berlin to go into the countryside, so I could do that easily. But I had also gotten pretty used to going across the border between the British and Russian zones. I would cross the border and barter with the farmers I met over there. The farmers would give me all kinds of food stuff. They needed money, and we needed food in Berlin. So I could get almost anything I wanted from them.

For example, I could pay about 1,000 marks for 100 pounds of wheat, or make the same deal for peas. In the city, I could sell the food for about three times what I paid for it. Some things, like a pound of meal flour, would sell for 40 marks in Berlin, but I could buy the meal for 10 marks in the country. Of course, that meant I had to grind the wheat to make it into flour.

To do that, I bought a shredder. I connected it to a device, like a huge iron, the kind of thing with rollers that you use to take stiff laundry out of the washer and to make it soft. So I ran the wheat through the shredder, then through the iron rollers, and finally I connected a mill to it so that I could make flour.

After I sold the flour I took the money back to the farmers and paid them for the wheat, and also bought new stuff that I would carry back to Berlin. One farmer offered me a half a cow, which was a lot of meat. I don't even remember what I had to pay for it. It wasn't easy to transport, but I think I made it in two trips, bringing as much fresh meat as I could carry in my biggest satchel while he kept the other part of my share cool in his cellar. As soon as I delivered the first part to Berlin, I turned around and went back and got the rest. Beef was always in demand.

There was another farmer I met in the British zone, and he always said he could get me piglets if I wanted. So one day I got two piglets from him, little tiny ones. I knew that if you fed them they would gain like a pound a day. After ninety days, you have a 90-pound pig – and that is good eating! So I put the little piglets in my backpack, and I went back to the border.

Now there was often a Russian guard at this one spot, and I knew he was there, so like usual I decided to go around. But it had been raining a lot, so I got pretty close to him on the road, because I didn't want to walk so far in the field. You know, that was all clay, and it was wet so you'd get stuck, and have that clay stuck all over your shoes. I was sneaking off of the road pretty near the guard post, and those little pigs were snoozing in my backpack. There was a really deep ditch that I tried to jump over, but I slipped and fell, slid all the way to the bottom. I landed on the piglets, and they were squealing – like 'wee, wee, wee' – really loud.

So the Russian soldier starts shouting: '*Stoy, stoy, stoy!*'

I knew he was telling me to stop, and I could hear that he was very close by. I really couldn't get away with those piglets making all that noise. He saw he and pointed his rifle at me and made me come up to the road. He arrested me, and he stole all the money that I was carrying.

He threw me in their little jail there at the guard post. It was like a cellar, with a lot of Germans in there. We were pretty hungry, and I still had some herrings in my pack that I had been travelling with, a bunch of them, maybe a few pounds. There was a woman there who had some bread, and I said, 'How about it? I'll give you one herring for one slice of bread.'

And she said, 'No.' She didn't trust me, somehow, or maybe she didn't want any herring.

'You give me a slice of bread, and I'll get you a whole loaf when we get out of here,' I told her. She didn't think I could do that, but I kept trying to persuade her and she ended up giving me a piece of bread. I ate one of those herrings on it – it was really, really salty!

I learned later you're supposed to soak those herrings for a day to get some of the salt out. But I remember I kind of liked it at the time. I'm glad we had water in there, though, because it sure made me thirsty. But finally they let me out after, I don't know, not even a whole day in there. That guard even gave me my piglets back, though he kept all my money.

So I took the pigs to the farmer in East Germany, right there near Osterwieck, and I told him to feed them both, and to keep one for himself and to save one for me. He was happy to do that. There was a baker there too, and he gave me a loaf of bread since I didn't have any money right then. But I was always doing business with him, so he let me have it, and I gave it to that woman who had given me a slice of bread in the jail.

I went back again and met more farmers, and one day one of them came to me and asked if I wanted to buy some peas.

I said, '*Ja*, how many are you selling?'

'I've got 300 pounds for 3,000 marks,' he said.

'I can't carry that much!' I told him.

But I had another farmer down there, and he allowed me to put stuff in his attic or his barn. So I put those 300 pounds of peas there when I went back to Berlin. I knew I could come back and get them the next time I came to the country.

But before I got back there, something important happened: I met a girl.

– Helmut Jacobitz

The Marshall Plan

One of the greatest peacetime programmes in the history of international diplomacy was the brainchild of one of the US army's greatest soldiers. General George C. Marshall was the Chief of Staff of the army during the Second World War, President Roosevelt's closest military adviser and General Eisenhower's direct (and only) superior officer in the US military hierarchy. It was he who guided the American army through the unprecedented expansion of 1941–45, and he who oversaw the land campaigns of Eisenhower in Europe and of General Douglas MacArthur in the Pacific.

Yet it was after the war ended that Marshall created perhaps his most important legacy. When Vice President Harry S. Truman ascended to the highest office in the land upon Roosevelt's death, the war in Europe had little more than a month to run before Hitler's death and the capitulation of Germany. Shortly after the conclusion of hostilities, Truman asked Marshall to become his Secretary of State.

Like all educated observers, Marshall knew that most of the nations of Europe had suffered devastation on an unprecedented scale during the Second World War. The new Secretary of State and his deputies came up with a plan to restart the economies of the countries ravaged by war. Announced in early June 1947, the plan made huge amounts of aid available to European nations. It benefited France, Britain, the Low Countries, Italy, Greece, Turkey and the British, French and US occupation zones of Germany, among other states. The same benefits were offered to the Soviet Union and its satellites, but on behalf of his puppet regimes Stalin declined to accept. (It is also likely that if the plan had included a lot of aid to the USSR, it never would have been approved in the US Congress.)

The plan went into action in March 1948, and disseminated $13 billion over the next four years – this, in the context of a United States GDP of about $250 billion in 1948. The emphasis of the Marshall Plan lay upon future economic progress, not simply rebuilding the damage caused by the war. Efforts were directed toward reducing or eliminating barriers to international trade and to creating a strong business infrastructure.

By the time the plan ended, in 1952, every participating nation's economy had improved to levels beyond what they had been before the start of the Second World War. History continues to regard it as one of the most generous and successful programmes of international aid ever attempted anywhere in the world.

It was after the war, in the summer of 1945, that my I learned what had happened to my relatives who'd lived in Pomerania, which had been near the Polish border and now was a part of Poland. My grandparents, my Aunt Elizabeth and her 4-year-old, Regina, and my Aunt Berta and her 20-year-old daughter Gertrude, who was pregnant, had suffered terribly.

They had to flee in January of 1945 when the Russians came. The Russians shot at them and chased them off of their land, along with just about every other German who lived in the whole province. They were all trying to get to Berlin, but it turned out that because of the war they had to flee north, to the Baltic Sea – in January, when it was freezing cold. They were walking and pulling a cart behind. My grandpa was sick, so he and Regina rode in the cart, while the rest of them walked.

In all, they went more than 250 kilometres, and were living outside, as refugees, for half of a year. I think it wasn't until July of 1945 that they finally made it to Berlin. My grandpa died not too long after that; and my grandmother didn't live very long either. They were both just despairing about what had happened to Germany, and to Pomerania where they had always lived.

From my aunts I heard about Berta's son, my cousin, who had been in a school for musicians. His name was Erwin Koeppler. He was 14 years old and he attended this really nice school in Pomerania, a boarding school. Those kids all wore uniforms, and studied to be good musicians. You had to audition to go there. Can you imagine: the Russians came in and took the whole school, students and teachers and everything? Berta didn't even know if her son was alive. It turned out that he and all those kids had been shipped to Siberia. They kept him there for five years, and Berta only learned that he was alive when he came home in 1950.

The winter of 1945/46 was the most terrible winter I ever lived through. There was very little food, and no milk for anyone except for babies. I don't think I had milk for more than a year! Mostly we didn't have electricity either – we'd get power for maybe two hours out of every day. You never knew when it was going to come on, so if we got it in the middle of the night my mother would get up and do the ironing, or boil water so we had some warm water.

And there wasn't enough coal for heating, so every building in Berlin, it seemed, was really, really cold. There had been lots of nice parks in Berlin, but now people had cut all the trees down to burn them for firewood. They even cut up the park benches, and wooden signs, to burn that stuff to make heat. We had a little bit of gas, but that was really tightly controlled. If anyone in the building used more than they were supposed to, they cut off all the gas!

So my mother was really strict about it, and we could hardly ever use gas for cooking. For a long time we didn't have any candles either – they weren't even for sale if you had money. After a while they did come out with these awful little candles, they were round, smelled bad and were very small – but I thought, 'Oh, I've got to have some of those!'

We did get a few, and though I wasn't supposed to I would sometimes put one next to my bed and use that little flicker of light to read at night. I loved reading, so I put up with those awful smoky candles so that I could do a little reading after dark.

It happened that my uncle, my mother's brother, lived in a part of Germany where there was a candle factory, and my mother had a chance to go and visit him. I don't know where she got it, but she saved up a little food for bartering. She traded it to her brother for a box of candles, like ten long, white candles. They were beautiful! I was so happy to see them, but my mother said, 'These are not for you! They are for cooking!'

In the end she gave me one candle, and I had to make that one last a long time. The others she used to cook – she would fry things using the candle wax as grease! It wasn't digestible, at all, but that's how desperate we were to have something in our stomachs.

As for me, I hadn't been working since the Reichsbank had been bombed, but I knew that I had to get a job that winter. I started looking in the newspaper for work, and I found a job as a bookkeeper. But I had no shoes at all, none to wear to work or anything. So I took a pair of my father's old boots, and I stuffed newspapers in them to make them fit a little better – but they still were way too big for me. Then I wore them to work.

And do you know what? People in the office, the other girls, they were very jealous of me because I had real shoes! One girl that worked with me there, she just had boards under her feet, and wrapped some cloth around the boards and her feet. But I had real boots, so I didn't get frost on my legs.

One day, I remember, we went to work. Our office was in an apartment that had been turned into an office. There wasn't even any glass in the windows;

they were just open to the outside. We were bookkeepers, of course, and we used old-fashioned fountain pens – well, they weren't old-fashioned then, it was what everybody used. But in that winter the ink froze and some of the little glass jars broke – that's how cold it was. For a while we put the ink in the oven and warmed it up enough to thaw it out, and we could work for a while, but then it froze again and there was no gas for the oven. So we just had to go home when that happened.

The toilet at that office was in a corridor, and a lady hung some curtains because the wall to the outside was badly damaged. It was pretty awful. I would take one, sometimes two, slices of bread to work with me, and I would eat that right away. Then I didn't have any more food until I went home. I think that whole winter I didn't see my mother except on weekends, because by the time I got home from work it was dark, and it was dark when I left in the mornings.

Food, our dinner, was usually one potato. I'd come home and my mother was grating that potato and putting it in water. Maybe sometimes we also had a carrot or something to put in there, but usually it was just potato and water. Just one potato for the whole family, then with maybe one slice of bread, nothing on it, to go with it. I was always eating dinner in the dark.

We got ration cards every ten days. I remember my mother would sometimes get a cup of sugar right away when she got the ration cards, and she would make jam. But I would eat my ration up right away. It made my mother mad, but she couldn't stop me – and I couldn't help myself, that's how hungry I was.

On Sundays, we would eat dinner together. My mother had a pound of food for Sunday dinner, which wasn't much. But she would make a soup with it. She said it wasn't enough – she knew that we needed fat, but there wasn't any to be found.

It was getting so cold that my mother said we needed to go to the forest and get wood to burn. We did that before I went to work at 8.30; once every week we'd get up at 4.00 and take the sub-train to this place where there were still some trees. My mother had a saw, and we went with this other woman from our building to get wood.

The forests were so clean! You couldn't find any old trees or branches, so we had to cut live trees. We looked for trees that were thick at the bottom. I learned that I could carry about 50 pounds of firewood. There were rangers there, and of course it was forbidden to cut trees, but they just looked at us, and let us do it.

But we put that green wood in the oven and it just started smoking like crazy. It wouldn't burn, so we knew we had to dry it. We put it under the beds, since that was the only place we had any space. And pretty soon my mother's bed cracked and fell apart, and then mine did the same thing. It was from the moisture in the wood – it just softened the glue that held the beds together and they came apart.

My father was still gone that winter. We hadn't seen him since 1944, and we didn't even know if he was alive. The last we knew he'd been working on a train, in uniform, checking for deserters. Before that, he'd been sent to the Russian Front!

He was so sick, and his legs were so weak, that he wasn't supposed to have to be in the army. But what did they do? In the middle of the war they drafted him and sent him to Russia, the worst place to be. He was working in the kitchen, making tea for his company. And when those men had to get out of there, because the Russians were coming after them, he just barely got into the truck – he was the last man to jump on, because his feet were so bad.

We saw him a little bit when he came home, but then they put him to work on the trains. Before the Americans and British invaded he rode the train between Berlin and Paris, and had to check young men who looked like they should be in uniform. Sometime after the Allies invaded France he disappeared, and we didn't see him again for a long time.

My father finally came back more than a year after the war had ended. It turned out that the French had been holding him in a camp. He was captured, I think, in the summer or fall of 1944, when the Germans were pushed out of France and that train to Paris stopped running.

When I finally saw him back in Berlin, when the French had released him, he was so sick, he looked like a walking skeleton. I remember his hand, it was just bones. I guess the French had tried to get him to sign up for the Foreign Legion, but he wouldn't, so they didn't feed him, and didn't let him see a doctor.

When he was finally released, they put him in a hospital in Berlin because he had terrible infections in his feet. He had already been so sick, with lead poisoning, and now he was terrified that he might end up losing his feet, or even his legs.

Things were still very hard everywhere in the city. There wasn't much food available in the stores. I remember one time we got a can of plums, and we opened it and my mother said it was full of worms. I said, 'Don't show it to me!' And I ate them with my eyes closed.

I also remember that at that time you didn't see any dogs or cats in Berlin. It had been full of animals before, everyone had pets, but they were all gone. One time I saw an old woman with a cute little dog on a leash, and all these people were looking at that dog, and they were hungry. I thought, 'Oh my god, lady, you better take that dog somewhere else, or get it home – or it will get eaten!'

On the black market another time my mother went and bought what was supposed to be a bunny. The skin was off of it, you know, but it had a long tail. I'm pretty sure it was a cat.

'I don't care,' my mother said, as she chopped off the tail. 'A bunny looks the same as a cat, once you take the skin and the tail off.'

It was awful! Years later, when we had just moved to Vancouver, Helmut said, 'You know they have awfully good bunny in the stores here, in the Safeway. That meat looks so lean, and I remember my mom used to cook it and it tasted good. It was cheap, too.'

So I bought it, and I cooked it. But I couldn't eat it. It turned out that no one else in the family would eat it, and I had to throw most of it out.

'Why didn't you eat it?' Helmut asked me.

'I don't know,' I told him. But I couldn't. I looked at it, and thought to myself, 'Well, it could be a cat.' I never bought it again.

The way most people got food, at least anything more than the government rations, was to trade on the black market. Everything we had in our house that was still in one piece was tradable. My mother traded things for one loaf of bread. The last thing she wanted to trade was my one coat, but I said, 'No – I'm keeping that!'

The Russians would come and we Berliners would meet them, like at a big swap meet. It was illegal, and sometimes the police would come and clear everyone out, but we would still do it. Once I traded my best dress to a Russian woman. I don't even remember what I got for it, but I remember that it looked so funny on her – I was so skinny and she was so fat!

I worked for that bookkeeper for about a year, and then I got really sick and had to stay home. I was in bed for a while and couldn't go to work. Finally I started to feel a little better. I got up and was getting ready to go to work. And here comes my boss lady, to my apartment! She saw me up and she thought I was faking, so she said I was fired. And I said, 'I quit!'

So once again I didn't have a job. But right away after that, I met Helmut.

– Charlotte Jacobitz

12

A Cold War Courtship

I saw his luggage, when he was loading up the peas to put them on the train, and his satchel was all full of blood! If I had seen that before I went on the train, I never would have gone with him. I would have run!

– Charlotte Jacobitz

No nation suffered greater civilian and military casualties, or a more stunning surprise attack, or more disastrous and catastrophic battlefield results than did the USSR during the Second World War. Yet Russia rebounded in a big way, employing her traditional defensive advantages: vast territory, brutal winters and incredible human resilience. These historical factors were augmented by an increasingly productive and muscular manufacturing base, centred around vast factories that were entirely devoted to creating war material.

As soon as the scope of the Nazi invasion was recognised, the Soviets began the process of transporting their key industrial facilities, lock, stock and barrel, to the Ural Mountains and beyond. There they were safe from even the longest-ranged German bombers, and were quickly up and running again. Driven by fear and hatred of the Nazi foe, the Soviets eventually built the largest army the world had ever seen, an army that repaid the costs of aggression with considerable interest.

By the time the dust settled over Europe at the end of the Second World War, Josef Stalin had attained just about every political and military objective that his paranoid and ambitious mind could ever have imagined. The

USSR had absorbed parts of Finland, Poland and Romania, as well as all of Lithuania, Estonia and Latvia, into its own borders. It created a wide buffer zone of puppet-controlled nations along its western border, with what was left of Poland, Czechoslovakia, Hungary, Romania and Bulgaria governed by regimes under the Soviet Union's direct control.

These states would eventually form the Warsaw Pact (in May 1955) and throughout the Cold War they would remain utterly dependent upon Moscow for military protection and financial aid. Of course, they would not always be willing or happy partners: in 1948 the Czechoslovakians revolted against Soviet rule, an uprising that was brutally suppressed by Russian tanks. The Hungarians did the same thing in 1956, suffering more than 10,000 deaths before the revolt was put down; and the restive Czechoslovakians again rose up, and were defeated, in 1968. In every case, the challenged communist government and solid Soviet control were completely restored.

To the south, the nation of Yugoslavia was a communist state, albeit a quasi-independent one. At the end of the Second World War, Yugoslav partisans, under the command of the powerful and charismatic Marshal Tito, had essentially ejected the Nazis by themselves, without the aid of a Soviet invasion, so the Russians did not establish as strong a foothold there as they did in the nations of their own bloc. However, Tito's government was based on the communist model, and it consistently aligned with Moscow over the west.

In Asia, Chairman Mao's Red Chinese were well on the way to ousting Chiang Kai Shek's nationalists and establishing in Peking (now Beijing) a communist dictatorship in the most populous nation in the world. Another Soviet puppet, Kim Il-Sung, was installed in North Korea, where he ruled with an iron fist and covetously eyed the democratic and American-supported regime in South Korea, just beyond the 39th Parallel. (In fact, the Stalinist regime in North Korea would outlast not just Stalin himself, but the entire Communist Bloc, by more than twenty years!) In any event, by the late 1940s Josef Stalin's Communist Party, with himself as unquestioned master, looked to be in control of about half of the globe.

There was only one thorn in his side, but it was a big one: the city of Berlin still bristled with American tanks, British and French soldiers, and thrived with a proud and independent population. Its very presence was an intolerable insult to the proud and ruthless Soviet dictator, and Josef Stalin was determined to bring the city to its knees.

It wasn't long after I got back to the city before I was going back and forth from Berlin to the countryside, bartering money and city goods for food from the farmers. As I said, mostly I would go into the Russian zone of Germany, which the city of Berlin was in the middle of. But sometimes I would cross the border into the west to barter in the British zone.

There was a difference between a 'sector' and a 'zone'. Berlin was divided into sectors, so there was an American Sector and a Russian Sector, and so forth, in the city itself. The whole country of Germany was divided into occupation zones, so the American zone referred to the part of Germany held by the Americans; while the American Sector meant the same thing, but only in the city of Berlin.

One time, back in Berlin, I met a girl near the cinema. I guess that was about May of 1947. Actually, I didn't so much as meet her, as I liked her looks when I saw her on the street. I think she smiled at me!

She turned to buy a ticket to the movies, so I bought one too. I went in and saw that she was in the middle of a mostly empty row, so I first sat four seats away from her, then three seats. Finally I moved two seats away from her, and asked, '*Fraulein*, do you mind if I sit next to you?'

'It's a free seat,' she said. 'You can sit wherever you want.'

So I sat next to her. We started talking about food, and I could tell she wasn't eating very well. So I suggested that she come with me the next day, and I told her that I would give her all the peas she could carry.

She probably thought, 'That guy's crazy!' But for some reason she agreed to meet me the next day, at the train station. She did, and she was there when I came in on the train. We travelled together to the countryside. I was disappointed when the farmer didn't show up to meet me, like he was supposed to do. But I promised her that it was okay, that I knew where the peas were, and that I could get them.

I learned that she had been working for, I don't know, maybe 160 marks per month, as a bookkeeper. I told her she was crazy working for that, that I could help her make a lot more on the black market. Already I was thinking that the two of us might be together for a long time.

– Helmut Jacobitz

I met Helmut right after I quit my job, when that boss lady accused me of pretending to be sick. I was kind of surprised myself that I went to see him at the train. It wasn't like me to do that, but that's how I trusted him, from our first meeting. I was supposed to be going back to my mother's, but I said, 'Mom, I'm not going home. I'm going outside of Berlin. I met this guy, and he's going to give me 40 pounds of peas.'

'Who is he? What's his name?' my mother wanted to know. 'Where did he get all those peas he claims to have?'

'I don't know,' was all I could tell her. 'But I met him at the movie, and I trust him.'

'You're not going! He probably won't even be there!' she told me.

'If he's not there, I'm coming home,' I said.

My mother used to drive me nuts. She would make appointments, dates for me – sometimes with guys I had never seen. She would make dates for me with guys she met on the train! The same day I met Helmut she did just that: arranged with some fellow she met that he would take me to dinner. I didn't want to go, and I didn't plan to go. Instead, I went near the place we were supposed to meet, and I saw a man, and I'm not even sure it was the right guy. I had only gone out so as not to argue with my mom. So I didn't go and try to meet him.

I decided to go to a movie instead. I passed this nice-looking man who smiled at me, and I smiled back, and then bought my ticket. Pretty soon I saw that the man had followed me into the theatre. We started to talk right there in the seats, and made a date for the next day.

But my mother didn't trust me enough to let me go with a man I met myself, a man that for some reason I liked and trusted. She was mad at me, but I wasn't going to change my mind.

So I went, and there he was. The train came in with the door already open, and I saw his head sticking out – he was looking around for me. So I went on to the train with him. He had a ticket, but I didn't have one. It wasn't easy to get a ticket. You had to have a permit from the city hall. If you wanted to travel somewhere, you had to get in line there, so that you could get a ticket. Everybody wanted to go to see the farmers so that they could get food.

But he got his permit in Osterwieck. I guess it was easy to get a permit there. And then, since he had a ticket to Berlin, he could get another ticket going back home. He always had tickets, but I couldn't get one.

Once we were on the train, he told me that he would make me a ticket. He had a whole shoebox full of tickets! They were just little pieces of cardboard that were printed on one side with where you have to go. The conductor had a tool, kind of like a pliers, that he stamped the ticket with.

But once you were on the train, he'd never look at the back of the ticket, just the front, to see where you were supposed to go. The trains were really crowded – they even used the toilet for a seat, instead of for a toilet! The conductor didn't take the time to check each ticket; he'd just push his way through the crowd and punch the tickets that were handed to him. Sometimes he would just put a mark on them, in pencil.

One time we travelled three people on one ticket! We just passed it around. But when we had a real and a fake one I always made sure I had the real one – I told Helmut: 'I don't want the other one, the fake one. I want the real ticket!'

That first day we went together I had a bite to eat while we were on the train, two slices of bread that my mother gave me. It was just bread, no butter or anything between them.

He said to me, 'What's that you're eating?'

I put the bread together like a sandwich and told him it was none of his business. But he figured it out. And when he finally met that farmer, he made sure to give me those peas. He had to go look for the man, since he wasn't at the train station where he was supposed to be waiting, but it didn't take long for Helmut to go to his farm and get this huge sack of dried peas.

But then I saw his luggage, when he was loading up the peas to put them on the train, and his satchel was all full of blood! If I had seen that before I went on the train, I never would have gone with him. I would have run!

I learned it was because he had brought half a cow back to Berlin, but only one part at a time. There was no wrapping paper, no plastic or anything. So he would just put the meat in his satchel, and carry it to Berlin, and then hurry up and go back and get the rest of it. It looked like he had butchered someone and put the body in his luggage!

But he gave me as many peas as I could carry, and I took them home to my mother, and it was the most food we'd had in a long time. After that, I started to go with him often. We would take the train through East Germany all the way to the border. He usually went to Osterwieck, which was in the Russian zone, but it was right across the frontier from Vienburg, where his brother Hermann lived. That was in the British zone.

Sometimes we would ride on top of the train – that was fun, on a nice day. You had to be careful, though – the bridges were really low, close to the train, so when you were on top of the train you had to lie down every time it came to a bridge.

I remember once a girl got knocked off the train because she was sitting up when it came to a bridge. She tumbled to the ground, but was lucky enough to fall next to the train – at least she didn't get killed! The train stopped, and backed up, and some men, including Helmut, climbed down and carried her into a freight car. At the next town they stopped a little longer, so those men could carry her to the hospital.

Lots of times Helmut would barter with the farmers in the Soviet zone, but sometimes he would cross the frontier into the west – that was the British zone, near Hanover. He would go through at Vienburg. I met some of the people he dealt with in Osterwieck and some of the places in the Russian zone near there. I never tried to cross the border into the west with him, though.

It could get a little scary at the border. When Helmut went across the border I would wait for him on the bench, in a little park in Osterwieck. Osterwieck is on the River Ilse, and the bench was right by the river. One time after I had gone with him a few times I sat there on the bench all day, while he was in the west dealing with the farmer. I didn't have any money, or even a train ticket, and it was getting dark and I started getting worried.

I wished I'd gone with him, but he said crossing the border was too dangerous, so he had me wait for him there. I had met one of the farmers he stayed with in East Germany, the family Winter. And I tried to remember where they lived, which was just outside of town. I finally did, and I walked over there when it was night.

'I'm waiting for Helmut,' I told Frau Winter. 'But he didn't come back yet.'

'You just wait here,' she said. 'He'll come by to get you.'

And he did – he was a good boy! He had to bicycle out in the country to find me, and I guess he had some trouble getting back across the border. But he found me, and we went back to the city with more peas. He could carry about 150 pounds of peas by himself! I was too skinny, though; I could only carry maybe 50 pounds. But we brought it all back to Berlin.

– Charlotte Jacobitz

A Question of Currency

In the immediate aftermath of the Second World War, Germans in both the eastern and western zones used the Reichsmark, the currency of the Nazi regime, as their monetary unit. Reichsmarks were commonly employed in the black market, but a strong barter economy existed as well. There was no possibility of negotiating a new currency between the western democracies and the USSR. The authorities in each occupation zone introduced their own currency, the equivalent of Reichsmarks, and the money was more or less freely exchanged between all of the zones of Germany.

In fact, United States occupation policy expressly forbade the occupying forces from taking any steps to improve Germany's financial strength. Many Germans, meanwhile, remembered the hyperinflation of the Weimar Republic, and were very worried about a resumption of that trend – one that could, almost overnight, render the currency of the realm essentially valueless.

In the meantime, the country existed on a cash and black market or barter economy. People attended 'swap meets' (rather like 'flea markets') in great numbers, and were as likely to trade services or products as they were to exchange marks. This casual economy made it difficult for the government to collect taxes and regulate trade. Furthermore, because of the large amount of cash in circulation, fears of inflation continued to haunt the German people.

Already it was becoming clear to all sides that the post-war partition of Germany into western and eastern occupation zones was, despite the wishes of a vast number of Germans, going to be a fairly long-term arrangement. Since the capitalist economies of the west relied on a distinctly different model than the communist east, the democracies collectively decided to reform the German mark, replacing the Reichsmark (RM) with the Deustche Mark (DM, or 'D-Mark'). In one move, they would put a heavy burden of restriction on the black market – because people who had been hoarding RM would have the value of their cash dramatically reduced – and create a huge obstacle to trade between east and west.

This currency reform was a primary reason behind the Russian blockade of Berlin; both the reform and the blockade commenced in June 1948. At first the reform affected just the occupation zones that would soon become West Germany, but in the face of Russian hostility the Allies swiftly imposed the reform into (West) Berlin as well.

As a practical matter, official transactions such as wages, rent and prices in retail stores were simply translated, so that 1 RM became 1 DM. In addition, each private citizen in the western German occupation zones was awarded two direct cash payments, of 40 DM and, a little later, 20 DM. This direct payment did not extend to the citizens in Berlin, since the reform happened later in the city than in the western part of the country.

People who were hoarding a lot of off-the-record RM, including for example prosperous black-marketeers, suffered a very disadvantageous exchange rate. Half of such funds, in RM, were frozen, and the other half exchanged at a rate of 10 RM to only 1 DM. Very large sums were further penalised, with an exchange of nearly 20 RM to 1 DM. Almost immediately, trade on the black market was severely curtailed, and people were forced to look for more conventional sources of income.

The next time Charlotte and I went to the countryside together, I went over to pick her up at her apartment for the first time. I remember looking up at the building, and there was someone looking out of every window! They were trying to size up this guy who was taking her out to deal in the black market.

Before the currency reform, most people would go to the farmers, and they would barter for a loaf of bread, or a pound of flour, or a small bag of peas. We called those people 'Hamsters' because they reminded us of little hamsters in cages, running around and around and just hardly getting anywhere; and because they made us think of little rodents with their cheeks packed with food. But they couldn't carry much in their cheeks!

I would go and get 100 pounds at a time, sometimes more. I would try to get those farmers what they needed from the city, because it was often bartering. Sometimes I would bring a tool, or soap; and once I even bartered a bicycle.

Other times I would pay Reichsmarks, because the farmers needed money too; and I was doing so much business that I had access to a lot of RM.

The best deal I ever made was for a radio tube. There was a farmer I used to stay with – he let me sleep in his living room when I was there, so I knew him pretty well. One time he told me that the police chief from his town needed a tube for his radio, because it wasn't working, and there was no place to get another one.

So the next time I came from Berlin, I brought him the tube he needed. I went to meet that chief and I gave him the tube. He asked me how much I wanted for it, and I said, 'Just take it, you don't have to pay me.' It would have cost about two months of his wages on the black market, so he was glad I let him have it. But he did give me a piece of paper that said I was helping out the police. It was a pass from his village – not something that would let me cross the border, but it was an ID card that allowed me to carry food without having it be confiscated. The card told people that I was a legal resident of the village of Wuelperode, which was right outside of Osterwieck.

It wasn't much later that I was coming to the train station in a different town, pretty near there. Charlotte was with me, and we had a wagon that I had borrowed from a farmer. I had several hundred pounds of flour on that wagon that I was taking back to Berlin – I borrowed the wagon because it was more than we could have carried ourselves.

We got to the train station and saw that the police had set up a checkpoint there, and they were inspecting everyone to see if they were smuggling food. These poor women who were there, if they had a pound of flour or a little bag of peas, the police would take that away from them.

I thought, 'Oh my god, I'm going to lose this whole wagon full of flour!'

I almost turned around, but the policeman had already seen me so I decided to bluff on through. I got off the wagon and asked who was in charge, and they took me to a police officer. I told him I had done work for a farmer, and instead of paying me with money, he paid me in food. Then I showed him that ID card, and told him the name of the police chief from the other town – I said the chief told me they can't take the food away from me, because I worked for it. 'I'm not smuggling on the black market!' I told them.

So the policeman said, 'Just wait here.' He came back and he let me put the flour on the train – the police even helped me load it on there! I asked him if someone could take the wagon back to the farmer, and he said no, they all had to stay at the station and watch for smugglers. But they agreed to wait for me while I took it back. So I returned the wagon and came back and got on the train – that train was an hour late because they waited for me!

Another time I bought a whole deer from a farmer. He put it in a smoker and dried it, and offered to sell it to me. He needed cash, and like lots of other times I had cash from the city, so I was able to buy it from him. He was in East Germany, so I didn't have to cross the border to get there.

All those farmers, they had just a little bit of land, because when the Russians came in they took the land away from the rich guys who owned huge farms. Everyone got like a little acre or two, but everything they grew was regulated. They had to give so much to the government.

But some of those guys were clever. One farmer had maybe 100 sheep. In the spring the ewes would drop lambs, and the farmer hid some of the lambs so the government guys didn't know how many sheep he really had. Or he would butcher a full-grown sheep when a lamb was born, and when the inspector came back he would still have 100 sheep. I used to buy a sheep from him now and then.

Another guy had a cow, and when that cow had a calf he hid the calf in a secret room in his barn. He'd park his hay wagon in front of the door, and you couldn't even tell there was a room in there. He's the one I bought half a cow from, that meat that made my luggage all bloody.

But the currency reform, when it came through, put a stop to the black market basically overnight. Most people didn't have much money, so for them it was no big deal. In Berlin they let you exchange up to 60 RM for 60 DM, and you could do that for every person in the family. So if there were four kids and two parents, you could get up to 360 DM by turning in 360 RM. If you had more than 60 RM per person, they would only pay you 1 DM for 10 RM, so you really lost a lot of the value of your money.

People who had large families, especially, didn't have enough RM to take up the full offer. On the other hand, I had a lot of RM stored up, because I'd been dealing in the black market for so long. I made deals with a lot of families who had more people than marks; I would say (for example), 'Here's 120 RM. You take it in and trade it for your 120 DM, and you can keep half and give me the other half.'

A lot of people took me up on this offer, which was good because 50 per cent of the value is a lot better than 10 per cent. I made the deal with a couple of people, though, who just took off with my RM. They were gone, and I never saw them again.

– Helmut Jacobitz

13

Blockaded and Betrothed

In the east, there was no business going on. You couldn't go into a store and buy a new bicycle, for example. In fact, most of the time you couldn't even buy a nail! If you wanted to buy something practical, you could try and go to the hardware store. Sometimes the storekeeper had a few things for sale, for cash, but other times he'd ask, 'What do you have to trade?'

– Charlotte Jacobitz

During the Second World War the USA accomplished one of the most amazing feats of science and technology in all the history of the human race – and they did it under a tight deadline, under conditions of incredible security. The Manhattan Project gathered the most brilliant scientists of the free world – including many who had fled fascist tyranny in Germany and Italy – and put them to work, first to solve the mystery of atomic fission, and second to turn that solution into a workable, and incredibly destructive, weapon of war.

If not for Adolf Hitler and the fear that his Nazi regime provoked in the rest of the world, the atomic bomb would probably not have been invented during the twentieth century – and maybe not at all. The theory of atomic power had been around for a long time, but it was just a theory. However, when rumours that the Germans were working toward atomic fission began to reach the west, President Roosevelt could not ignore them. No less a personage than the expatriate German/Jewish scientist Albert Einstein, the foremost theoretical and practical physicist in the world, informed Roosevelt that such a weapon was indeed feasible. Clearly, it would have been rash to the point of suicide to let the Nazis be the first, and only, power in the world to possess an atomic bomb.

So the President authorised the Manhattan Project, which would eventually draw billions of dollars from the US military budget, and consume the attentions of thousands of the world's most brilliant scientists. Begun in New York City (hence the name) and continued in Chicago, Tennessee and the Columbia valley in Washington State, the brain trust of the project would eventually become concentrated on a remote mesa in New Mexico, a place called Los Alamos. There they would complete the final calculations and actually assemble the components of the bombs.

The project used up not just money and brainpower, but virtually all of the uranium 235 and plutonium (both new elements, created by the manufacturing facilities supporting Los Alamos) that existed in the world. The USA had created enough fissionable material to build exactly three atomic bombs by the summer of 1945. By this time, Germany had surrendered – and even before that, it had become clear that the bombs would not be needed to defeat the Third Reich. (Einstein even begged the President to cancel the project when the latter fact became apparent.)

Nonetheless, the development of the atomic bomb had taken on a life of its own. In July 1945, at a site near Alamogordo in the New Mexican desert, the first man-made atomic explosion occurred. It was called the Trinity test, and proved that atomic theory had become reality. The two remaining bombs were then carried by ship to the island of Tinian in the Pacific Ocean; from there, in early August, B-29 bombers carried one to Hiroshima and the other to Nagasaki, destroying both cities. Within days, Japan sued for peace.

It seemed (for an amazingly short time) that the United States had developed a weapon that might render war obsolete, for who would dare to challenge the only nation in the world with an atomic arsenal? However, the Americans didn't know that Soviet spies had infiltrated the Manhattan Project from the earliest days of the great enterprise. Within a matter of months after the end of the war, the secret of the bomb's design had been carried to Moscow, and by 1947 Russia was working on an atomic bomb of her own. The Soviet device was exploded a little more than a year later, and by 1949 the United States was forced to admit that there were two atomic powers in the world.

Now, instead of ensuring world peace, atomic power was a genie out of the bottle, and it was a genie capable of destroying the entirety of human civilisation on the planet Earth. This balance of fear and power, soon amplified by the even more destructive hydrogen bomb, would shape the whole of the Cold War that would define the relationship between the United States and Soviet Union for the next forty years.

Helmut liked to do things for fun, even though he was a hard worker. Once he invited me to come with him to have a picnic by the lake, on a weekday in summer. My mom said I couldn't go – I had to stay and help her clean the apartment (which was already pretty clean). Mainly, she just wanted to keep control of me. But I told her no, and I went with Helmut anyway.

I remember once I had a big fight with my mother – her temper was always ready to blow up, it seemed. She was shouting at me, and telling me I was a terrible daughter, and she never wanted to see me again. I stormed out of the apartment and went to Helmut's. His mother let me stay over there one night, in his sister's room. But then she talked to me, gently, the next day, and said that I had to go home and patch things up with my mother.

When I got home, my mom cried, and said she was so glad to see me! That night and day kind of changed our relationship, because from then on she stopped bossing me around. She let me be an adult.

It wasn't long before my mother stopped being suspicious of Helmut; she liked him pretty much, and she could see he was making me happy. Actually, both of our mothers eventually learned to like each other. I got along well with Helmut's mother, too.

I was wondering how I would find a job again because I had been out of work for a year by then. But Helmut said I shouldn't work for someone else, where I would only make enough to buy a loaf of bread or something for a day's work. He told me that he and I should go into business together.

He made a mill in the cellar underneath his father's store. It was about eight or ten steps down steep stairs, and he built this machine, made of metal, that would grind corn [wheat] into flour.

He would buy grain from the farmers, as they didn't have any way to mill the corn. You needed a government permit to do that, and even if you got a permit the communists would take most of your flour, and you wouldn't make any money for doing it. So Helmut had a machine, like that big iron for steaming clothes – a dry-cleaning press, I guess. It was heavy, with rocks in it, and he connected it so I could grind the corn into flour. But in the beginning he didn't know how to separate the shell, so I was always shaking it to get the flour out.

So everything was white. I was white! Later on he connected the mill to some kind of sifter, so that it would separate. I would get flour, and also cream of wheat. He was going to build it even bigger and give me more to do. I said, 'You know, this time is over one day, I hope!'

But we had to do it ourselves, because you had to have that permit to grind flour from the government. I think it was about three or four months that we milled flour. Then he started on the oil – that was so greasy!

– Charlotte Jacobitz

We got tired of making flour all the time so I built another machine to squeeze oil out of seeds. It used a screw press to compact the seeds, and that was much cleaner, and also was worth a lot more money. The kind of oil you got depended on what kind of seeds you used. We would make linseed oil, or poppy seed oil, and sometimes rapeseed oil, which was used for margarine. Sometimes we'd make sunflower seed oil, too. We'd bottle it up and sell it, for a good price, on the black market.

The leftover 'cakes', the hulls of the seeds, from both the linseed oil and the poppy seed oil were popular with dairy men. These cakes were little round balls of compressed hulls that were left after the oil had been squeezed out. I think they added it to the feed to make better milk.

The dairy men we dealt with were not actual farmers, with pastures and barns in the country. They lived in the city, and would keep maybe ten or twenty cows in courtyard stalls, like stables. They would sell milk and other dairy products, like butter and simple cheese, from a store in the front of the stable. We called these little dairy shops *Kuhstall*, which literally translates as 'cow stable'.

So those were the kinds of oil we made the most; I could sell every bottle right away, and we were able to make a little money off of the leftover by-products, too. I had some regular customers who liked the oil so much that, when I got too busy to deliver it, they came to me to get the oil rather than do without it.

The poppy seed oil was another good deal. After I got the oil out of the seeds, I could sell the seeds to the bakeries, because there was enough flavour left in them that they could still use them in cakes and breads.

For all these kinds of oil, you first had to smash the seeds and then squeeze the oil out of them. Then later on I got another machine that was much easier. Charlotte didn't have to do any heavy work any more – even she admitted that new one was quite a machine.

It worked kind of like a meat grinder. Electricity would turn the crank and the oil would come out in one place, and the leftovers would come out in a different place. I put a hopper on it that would hold a lot of seeds, so I could turn it on and go do something else for a while. I rigged it up so a bell would ring when it was out of seeds, and I would go down in the cellar and fill it up again. That oil really made a lot of money for us.

But then came that currency reform, in June of 1948. I guess it was the same time as the airlift, but actually, the currency reform had a lot more impact on our lives than the Russian blockade did.

That was about the time that my father decided to sell his store. He decided he would go into the sign business again. He wanted my older brother Hermann to go into business with him, but Hermann said, 'No! I'm never going to lift a hammer again!' So my father asked me to work with him instead.

He had sold his original sign business right about when the war started. The guy that bought my father's business promised me a job when I was able to work, meaning after the war, when I got out of the military. He had all of my father's tools, and his workshop, and it was all set up to go. I had learned a lot about cutting and shaping sheet metal by then, and about sign-making, so it would have been a good job for me. But the building got totally bombed out during the war. He still started up a sign business, but he didn't need me to work for him; it was a pretty small-scale operation.

So I decided to work with my father again. It turned out to be one of the worst decisions I ever made!

– Helmut Jacobitz

Blockade and the Berlin Airlift

By early 1948, Stalin had had enough of the Berlin problem. The fact that Germany was divided into occupation zones was enough of an irritant for him, but to top it all off there was this 'island' of West Berlin: Allied control-led territory right in the middle of the Soviet Empire. Its very existence was an affront, and it was an insult that was apparent to him every time he looked at a map.

Since the Western Allies had decided to go ahead and remake the German currency, Stalin also knew this was about to create a huge disadvantage to Germans in the east who wanted to trade or do business with the west. This wrenching change in the status quo was announced as first affecting only western Germany, but as the Soviets grew more intransigent the Allies applied the currency reform to Berlin, as well. At this time, there was no significant barrier between the east and west sectors of the city; people were free to move back and forth for jobs and socialising. However, more people were leaving jobs and rental properties in the east, and going to the west, where the economy was much better, and jobs paid better, too.

The Soviet Chairman wasn't ready to go to war with the west – although Russia was nearly ready to test an atomic bomb using the design his spies had stolen from the Manhattan Project, he knew that the Americans had an arsenal of these potent weapons. Instead, he thought he could gain control of Berlin by starving the city out. He reached his decision as the winter of 1948 moved into spring. The Soviets began by harassing the Western Powers dip-lomatically, first by having the USSR delegation walk out of the meeting of the Allied Control Council (20 March) in Berlin. This was the body that met periodically to agree on the joint government of the city, which remained divided into zones controlled by the four victorious powers.

On 1 April Stalin ordered his men to interfere with British and American access to the city, which had been granted by treaty along three railway lines and two limited access highways (*Autobahns*). They did this by creating additional checkpoints, roadblocks and delays along what had generally been rather smoothly operating corridors. Some trucks and trains were turned back, while the rest were halted and delayed for at least a few hours, sometimes for days, because of newly installed 'red tape'. By 24 April, the United States Air Force (USAF) had begun flying supplies into the city by air, though the trains were still running sporadically, around frequent Soviet harassment.

On 16 June the Soviet officer who was a member of the four-person Kommandatura, the overall military authority in Berlin, walked out of the meeting, thus isolating the Russians from the other three military commands in the city. It was this crisis that caused the west to extend the currency reform to Berlin itself.

In response, on 22 June 1948, Soviet authorities abruptly and completely shut down all three of the rail lines connecting Berlin to the west, and closed the two highways as well. There was less than one month's food supply in the city of 2 million people in the western zones alone. (More than two-thirds of the city's population lived in the western-controlled sectors). US army general Lucius Clay urged that the Allied military garrisons stay in the city, and that food be brought in by air.

Clay urged the Berliners to expand the city's two existing airfields and commence work on a third, which was soon completed. At the same time, all available western military aircraft began what came to be known as Operation Vittles, considered by many to be the most amazing peacetime military accomplishment in history. Transport planes were the most important to the effort, of course, though they were frequently provided with fighter escorts; and the Soviet air force often sent interceptors to shadow and sometimes buzz dangerously close to the supply flights. Most of the planes and fliers were American, though the British and French contributed aircraft and crews as well.

The Americans did not want to let Berlin get taken over by Russia. So the Russians closed off the city. The trains stopped leaving, and you couldn't get to West Germany any more. The Russians never thought that they would lose, but they did. The whole thing was a fight between America and Russia. The Russians were trying to separate Berlin from West Germany, to get the

Americans and English out of Berlin. It was against the treaty they all signed at the end of the war, but the Russians didn't care anything for the treaty.

The thing that was different during the blockade was that you couldn't get food to the city by train, but the Americans brought it in by aeroplanes. We didn't see the planes much because we didn't live near the airports, but they were flying planes in all the time, day and night. Tempelhof Airport, which was Berlin's busiest airport for a long time, was full of aeroplanes and supplies all the time. We thought a lot of that airlift, because it kept us from becoming Russians.

They still put the food in the stores, though, and rationed it. It wasn't like they just piled it up off the planes and gave it away. For Helmut and me, because we continued to get some of our food on the black market, I guess it wasn't that different. But some things we could only get from the Americans. Helmut called it lousy food, but maybe that's because he knew so many farmers. I was glad to get it!

We had to line up. We had ration cards and you could get so many things per card. Some things, like butter or margarine or lard, you could only get at the stores. My mother made me get in line at 2 a.m., because the lines would get so long that the people at the end wouldn't get anything. Then she would come two or three hours later and take my place in line. She hoped to get butter, but if that was gone she'd take margarine. Sometimes there was meat, like you got a pound of meat with your ration, or maybe ten eggs. Whatever they had, you would try to get it.

The food wasn't that different than what we got in stores before the blockade. It's just that it used to come in by train, and now it was brought in by aeroplane.

– Charlotte Jacobitz

Stalin Blinks First

From 26 June 1948 until 30 September 1949, the planes of the Berlin Airlift flew constantly, day and night, on a crushingly tight schedule that had aircraft landing and taking off practically in each other's slipstream. By the spring of 1949, one plane was landing in Berlin every minute of every day and night. In all, more than 275,000 flights were made, bringing in 2.3 million tons of food (and coal, which was desperately needed during the winter). Seventy-five British and American fliers lost their lives in the process, more than half of them being the victims of a collision when a Soviet fighter pilot zoomed too close to a British passenger plane and brought both aircraft down. Surprisingly enough, the Soviets formally apologised for this tragic accident.

By the summer of 1949 Stalin, most displeased, was grudgingly willing to concede defeat. Already the western democracies were working on plans to unify their three occupation zones into one 'West German' nation. Further, the Western Allies used their only piece of economic clout and broke off all trade with East Germany, which created unpleasant hardships for East Germans and Russians alike. Stalin officially lifted the blockade in May 1949, but the relief flights continued on through the summer and the entire month of September. Even though the trains were rolling, the Allies brought in plenty of extra supplies, so that if the blockade was restored Berlin would not be caught with a mere month's worth of provisions.

The Russians agreed, finally, to a meeting of the four occupying powers' foreign ministers, and announced that they would drop their opposition to the creation of West Germany as a new nation. All four powers agreed to grant Berliners more autonomy over their day-to-day lives, though the militaries of both east and west would retain tight control over security matters and any new constitutions.

In retrospect, the Berlin Blockade and Airlift had been the first showdown of the Cold War, and it proved that Josef Stalin had underestimated Harry S. Truman.

We were doing so well by this time that I even bought a bar of chocolate, for 200 D-marks! I hadn't bought chocolate for years – we'd had only a little money, so we bought other stuff. But the production of the oil had made us pretty well off, and we started to look around for other ways to make money. Of course, Helmut was going to work on signs again with his father – he would make the signs, and his father would hang them. But that wasn't steady work. Besides, we had decided to get married, and we wanted some kind of business of our own.

In the east, there was no business going on. You couldn't go into a store and buy a new bicycle, for example. In fact, most of the time you couldn't even buy a nail! If you wanted to buy something practical, you could try and go to the hardware store. Sometimes the storekeeper had a few things for sale, for cash, but other times he'd ask, 'What do you have to trade?'

There was a corridor you had to go through, to take the train from Berlin to West Germany. The Russians controlled it, and even when they let people travel there again they were pretty mean about it. You could get a pass to go for like three days, a holiday. But the Russians made sure it took a whole day to get there, and another whole day to get back, so you really only got one day in West Germany.

So you could just look around a little bit, maybe do some shopping, then you had to catch the train back to Berlin. Still, they had some nice little stores, and lots of things you couldn't buy in Berlin. I learned to buy potatoes from the United States. They were in a can, and I really liked them.

Helmut said they tasted awful, but I told him, 'I ate candles during the war. If I can eat candles, I can eat potatoes from America!'

And then we ended up buying a stationery store. We used the profits we had made from the oil. Helmut even traded a bottle of oil to the worker at city hall, so that he could go in and get a permit to start the business.

My Aunt Elizabeth agreed to run the store for us. It was in East Berlin, but it was still easy to go back and forth from east to west, at least inside the city itself. You could still cross back and forth, pretty much whenever you wanted. The Russians were upset that so many people were going to the west, and they said you can come over here to the east. They were trying to get people to move from West to East Germany.

They even offered us a nice apartment, larger than we could have gotten in the west. It would have all the furniture, dishes, and things you would need, because it had been left that way by some family that fled to the west.

But we didn't want to live in the east, nobody did. For one thing, it would have been kind of creepy to be in someone else's home, using all their stuff. But for the other thing, the main thing, we were always worried that the Russians were going to try and take over Berlin, and make everybody a Russian.

– Charlotte Jacobitz

Two New Nations

In May 1949, after the blockade had officially ended but while the Berlin Airlift continued, the occupying powers of the Western Allies authorised a momentous step: the creation of a new and at least moderately independent state. Formed from the parts of Germany occupied by the British, Americans and French, the Federal Republic of Germany, or West Germany, was established as a new nation. While most Germans wished the national capital to be Berlin, that was deemed impractical under the current division; so the city of Bonn, on the Rhine, was declared to be the new capital.

The first chancellor of the new nation would be Dr Konrad Adenauer, an esteemed German who had been a critic of the Nazi regime, having been imprisoned twice under Hitler's order. A well-known and admired centrist and founder of the Christian Democratic Union, he was a popular choice. At the ceremony to announce the formation of the new nation, he was joined by West Berlin's mayor, Dr Ernst Reuter. The gathered crowd broke into applause when Reuter signed the document, clear proof that West Germans very much considered Berlin to be part of their own nation. Not surprisingly, the Soviet delegates refused to sign.

The communists in the Soviet occupation zone responded in kind on 12 October of the same year. The German Democratic Republic (East Germany) officially came into being under the leadership of a communist government. The capital of the new nation would be East Berlin. Wilhelm Peck was appointed president of the new 'republic', which despite its name would still be ruled by the Communist Party and its master in Moscow. Within a matter of months, East Germany would create its own secret police force, the dreaded Stasi, which would prove to be a ruthless and able enforcer of the regime's will for the next forty years.

The German people expressed their opinions with their feet, as the population continued to flow from east to west. In the city of Berlin, alone, some 125,000 people were estimated to have fled from the Soviet-controlled East Berlin into West Berlin during 1949. From West Berlin, many of them emigrated further, into the cities and rural areas of West Germany itself. Naturally, the Soviets abhorred this flight, both as a practical matter (many of those who left were among the most skilled workers in the city, including doctors, accountants and other professionals) and as an embarrassing bit of propaganda: if the communist state was such a 'Workers' Paradise', why did so many workers want to leave?

We got married almost at the end of the decade of the 1940s, on 26 November 1949. It was a small ceremony, at the city hall, with just our families and a few friends there. We did have a dinner celebration back at my mother's apartment building, in a bigger room that people from that building could use for special occasions. We had a pretty nice time: Helmut was able to get us plenty of food, and my mother made us a nice feast.

My father, who was in the hospital and very sick, was able to come, in a wheelchair. I borrowed my father's wedding ring to give to Helmut during the wedding, but then we gave it back – Helmut was never going to wear a ring!

Helmut did make me a brass ring when we got married – I had to polish it every day or it got tarnished! He didn't see anything wrong with that, but I got fed up with it. I finally threw it out and got a cheap silver one, which I still wore when we moved to Canada. Finally I told him, 'It's about time, after forty years, that I get a nice a ring!' So he got me this one. He paid about $1,000 for it – he said that was crazy, to spend that much for one finger.

But really, at the time we got married, we were pretty well off, compared to a lot of people. The thing about jewellery was really just the normal state of life then, since just about everyone had traded their jewellery and other valuables away during that really hard winter after the war, if not before. My mother, for example, once owned an expensive gold necklace, but after the war she traded it away for a loaf of bread and a pound of peas or flour.

I still teased Helmut about not wearing a ring, but I know it was because of his work. When you are dealing with saws, and drills, and ladders and all that, having a ring on your finger can be kind of dangerous. At least, that's what he always said!

– Charlotte Jacobitz

14

To the West and the Wall

We went to visit our friend Fritz, in East Berlin. We were nervous going over there, through the Russian checkpoint. They made us leave our camera there. We had the two boys with us – Reinhard was 10 and Helgo about 6 – and since they'd lived in Canada for so long we were worried about them speaking English while we were around the Russians. Charlotte told them both just to stay quiet, which, kind of amazingly, they did.

– Helmut Jacobitz

As the decade of the 1950s opened, Josef Stalin had been the absolute ruler of the Soviet Union for more than a quarter of a century. His hold on the reins of power showed no sign of easing, and his paranoia, if anything, was increasing. Deeply insulted by Marshal Tito's independent leanings in Yugoslavia, he was determined to prevent any similar wavering in his puppet states. He ordered a series of show trials to be held in Germany, Poland and Czechoslovakia, wherein politicians accused of 'Titoism' were charged with crimes against the state and, in most cases, executed. The lid of communist rule was pressed very tightly on to the populations of the Soviet buffer states.

In the summer of 1950, one of Stalin's puppets, Kim Il-Sung, launched his North Korean army on a surprise invasion of South Korea. It does not seem that Stalin actually ordered this attack, but it is clear that he approved. The North Koreans were armed with Soviet equipment, including the T34 tanks that had proved to be such an effective weapon against German panzers.

While there were initial rumours that the tanks were manned by Russian soldiers, they were in fact operated by North Koreans who had been trained by Russians. (Later in the war, Soviet pilots flew MiG fighters against American fliers, in the first jet–to–jet battles in world history.)

The Korean War raged for three years, with the first year characterised by dramatic successes and catastrophic setbacks for each side. The North Koreans almost conquered the entire South in a stunning summer campaign, and then the United Nations forces (under the command of US army general Douglas MacArthur) outflanked the communist forces with an amphibious landing. Moving into North Korea, the UN forces almost occupied the entire country – until the Red Chinese intervened in a shocking surprise attack. Early in 1951 Truman relieved MacArthur for insubordination. The general, among other things, wanted to bomb bases and depots in Red China, while Truman strived desperately to keep the war from exploding into another global conflagration. For two more years the war settled into a bloody stalemate while the sides negotiated a settlement that left the border very near to where it had been at the time of the North Korean invasion.

Also early in the 1950s, Stalin initiated another of the purges that had been such a regular part of his style of rule. This time it was targeted against artists and intellectuals, many of whom disappeared into the gulags because their work was deemed less than pure. Writers, painters and filmmakers who survived the purge worked very hard to make sure that their manuscripts, artworks and films all toed the party line. At the same time, the Soviets went to great efforts to proclaim that Russian artistic and scientific accomplishments were inherently the greatest in the world; this effort was accompanied by a co-ordinated plan deriding the accomplishments of foreigners in all fields.

Though he had been rebuffed in his attempt to isolate Berlin via blockade, Stalin continued to keep a wary eye on the island of Western power within his domain. He never accepted the democratic presence on communist soil, and continued to seek a way to use his power to gain control of the German capital.

We moved into a one-bedroom apartment after we got married, and we felt lucky to have it. We actually traded for the apartment, exchanging with the couple who had moved into the apartment that was attached to Helmut's father's store (which had just been sold). That was where Helmut had been living. We were very fortunate to fall into this arrangement, which was also in the Wedding neighbourhood – really just a few blocks from my own family's apartment.

Much of Berlin was still in ruins from the war, so there was a great shortage of apartments. Most people still had to live with their parents even when they were married. The bedroom in our place was so small there was just room for the bed – you couldn't even walk around in there! But it had a bedroom, and a separate room with the living area and kitchen in it.

When Helmut's father had owned that store before we got married, one of the main things he'd sold there had been soap. So we knew a wholesale soap dealer, and during that first winter when we were married we would go to that dealer, buy soap, and take it to an open market that they had about two days a week.

For a short time we sold our soap there, and made a living, mostly getting paid in cash. It was nice soap and soap was still kind of hard to find in the city. Helmut would polish it since it would get dirty from being transported, and I would take it to the market. I got kind of dirty too. That part of it was disgusting – I tried to go to the market on days when none of my girlfriends would be there, because I didn't want them to see me.

Also, I was pregnant during that winter, and it wasn't long before I discovered that the smell of that soap made me physically sick to my stomach – I would actually throw up when I was near it! So I couldn't work selling that soap, and my mother took over for me during the first few months of 1950. I still remember her going to the market, riding on the back of Helmut's motorbike. They made quite a sight!

Finally, our son Reinhard was born on 1 May 1950. We were a small family, in a small apartment, but we were taking care of ourselves and making our way.

My father was still very sick from his time in the French prison camp, and he couldn't walk any more so he had to sit in a wheelchair. The infections in his feet and legs just kept getting worse, and finally the doctors had to cut the nerves in his abdomen. They started giving him some new medicine – penicillin, I think it was. They put sixty needles in his bad toe, which was awful. He looked terrible, and he was so sad.

Nothing worked, and it went on for a long time. They removed first his toes and then his foot, because of gangrene. But they had to keep taking more and more off of him, until his one leg was gone; and then the gangrene started in on his second leg.

My father had always been a very cheerful man, but this was terrible for him. The first time I ever saw him cry was when they took the last piece from his second leg. He lived for a few years after that, but it wasn't the same for him. He had a small disability pension, because he was completely unable to work after the war, and he and my mother stayed in their apartment on the fourth floor. My mother had a basket for washing, and she would wash him in it. She put him in it and pulled it around the apartment – it had no wheels – because that was the only way he could get around.

He didn't come down from the fourth floor until finally they came to visit us once, on a Sunday. Helmut carried him down four flights of stairs, and I remember my father was hanging on him all the way. Helmut drove him in the car, then carried him up to our place, which was only half a flight of stairs up.

That was his first time out of there in a long time, but after he came once he was willing to do it again. We'd have them over for the day every so often, whenever we could. Later he got a wheelchair for inside, and then another one for outside. At least he could get around a little then. On nice days, he would stay outside for practically the whole day.

– Charlotte Jacobitz

We had to stop the soap business, because we didn't have a business permit, and also didn't want to pay taxes on everything. Both the east and west governments were getting more particular about things like that, so we needed to do something else.

As I said, my father started up a new sign business, and I was his second choice for a partner, after Hermann turned him down. I needed work at the time, and I was good at making signs, so I went back to work with my father.

I had a little money saved up, and I invested it with my father's money to start that company. We got some work, and did jobs, and started to become successful. At the same time, Hermann was having trouble finding a job, and he ran out of money. After my father and I got our sign business up and running, Hermann decided that maybe he would be able to hold a hammer again, and he wanted to become a partner in our company.

I told him 'no' because he didn't want to do the work, and he didn't have any money to invest in the company. But my father said 'yes', and brought Hermann in to help make the signs.

That was too much for me. I think I mentioned before that in Germany, it was common for several companies to be involved in a single sign – a sign-maker, a painter, a sign-hanger, and so forth. Since I made the signs and my father hung them, I wanted to go into business for myself, so I told my father I would break up our company, and he could hang signs and I would make signs. We'd be able to work with other people if we wanted.

Well, I was pretty shocked by this, but my father and my brother took me to court, and tried to get the judge to prevent me from breaking up the company. Both my mother and my sister, Gretel, took my side in that argument, but my father was too stubborn to listen to them. He wanted to work with his oldest son.

Unfortunately, the judge agreed with them. He was kind of ashamed when he told me his decision, but he said that the law was written to prevent large companies from being broken up into small companies. So he wouldn't let me keep my share of the business and break away from my father, and Hermann was brought into the company as a full partner.

That was a bitter lesson to me. I left the company, and lost my investment. Also, I never spoke to my father again.

– Helmut Jacobitz

Death of a Dictator

As the year 1953 began, Josef Stalin showed no signs of relaxing his grip on power. Early in the year his paranoia found a new target, and the government began to purge a number of doctors, many of them Jewish, from their positions as working physicians and as teachers. This so-called 'Doctors' Plot' started to play out as most of the dictator's other purges: the accused were arrested and publicly accused of disloyalty to the state. Large, public trials were scheduled for later in the year.

However, on 5 March 1953, Stalin suffered a severe stroke while sleeping, and he died a short time thereafter without regaining consciousness. It was only natural, in the climate of accusation and suspicion that ran rampant throughout Moscow, that the death would be regarded as suspicious – it came so suddenly, and there were no witnesses in the room at the time he actually suffered the stroke. However, no feasible alternate explanation for the death was ever put forward. Thus, the man responsible for some of the greatest violence and terror in world history was fortunate enough to, for all intents and purposes, die peacefully in his sleep.

Despite the persistent rumours and lingering suspicions, the reaction to Stalin's death throughout the USSR, the rest of the Communist Bloc and indeed the world could probably best be summed up as 'relief'. The doctors who had been charged in the latest purge were quietly released, and the senior members of the Politburo went out of their way to praise the late dictator even as, behind the scenes, they began manoeuvring for power. General Georgy Malenkov, and the head of the state security service (the KGB), Lavrentiy Beria, were widely regarded as the two most likely rivals to take office as Stalin's successor. Western observers noted that the veteran communist apparatchik Nikita Khrushchev, another of Stalin's inner circle, was relieved of one of his posts upon Stalin's death. His influence was presumed to be on the wane.

Within a few months of Stalin's death, during June 1953, restive Berliners began to protest Soviet rule in the eastern sector of the city. These protests quickly spread to the rest of East Germany, and just as quickly they were squashed by the combined might of Soviet and East German security forces. (Unlike later uprisings in Prague and Budapest, this mini-rebellion did not rise to the level of tanks firing upon protesters in city streets.)

An objective analysis of Josef Stalin's career is difficult, if not impossible. In many ways he was a fitting contemporary of Adolf Hitler. Both men were masters in the employment of secret police forces to maintain their regimes, and they practised mass murder as an instrument of the state on an unprecedented scale. Each dictator ruthlessly exploited the naivety and idealism of his opponents, and held on to his power with absolute dictatorial control.

The primary difference, perhaps, is that Hitler's regime resulted in the catastrophic defeat of his nation in the world's bloodiest war, while Stalin died leaving his country as one of the two most powerful nations in the world – and, for all practical purposes, as the most triumphant victor in that same war. Furthermore, Stalin's nation had been much more economically backward than Germany when he ascended to power after the death of Lenin. Russian industrial production increased dramatically under his rule, and even after the war the nation continued to devote an almost incomprehensible proportion of its prosperity toward maintaining a massive military. This was not just the dictator's will, but a reflection of a grave national terror: after the horrific invasions of Napoleon and Hitler, all Russians were determined that such an attack would never again befall them.

Though Soviet industry flourished greatly during Stalin's reign, the same cannot be said of the vast nation's agricultural base. Indeed, Stalin's insistence upon collectivising small farms has to be regarded as a colossal failure. His edicts pushing peasants off of their lands and gathering them into massive government-owned plantations was directly responsible for the famine and starvation that cost the lives of more than 10 million of his people – and some estimate that twice that many, or more, perished as a result of these massive relocation programmes.

As for Stalin's most deep-seated legacy, history can now observe that the climate of fear and oppression that the Soviets carried with them into all of the lands they claimed after the Second World War would plant the seeds of a revolution and political convulsion that, less than forty years after the dictator's death, would bring down his regime and send shock waves surging into every corner of the world.

Charlotte and I still owned our store in East Berlin, which her aunt was running for us. For a while we were able to get products to sell, to keep the shelves stocked. We were worried about the Russians, but life seemed to be getting a little bit back to normal in the city. It was still no problem to travel back and forth between East and West Berlin, whenever you wanted.

Since my father and I were no longer in business together, I started doing some work for another fellow who ran a sign company, just to collect some pay. One day I was taking down some signs that had been put up with the Christmas decorations. I guess this would have been in January of 1951.

I was up above a huge metal sign from a shoe store, one that was shaped like a shoe, so I was about three stories up. I was taking down a sign shaped like a Christmas tree when my ladder broke, and fell down. I was holding on to one thing, like a big nail, but it was giving way and I knew I was going to fall.

I couldn't just let go because I would hit that sign from the shoe store and it would knock me sideways while I was falling, so I wouldn't be able to control myself. I pushed away from the wall and went past the sign feet first, and at least I was in control all the way down. But I hit the sidewalk hard and was banged up pretty good, with my pelvis broken, as well as some ribs, and I also had a lot of bruises. I was out of commission and in the hospital for three months of healing. And even after I got out I had to be careful.

– Helmut Jacobitz

I was home with my infant son and this policeman came to the house and knocked on the door. I thought maybe he wanted some taxes or something so I didn't open the door, and he went away. But then he came back, and this was after Helmut should have been home so I was getting worried. I opened the door.

He gave me a slip of paper that said my husband was in an accident. That paper told him, the policeman, to be careful how he told me the news, not to upset me because the fall had been so hard. I thought Helmut was dead! I took Reinhard to my mother's, which took an hour.

Then I took a train to see him in the hospital. I was so glad to see him! He was all wrapped up in bandages and a cast, but at least he was alive.

– Charlotte Jacobitz

New Man in Moscow

The world remembers Nikita Khrushchev as a stalwart Cold Warrior, the frightening Russian leader who banged his shoe on the table at the United Nations, warmly embraced Fidel Castro and tried to sneak strategic nuclear missiles into Cuba, igniting what most historians view as the hottest crisis of the Cold War. Less well remembered is the fact that this garrulous little man stood in stark contrast to Josef Stalin, and greatly reformed Soviet society in the aftermath of his predecessor's death.

In fact, Khrushchev was a consummate politician and survivor. He knew how to wheel and deal behind the scenes, and shortly after Stalin's death he aligned himself with the esteemed general, Malenkov. Together they convinced the rest of the presidium that Beria, the KGB man, was plotting a military coup. Beria was arrested and, with half a dozen of his cronies, executed in December 1953. He would be the last Soviet leader to pay this ultimate price as a result of a political power struggle.

During 1954 Khrushchev worked on marginalising Malenkov, and even then the military man didn't seem to grasp what was happening. By the end of that year Malenkov had lost his seat on the presidium, and Khrushchev had passed a number of reforms, including the 'Virgin Lands' agricultural expansion (not unlike the US Homestead Act of the previous century) and the opening of the Kremlin grounds to the Russian public.

In 1955 the new leader began to release many political prisoners from the gulags, and as more and more of these long-suffering souls returned to their homes, the people became increasingly aware of the excesses of security and terror wreaked during Stalin's reign. In February 1956 Khrushchev gave a secret speech to the Communist Party Congress, in which he criticised Stalin harshly, shocking many of those in attendance.

This speech did much to secure Khrushchev's hold upon power. He believed that if the cruelties of Stalinism could be put behind them, the Russian people would be able to move forward and embrace a true, eternal and ultimately triumphant form of world communism.

When I got out of the hospital I wanted to find a job. I had never taken any handouts from the government before, but we had no money, and I still didn't have a job. So I went to the welfare office and told them my situation, and asked if they could give me enough to get through one month. They did: they wrote me a cheque for 150 marks, and said I could keep getting that much until I got work.

I paid our rent, which was about 30 marks, and still had some money left. So I walked a few miles to save bus fare, and bought a piece of sheet metal for 20 marks. I went home and started making signs. I started out just by clearing out a little space in the cellar of our apartment building.

I got lucky, then. This man I knew, Nagel, had finally come home from the war, from Siberia. He came to me and said he needed a job. He was a really handy fellow, and he started working for me, and we set up an actual shop in that cellar. We had to hammer and saw and stuff, but the other people in the building didn't even mind about the noise, because I very soon had more and more people working for me. One man had a driver's licence, and he used to deliver signs. Another was a carpenter.

Unemployment was still pretty bad, but I was keeping busy working day and night. One fellow worked for me and I paid him 1 Western Deutsche Mark ['Westmark'] an hour, which was very cheap for me. But he was living in East Berlin, and that was worth maybe 5 or 10 Eastmarks over there, so he was doing all right – he actually was making a fortune.

I had to watch out though. It's kind of like with the IRS here [in the US]: if you get caught cheating they'll come for you. What we were supposed to do is I should have paid him a little more than 1 mark, like 1.5 or 1.6 Westmarks. Then he was supposed to go turn those Westmarks in to the East Berlin government, and they would keep two-thirds of his money and he would make less than I was actually paying him. So he was living like a king over there, but we had to keep it quiet.

In order that nothing happened I usually put in some regular pay in Eastmarks for him, which made him kind of mad. I think he understood why, though. We were working a lot, like forty-eight hours each week normal, and he worked a lot of overtime, sometimes even all night.

So I paid him some in Eastmarks, in case someone came and said, 'That guy worked here all last week – how come you didn't pay him?' I could say he only worked a few hours, and show that he'd been paid in Eastmark currency.

We had one really good customer, and made quite a few nice metal signs for them. It was called Schultheiss, and they were the largest brewery in Germany – if you can even imagine that! There was a lady who ran the company that was in charge of all their signs, and they put them up on just about every pub and beer hall in the city. And my company got the jobs to do all those signs!

We got pretty big then, and I hired quite a few men. We had our biggest apartment ever. And I had five guys working in a little room.

My brother Hermann tried to undercut me with his and my father's business, and he got some customers away from us – though not the work for the brewery. But where I was using mechanical ladders and doing the work safely, he would charge less and maybe not even use a ladder if there was a ledge on the side of the building to stand on.

He was pretty foolish and reckless, actually. He used to do handstands on the top rung of my father's biggest ladder, just to show off. It all turned out tragically for him. His son Harald fell to his death in 1956, when he was 18 years old, doing one of those crazy jobs for his father.

– Helmut Jacobitz

In about 1953 we took a four-day vacation to West Germany. We left Reinhard with my mother, and took the train through East Germany to the west. The

Soviets gave us a lot of hassle, because they didn't like people doing that, so like before we had to take a full day to cross to the west and another full day to come back. But for two days we had a nice time in West Germany.

Our second son, Helgo, was born on 10 January 1954. By then, the communists were taking lots of the stores and buildings away from their owners in East Berlin, with the government starting to own everything. My cousin Martha had a bunch of apartment buildings and made a good living collecting rent, but they took those buildings away from her. She was lucky she had a house in West Berlin, where she lived!

The East Germans also had their eyes on our store, which my Aunt Elizabeth was still managing. They offered us another apartment in East Berlin, an even nicer one than the first one. But they were also threatening to take our store away, and we didn't trust them.

It wasn't long after Helgo was born that the East Germans took the store over – they just took it away from us, with no compensation or anything. So we lost the store, which was a hard blow since we were still trying to make a decent living.

At the same time, we'd been hearing about Canada, and thinking a lot about moving. That country was actually advertising in Germany, encouraging people to come over there to live and to work. We were still worried about the Russians trying to take over all of Berlin, so we looked into it. We decided that the opportunity made sense, so we made up our minds that we would move to Canada. Even then we thought maybe we would end up in the United States, but we began by making plans to go and live in Vancouver.

It was April 1956, when we left for Canada the first time. My dad was really sad to see us, and Reinhard and Helgo, go. The boys liked to sit in front of my dad on the wheelchair and ride around.

There were a lot of men in wheelchairs around where my father was. He had one good friend, and they were always together. When that man died, it was almost like a relative had died. They were best friends.

My father was proud, too, and not always in a good way. I remember one time he was sitting on the curb in his chair, watching the traffic go by. It was almost Christmas time. This car pulled up and stopped, and a little girl got out and ran up to my father and gave him an envelope. I didn't see it, but it probably had money in it – she wanted to give him a Christmas present. And he took it and threw it down.

That was my father sometimes, after he lost his legs. He could be really mean. That little kid wanted to do something nice for Christmas, and he sent her running away in tears. I felt so sorry for her, and so mad at him.

Anyway, it was hard, but we ended up going to Canada in 1956. We moved to Vancouver and bought a rooming house, which I ran while Helmut worked other jobs. We had a lot of tenants come and stay with us, because there were a lot of Germans coming to Canada and we were well known as a place where Germans could stay and be comfortable. We helped a lot of other people from our country get settled over there.

– Charlotte Jacobitz

Years of Crisis

The end of the 1950s brought, if anything, an increased heightening to the tensions of the Cold War. Both sides, by then, had not just atomic, but thermonuclear, weapons. The United States had developed atomic-powered submarines that could stay underwater for months at a time, and both sides had fleets of bombers and were developing missiles that could carry these incredibly destructive bombs all the way around the world.

Although the US had a distinct advantage over the Soviet Union in terms of nuclear power, the Americans and their allies were not entirely sure of this imbalance, and of course the risks were too great to take any chances on actual aggression. Khrushchev played on this fear with his bombast and threats, assuring the world that the USSR was turning out nuclear-armed missiles 'like sausages'!

The Cold War flashed warm in May 1960, when an American U-2 spy plane, piloted by Francis Gary Powers, was shot down over the Soviet Union during the last months of Dwight Eisenhower's second term as President. The Soviet leader used this incident as an excuse to cancel a planned summit meeting between the leaders of the USA, Britain, France and the USSR. The new US President, John F. Kennedy, took office early in 1961, and when he met Khrushchev in Vienna a few months later the Soviet Premier bullied and berated the young President, leading Kennedy to predict 'it's going to be a cold winter'.

Berlin remained an aggravating wound in the flank of the communist state. The 'brain drain' that had been going on since the end of the Second World War continued, with no signs of abating. It was hard for the Soviets to proclaim the triumph of World Communism and the perfection of the 'Worker's Paradise' when so many of those same workers were fleeing to the west just as fast as they could get away.

However, Nikita Khrushchev was nothing if not creative. Thus, when it came to stopping the flow of people out of Germany, through Berlin, he came up with a plan that took the rest of the world by surprise.

So by 1960 West Berlin was doing pretty well, and East Berlin was poor. You could buy a car if you wanted, in West Germany, whatever kind of car you wanted and could pay for. In East Germany you could only by one kind of car, a Russian car called the Trabi. But you had to pay for it, and then wait ten years to get your car!

We had been living in Canada for a few years, and our rooming house was actually pretty successful, but we were both getting really, really homesick for Germany. By the summer of 1960 we were missing our old homeland so much that we decided to move back. We couldn't sell that rooming house by the time we were moving back, so we just walked away and left it.

We were both able to get really good jobs working for a company in Cologne. We decided that we would try moving back for almost a year, because if we were out of the country for twelve months we would lose our Canadian visas. We were also still thinking about moving to the United States, but we felt like we had to see what it was like going back to Germany.

We made good money, and liked living in Cologne, but there was an awful lot of fear of the Russians everywhere, even though we were not right on the border. Everybody was afraid that there was going to be a war, and we wanted nothing to do with that. We decided to go back to Canada at the end of our time in Germany, and permanently make our home on the other side of the Atlantic Ocean.

So our year in Germany was coming to an end in the late summer of 1961. Before we went back to Canada, we took a few weeks off, and went to visit our families who lived in Berlin. It so happened that we were in the city when they put up the wall. They did it overnight.

Everyone who could get away was still leaving East Berlin and going to West Berlin, and from there to West Germany. There were lots of jobs, good pay, in West Germany, and nothing in East Germany. That's why the Russians put the wall up.

The day before it happened we went to visit our friend Fritz, in East Berlin. We were nervous going over there, through the Russian checkpoint. They made us leave our camera there. We had the two boys with us – Reinhard was 10 and Helgo about 6 – and since they'd lived in Canada for so long we were worried about them speaking English while we were around the Russians. Charlotte told them both just to stay quiet, which, kind of amazingly, they did.

We visited Fritz and went back to where we were staying that evening. We were in West Berlin, and they put the wall up that very night! We could have been caught, trapped, over there.

A lot of people did get separated from homes and loved ones. I remember there was one building in East Berlin, but one wall of it was on a street in West Berlin. After they put the wall up people were jumping out of the windows on that wall to escape, to get to West Berlin. The West Berlin fire department came with a truck and raised their ladder to help people climb down from those windows. They did that until the East German police came and shut down the building until they could brick up the windows. Even then, people pushed out the bricks and jumped, until they sealed it off with solid concrete.

They didn't build the whole wall until a little later, but they blocked it off with barbed wire overnight, and had military guards there to keep people from crossing. They would shoot you if you tried to run across.

In the beginning, after the wall went up, you couldn't even write or phone or anything. There was no communication allowed. The really terrible thing was when direct families were separated, like parents and children who couldn't visit each other any more. They would meet at certain places and wave, but they were so far apart they couldn't even talk to each other.

People were just helpless – they couldn't do anything about it. It was awfully sad. The only people they would let leave East Berlin were the retired people, since they didn't want to pay them their pensions. But if you were still of working age, they wouldn't let you out.

Those people who escaped to the west got a bonus for coming, some money from the government to get them started. But you had to be lucky to get away, to come over.

My sister Gretel lived in the east, but she had it okay because she was a pretty famous actress there. She was able to buy things from a government store, with special tickets. She would give my mother and Reinhard some nice clothes that she got. She could also get typewriters and some nice equipment like that, but she wasn't allowed to bring them to West Berlin.

Then there was the Stasi, the East German state police. They were nuts. They were the guys who shot at you if you tried to escape over the wall. Charlotte's cousin, Gertrude, was married to one of those Stasi guys, one of the top men. They fired him from that job because Gertrude wrote to her mother in West Berlin, and they didn't like that. Then, when the wall came down, he was saying, 'Oh, I never hurt anyone! I had nothing to do with it!'

So we went back to Canada, on the way to the United States, and this time we had no regrets. Like all Germans, we were worried that the Russians one day would take over Berlin. Berlin was like an island, a little jail, in the middle of the communist world.

– Helmut Jacobitz

Epilogue

There are many people in the world who really don't understand, or say they don't, what is the great issue between the free world and the communist world. Let them come to Berlin. And there are some who say that communism is the wave of the future. Let them come to Berlin. And there are some who say in Europe and elsewhere, 'We can work with the Communists.' Let them come to Berlin! And there are even a few who say that it is true that communism is an evil system, but it permits us to make economic progress. Let them come to Berlin!

– Excerpt from President Kennedy's speech, West Berlin, 26 June 1963

The Berlin Wall solved Nikita Khrushchev's immediate problem, in that it almost completely stopped the emigration of East Berliners and East Germans to the west via the conduit of West Berlin. However, that short-term benefit must be weighed against the long-term propaganda cost, for the well-known barrier loudly and publicly begged the question: what kind of government needs to build a wall to keep its own population from fleeing?

When it was first installed, on the night of 12 August 1961, the Wall was, in effect, just a border closing, often enforced with coils of barbed wire and with armed guards everywhere. Throughout the rest of the year it took on its more permanent form, as the streets and roads crossing the border were torn up, actual brick, mortar and concrete gave the wall solidity, and gradually a wide no-man's-land was cleared on the communist side. Eventually the entire circumference of West Berlin would be enclosed, the barrier lit at night and constantly patrolled by sentries carrying automatic weapons, accompanied by guard dogs.

The West Berliners, led by Mayor Willy Brandt, protested the erection of the Wall vehemently, and were disappointed that the United States did not make a more vigorous objection. From the point of view of the Cold War, however, the Wall actually served to defuse the situation in Berlin. From 1961 until the fall of the Communist Bloc in 1989, the city would no longer be the flashpoint it had been since the end of the Second World War. The Wall allowed the communists to at least ignore the Berlin situation, if not forget about it entirely.

President Kennedy did not let the construction of the Wall proceed without response, however. Within days after the closing of the city's border, he appointed retired General Lucius Clay as a special ambassador to the city of West Berlin. Clay, who was regarded as a hero by most Berliners for his key role in conceiving of and commanding the Berlin Airlift, arrived in the city with Vice President Lyndon Johnson on 19 August. The next day a brigade of US troops, in a convoy nearly 100 miles long, proceeded from West Germany along the *Autobahn* through East Germany. The soldiers and vehicles were counted as they passed the checkpoint, and watched carefully by East German authorities as they advanced, but they were allowed to pass. The men of the brigade were warmly and enthusiastically greeted when they arrived in West Berlin to reinforce the three brigades (British, US and French) already posted there.

On 26 June 1963, President Kennedy travelled to Berlin. He planned to give a polite and diplomatic speech at the city hall. As his motorcade travelled through the city he was greeted by thousands of Berliners cheering deliriously. At several points the motorcade stopped, and Kennedy got out and climbed a watchtower to look over the wall at the grey emptiness of East Berlin.

By the time he reached the city hall, he had decided to throw out his prepared speech. He climbed to the rostrum and spoke to a crowd of hundreds of thousands of West Berliners, and he gave full and spontaneous vent to the outrage and disgust that the sight of the divided city had aroused in him. Giving this speech in the very shadow of the Wall – and using it as proof of his accusations – he included an historic phrase, a phrase demonstrative of the free world's solidarity with the city, when he firmly proclaimed: '*Ich bin ein Berliner!*' ('I am a Berliner!')

Kennedy was stunned by the reception his speech received, in Berlin and at home. As he left the city, he remarked to his advisers, 'We'll never have another day like this one as long as we live.' He told West German Chancellor Adenauer that he would leave a note for future presidents, advice for them when they encountered tough and demoralising challenges. The note would simply say that, when things got bleak, 'Go to Germany'.

We arrived in Canada, at Toronto, at the end of our year in Germany right after the Wall went up. Rather than return to Vancouver, we applied for, and were granted, three-month travel visas to the United States. With all our possessions in a trailer, we drove a long route that took us to Chicago, Florida and, eventually, Los Angeles.

Helmut, as always, went to work. Our visas were extended with his work permit, and he soon found himself managing a workshop in the layout department of Warner Brothers, the filmmaking company. Together we also bought a small apartment building that was in quite shabby condition. We renovated the building, rented out the units, and bought another, larger building.

Our boys Reinhard and Helgo, as they grew, became partners in our apartments and other real estate. In the mid-1960s, we founded a German-American club for ourselves and fellow ex-pats in the Los Angeles area; the club quickly grew to over 100 members. We would get together monthly, and plan trips and other events.

Our sons grew up and married, and now we have five grandchildren. Along with the rest of the world, we watched in wonder in November 1989, as Berliners finally tore down the Wall.

We finally returned to Germany for a visit in the summer of 1991. We took our grandson Jason and spent a memorable week or more visiting Berlin, where we still have siblings, cousins, nieces and nephews. The Wall was gone, but the contrast between east and west remained, visible in many places. But slowly, Germany was becoming one, again.

– Charlotte Jacobitz

The physically divided city of Berlin would remain a vivid symbol of communist oppression for as long as the Wall stood – it was there to see, clear proof of the failure of that system of government. The Cold War would wax and wane, and eventually the Soviet Union would bankrupt itself by trying to maintain a level of military strength that was simply beyond its ability to sustain.

In places the war turned hot. The Americans would shed much blood in Vietnam in the 1960s and 1970s, fighting North Vietnamese and Viet Cong soldiers armed with Soviet-supplied AK-47 assault rifles; then the Soviets bled and died when they vainly tried to expand their dying empire in Afghanistan during the 1980s. The Red Army lost thousands of helicopters and many more soldiers to *mujahideen* armed with US-provided Stinger missiles, lethal, shoulder-fired anti-aircraft weapons.

In Berlin, some Germans would brave the defences and try to cross the Wall; a few made it, and as many as a hundred were killed trying to do so.

Some used creative techniques, tunnelling under it or, in one case, building a home-made aircraft and flying over it. For the most part the Wall did prevent Berlin from serving as an escape route to the west, but it did not stop the flow of emigrations. As the years passed, the preferred path of exodus for Germans from east to west switched to Hungary and Czechoslovakia, from which many thousands escaped into Austria, and from there into West Germany.

During the late 1980s, with Mikhail Gorbachev as the General Secretary ruling the USSR from Moscow, the populations of the Soviet satellites in Eastern Europe grew increasingly restive. Elected in 1980, American President Ronald Reagan made the strategic decision for the United States to try to outspend the USSR in a military build-up, in an effort to drive the Soviet economy to the breaking point. As the decade passed, it became increasingly apparent that the Russians could not keep up.

In 1987, President Reagan visited Berlin and addressed a large crowd in front of the Brandenburg Gate. Like Kennedy, he used the physical presence of the Berlin Wall as the only evidence he needed in his challenge to the Soviet system. Also like Kennedy, he employed a memorable phrase, words that would resonate through history, when he demanded: 'Mr Gorbachev, tear down this Wall!'

Beginning on 9 November 1989, the Berliners themselves did just that, starting with a few small sections but swiftly destroying the entire, hated barrier. Sensing the change in historical tides, the East German police did not try to interfere. When the Wall came down, the two halves of Berlin were united, and soon thereafter Germany herself became one nation.

Inspired by the German example, the peoples of Poland, Czechoslovakia, the Balkans, the Baltic States, Ukraine and all of the Russian heartland rose up and demanded freedoms that were taken for granted in the west. The communist regimes of Europe, entrenched though they were, could no longer withstand the will of their people, and the Soviet socialist system, like Nazism, tumbled unlamented into the dustbin of history.

Index

Other titles published by The History Press

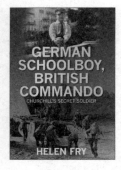

German Schoolboy, British Commando
HELEN FRY

£18.99

Colin Anson, born in Berlin, was forced to flee Nazi Germany and found refuge in Britain, where he went on to join the British army. He took part in the invasion of Italy and Sicily in 1943, in raids into Yugoslavia and Albania, and the liberation of Corfu. This is an extraordinary portrait of a son's determination to continue his father's legacy as he fought the Nazis.

978-0-7524-4996-8

The Other Schindlers
AGNES GRUNWALD-SPIER

£14.99

This is a touching collection of the stories of thirty individuals who rescued Jews, which provide a new insight into why these people were prepared to risk so much for their fellow men and women. With a foreword by Sir Martin Gilbert, one of the leading experts on the subject, this is an ultimately uplifting account of how some good deeds really do shine in a weary world.

978-0-7524-5706-2

Ein Volk, Ein Reich
LOUIS HAGEN

£14.99

Through the lives of nine ordinary Germans, tracing their experiences of Nazism from the first hopeful days until the horrors of the Russian occupation of Berlin, Louis Hagen provides a salutary and unforgettable record of the German people in the shadow of the swastika.

978-0-7524-5979-0

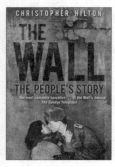

The Wall
CHRISTOPHER HILTON

£12.99

Across a 12ft wall, East and West confronted each other for nearly thirty years, yet it is the individual stories that are perhaps most telling. Leading world politicians, the American and British military, East German border guards and ordinary people on both sides feature in this book, their memories expertly interwoven into a remarkable, seamless narrative. This is an extraordinarily vivid, occasionally harrowing, sometimes touching story.

978-0-7524-5833-5

Visit our website and discover thousands of other History Press books.

www.thehistorypress.co.uk